Social Pluralism and Lithic Economy at Cerro Baúl, Peru

Social Pluralism and Lithic Economy at Cerro Baúl, Peru

Benjamin R. Vining

BAR International Series 1461
2005

Published in 2016 by
BAR Publishing, Oxford

BAR International Series 1461

Social Pluralism and Lithic Economy at Cerro Baúl, Peru

ISBN 978 1 84171 728 9

© B R Vining and the Publisher 2005

The author's moral rights under the 1988 UK Copyright,
Designs and Patents Act are hereby expressly asserted.

All rights reserved. No part of this work may be copied, reproduced, stored,
sold, distributed, scanned, saved in any form of digital format or transmitted
in any form digitally, without the written permission of the Publisher.

BAR Publishing is the trading name of British Archaeological Reports (Oxford) Ltd.
British Archaeological Reports was first incorporated in 1974 to publish the BAR
Series, International and British. In 1992 Hadrian Books Ltd became part of the BAR
group. This volume was originally published by John and Erica Hedges Ltd. in
conjunction with British Archaeological Reports (Oxford) Ltd / Hadrian Books Ltd, the
Series principal publisher, in 2005. This present volume is published by BAR
Publishing, 2016.

Printed in England

PUBLISHING

BAR titles are available from:

          BAR Publishing
          122 Banbury Rd, Oxford, OX2 7BP, UK
EMAIL   info@barpublishing.com
PHONE +44 (0)1865 310431
FAX   +44 (0)1865 316916
          www.barpublishing.com

LIST OF FIGURES

Figure 2.1	The Osmore Drainage and location of major archaeological sites.	4
Figure 2.2	Map of the Cerro Baul Archaeological Zone, and adjacent Middle Horizon sites.	5
Figure 2.3	Map of Sectors A through D, Cerro Baúl Archaeological Zone.	7
Figure 2.4:	Map of Sector F, Cerro Baúl Archaeological Zone.	8
Figure 2.5	Map of Sector H, Cerro Baúl Archaeological Zone.	9
Figure 2.6	Map of Sector L, Cerro Baúl Archaeological Zone.	10
Figure 2.7	Map of Sector N, Cerro Baúl Archaeological Zone.	11
Figure 2.8	Map of the Central Andean area, showing Middle Horizon sites mentioned in the text, and proposed core and provincial territories	12
Figure 3.1	Lithological Map for the Upper Osmore Drainage derived from remotely-sensed ASTER data	20
Figure 4.1	Geological column for the Upper Osmore Drainage.	24
Figure 5.1	Geological hand samples of local material that was exploited archaeologically at Cerro Baúl.	28
Figure 5.2	Bar-graph of the raw material variety that was exploited in each archaeological context.	30
Figure 5.3	Minimum convex polygons for sample excavation units Unit 9, Unit 24, and Unit 19.	32
Figure 5.4	Histograms of obsidian and local-material debitage based on the percentage of flakes represented in each class.	37
Figure 5.5	Principal components plot of material types based on the data from lithic debitage in all analyzed contexts.	39
Figure 5.6	Scatterplots of density of raw material in each excavation unit versus distance from the center of the site.	40
Figure 6.1	Density grids of local-material and obsidian debitage per square meter.	45
Figure 6.2	Density grids of local material debitage per square meter.	47
Figure 7.1	Expedient bifaces at Cerro Baúl.	50
Figure 7.2	Bifaces that fit the provisional type A, with triangular bodies and concave bases.	52
Figure 7.3	Bifaces that fit the provisional type B, with lanceolate bodies and concave bases.	53
Figure 7.4	Bifaces that fit the provisional type C, with straight, triangular bodies and straight bases.	54
Figure 7.5	Bifaces that fit the provisional type D, with lanceolate bodies and straight bases.	55
Figure 7.6	Bifaces that fit the provisional type F, with excurvate and convex bases.	56
Figure 7.7	Bifaces that fit the provisional type G, the "Tiwanaku" type, with triangular bodies and stemmed bases	57
Figure 7.8	Bifaces that fit the provisional type J, which are probable preforms.	57
Figure 7.9	Bifaces from Unit 21, artifacts in left column fit provisional type G, and those in the right column fit type I with basal notching.	58
Figure 7.10	Scatterplots of biface length (mm) versus width (mm) for each morphological type as provisionally defined.	60
Figure 7.11	Principal components plot of bifacial types based on their technological and material attributes, per excavation unit.	60
Figure 7.12	Unifacially-retouched flakes.	62
Figure 7.13	Unifacially-retouched flake of local rhyolite.	63
Figure 7.14	Unifacial implements.	64

Figure 7.15	Unifacial implement flaked on a cobble of rhyolite.	65
Figure 7.16	Bivariate correlations for the length, width and thickness (mm) of unifacial implements.	67
Figure 7.17	Scatterplots for the length and width, and thickness and width (mm) of all unifacial implements, with regression fit lines.	68

LIST OF TABLES

Table 2.1	Excavated units from Cerro Baúl Archaeological Zone and interpretation.	6
Table 3.1	Typical stratigraphic sequence for archaeological deposits at Cerro Baúl (from Williams and Ruales 2002, 2004).	18
Table 3.2	Advanced Spaceborne Thermal Emission and Reflection Radiometer (ASTER) system parameters.	22
Table 5.1	Percentage of raw material types that were found in each excavation context as lithic debitage.	28
Table 5.2	Indices for diversity and evenness for lithic debitage within each excavation unit.	31
Table 5.3	Euclidean distance between each excavation unit and Unit 9 at the summit of Cerro Baúl, and the resource area for each context estimated from the Minimum Convex Polygons.	33
Table 5.4	Pearson's r correlations for resource area, distance, and diversity indices from Tables 5.2 and 5.3.	33
Table 5.5	Comparison of the five percent trimmed-mean statistics for obsidian and local materials, in weight in grams.	35
Table 5.6	Observed versus expected frequencies for cortex morphology based on χ^2 analysis.	35
Table 5.7	Observed versus expected frequencies for flake technological attributes based on χ^2 analysis.	36
Table 5.8	Densities of exotic and local raw material per cubic meter in each excavation unit.	38
Table 5.9	Coefficients for the correlations between the Euclidean distance from Unit 9 and the average density of raw material per cubic meter in each excavation unit.	39
Table 6.1	Density indices for each excavation unit based on the mean and variance of debitage frequencies per square meter.	44
Table 7.1	Contingency table of nominal morphological data observed on bifacial implements.	51
Table 7.2	Observed versus expected frequencies for the major bifacial morphological attributes based in χ^2 analysis.	51
Table 7.3	Provisional biface typology based on frequent attribute combinations observed among the formal bifacial implements at Cerro Baúl.	59
Table 7.4	Descriptive statistics for biface length and width.	59
Table 7.5	Observed frequencies of raw material types used for formal bifacial implements by morphological type.	59
Table 7.6	Summary descriptions of the 10 provisional biface types at Cerro Baúl that are outlined in Chapter 7.	59
Table 7.7	The observed frequency of biface types per excavation unit.	61
Table 7.8	The average density of bifacial points per cubic meter.	61
Table 7.9	Observed frequencies of raw material types that were used to fabricate unifacial implements.	65
Table 7.10	Mean values for measurements on unifacial implements, organized by material properties.	65
Table 7.11	Spearman's r correlation coefficients for measurements on unifacial implements.	66

LIST OF ABBREVIATIONS

AD	anno domini
ASTER	Advanced Spaceborne Thermal and Emission Radiometer
ENSO	el Niño Southern Oscillation
GIS	Geographic Information Systems
IDW	Inverse Distance Weighting
kybp	thousand years before present
Landsat TM	Landsat Thematic Mapper
masl	meters above sea level
mybp	million years before present
PCA	Principal Components Analysis
SWIR	Short-wave Infrared
TIR	Thermal Infrared
UTM	Universal Transverse Mercator
VNIR	Visible-Near Infrared
WARP	Western Andean Escarpment

ABSTRACT

Pluralistic communities offer the opportunity to explore the complex set of factors that effect the composition of social groups. Excavations at the Middle Horizon site of Cerro Baúl near Moquegua, Peru have shown that this community was predominantly Wari, but in the later Middle Horizon Epoch B the occupation included a significant contingent of Tumilaca residents, related to contemporaneous occupations of Tiwanaku colonists elsewhere in Moquegua and the central Andes. This study examines over 1,979 flaked lithic artifacts from multiple domestic contexts that represent both Wari and Tumilaca residents. The lithic data reveal that economic differentiation was an important factor that determined material use and economic differentiation also strongly characterized social interaction at Cerro Baúl. Differences in local and exotic material use reflect participation in socially-organized procurement networks of varying scale, and economic and mechanical considerations figured strongly in lithic implement usage. Furthermore, the membership of economically-characterized social groups crosscut ethnic boundaries. This variability in resource exploitation and manufacture modes most likely can be linked to occupational differentiation among the presumed social classes at the Wari center during its Middle Horizon (c. 600-1000 AD) occupation. Ultimately, these interpretations contribute to our understanding of the socio-economic dynamics between Wari and Tiwanaku cultural groups and support the hypothesis that class-organized inter-ethnic interaction was a probable development of the dynamic contact between the Wari and Tiwanaku expansive states during the Middle Horizon.

Chapter 1: Introduction

The effort to define archaeological cultures has depended on considerations of behavioral and material styles in order to delineate groups and to sketch the dynamics of their interaction. Particular styles, through either deliberate agency or habitual reproduction of norms, express group affinities that are frequently social in nature: the members of groups use and exhibit homologous formulations of traits within a larger structure that accommodates standardization or occasional personal innovation (Wobst 1977; Weissner 1990; Sackett 1986). Clusters of similar attributes, including stylistic elements and modes of behavior, within social units contribute to the concept of a representative type for that entity. Together, the repetition of redundant or similar material and behavioral elements constructs "trait inventories" that are recognized as unique to the abstract and material culture of a given social group, and which comprise a group's standards for comparison and evaluation—an "assumed common understanding"—of individuals and events (Barth 1998: 12, 15). On a gross scale, differences between groups are manifested as differences in trait inventories, particularly when disparate sets of traits are compared in areas of inter-group interaction.

The theoretical assumption that material and behavioral styles can serve as a marker of social boundaries is only partial, however. When restricted to an analysis of material, the utility of style as a correlate for social entities is limited by phenomena that impact the composition of artifact assemblages but which do not reflect substantive variation in the membership of culturally or ethnically defined groups. On occasion social groups that can take precedence over ethnic categories (for example) are formulated on the basis of other, "instrumental" criteria, and material culture is used in these situations in reference to political affiliation, membership within ideological groups, or class-based societies (Barth 1998: 29). Economy can be and often is a key criterion for defining interactions that supercede or complement apparent ethnic categorizations (Haaland 1998). In Andean South America, far-extending economic and social networks frequently mean that artifact style cannot be used as a direct correlate for ethnic affiliation, particularly if the item is considered outside of its social context (Aldenderfer and Stanish 1993: 2; Julien 1993: 226; D'Altroy and Hastorf 2001). Instead, material is also indicative of extensive scales of both direct and down-the-line interaction and they define networks that are structured by political, ideological, and social concerns.

Plural societies—such as those that have recently been proposed for Middle Horizon (ca. AD 500–1000) Andean communities (e.g., Janusek 1999, 2001; Williams and Nash 2001) provide the opportunity to evaluate group membership that is formulated with variable and compounded criteria. Plural societies are organized through a nested series of closed and open social spheres that accommodate interactions where the variable that characterizes these interactions is the degree of social intimacy, defined by shared standards of evaluation. Economic concerns, primarily material-driven exchange, are associated with the development of open, poly-ethnic social spheres which encourage dealings between disparate groups and individuals (Blanton 1994: 156; Eidheim 1998). Boundary maintenance, however, is not precluded by shared economic interests since these comprise a limited area of activity and a group's distinctiveness can simultaneously be sustained by more durable cultural characteristics while engaging in poly-ethnic transactions (Haaland 1998: 61–63).

The site of Cerro Baúl during the late Middle Horizon was just such a socially heterogeneous community with ethnically distinct households of Wari and Tumilaca residents. Excavations have shown that the site was predominantly occupied by Wari residents, tied to the expansive Middle Horizon state. Williams and Nash (2002: 261–262) propose that by the 10th century AD, Cerro Baúl was an integrated multi-ethnic community held together by institutionalized socio-ritual activities and economic organization. Diverse material culture at the site suggests that while residents maintained close cultural and social ties with Wari populations in Ayacucho and elsewhere in central Peru, the local populations originating from Tiwanaku, the Tumilaca, also maintained relations to the highland communities. Many elements of material culture, including ceramic styles and other traditional analytic indicators, show the reproduction of distinct cultural identities during this period of cohabitation, and economic indicators—including residential patterns—indicate that this community was strongly segmented (Williams and Nash 2002: 261). Importantly, the economic evidence also indicates that much of the social segmentation did not follow ethnic divisions.

This study presents the analysis of lithic artifacts from twelve contexts, predominantly residential, at Cerro Baúl. Six of these contexts have been characterized—on the basis of the preponderance of material culture encountered during their respective excavations—as occupied and used by Wari residents while the remainder have been attributed to Tumilaca inhabitants. Additionally, these contexts represent the spectrum of socio-economic differentiation at Cerro Baúl, from the most opulent household to the most rustic. The lithic analysis indicates patterns of differentiation which do not conform strictly to the inhabitants' presumed ethnicity but rather can only be explained as economic in quality. Multiple levels or spheres of social interaction are implied by the juxtaposition of the lithic data and other material used to define ethnic groups, such as ceramic styles. These data, consequently, suggest that other social spheres were active at Cerro Baúl that cross-cut ethnicity and where economy was a primary concern. These conclusions have significant implications for the proposal that quality of interaction between Wari and Tiwanaku groups changed substantially and substantively in the late Middle Horizon. Further, it suggests the need to closely examine the possibility that mutually supportive interaction that was economically realized developed as a product of status-based social groups.

These aspects of the social structure are explored vis-à-vis lithic artifacts in the following chapters. Chapter Two discusses the archaeological contexts that are examined in this work, and sets the theoretical background for the development of class-oriented social segmentation during the Middle Horizon based on long-distance elite interaction and hierarchical social interaction within a site.

Chapter Three describes the specific analytical approaches that were taken to elucidate social information from tacit rocks, including the excavation strategies which impacted sample composition. An important element of this study is the spatial variability that can be understood from the use of material culture at Cerro Baúl, and this variability can be linked to the geological environment. The analytical steps that were taken to model geological and cultural spaces at Cerro Baúl are also outlined in Chapter Three, including brief discussions of data interpolations and the application of remotely-sensed data. These tools are used to establish the physical and cultural contexts of lithic material use throughout the analysis and are also addressed in later chapters.

Lithic material use can be divided into two basic strategies, one of which was the exploitation of local material. As such, the geological heterogeneity played an important role in determining the quality and character of material that was used archaeologically, and these geological environments and their relationship to archaeological contexts are described in Chapter 4.

The remaining chapters present and discuss the data for lithic artifacts, including local and exotic debitage (Chapter 5), the spatial dynamics of material use (Chapter 6), and finely flaked bifacial and unifacial implements (Chapter 7). These chapters develop the notion that material use at Cerro Baúl was strongly economically determined, more so than ethnically or culturally.

As this presentation of archaeological data deals only with one class of material, the implications for society and economy at Cerro Baúl are necessarily provisional, but it will constitute—I sincerely hope—a significant contribution to illuminate many aspects of a site that can truly be considered socially pluralistic and at the border between two major cultural entities. Such a topic—the understanding of intercultural border dynamics—is relevant for any age and is vital particularly for understanding the development and quality of Wari and Tiwanaku during the Middle Horizon.

Chapter 2: Archaeological Background

The Site of Cerro Baúl

The Cerro Baúl Archaeological Zone sits in the upper Osmore Drainage of southern Peru, above the modern city of Moquegua (Figure 2.1). The zone is a constellation of archaeological sites with contemporaneous occupations primarily during the Middle Horizon (ca. AD 500–1000) and which are dispersed along an inter-valley ridge between the Tumilaca and Torata Rivers. Including the core site of Cerro Baúl, the archaeological community included several other spatially discrete but culturally and temporally related settlements within this same inter-valley area. In addition, two adjacent hills, Cerro Mejia and Cerro Petroglifo, also were occupied at this time.

Cerro Baúl has been organized by archaeologists into fourteen sectors (Figure 2.2). The site is unique for the Middle Horizon, as it perhaps was the only site cohabited by residents from two coeval but otherwise separate polities, the Wari and Tiwanaku. Based on the character and type of archaeological deposits, each sector has been classified according to a functional type as well as the apparent cultural affiliation of the individuals that inhabited it (Table 2.1).

A preponderance of material that is technologically and stylistically similar to Wari artifacts throughout the Peruvian sierra can be found in most of the site sectors as well as at the archaeological sites at Cerro Mejia and Cerro Petroglifo (Moseley et al. 1991). Tumilaca material appears at discreet sites adjacent to the Cerro Baúl Archaeological Zone and is also interspersed with other residences at Cerro Baúl itself. Tumilaca is a local expression of Tiwanaku culture that has ties to earlier Tiwanaku settlements in Moquegua and in the Bolivian altiplano; its development may be linked to the declining influence of Tiwanaku away from its core area during the late in the Middle Horizon, ca. AD 950 (Bawden 1993: 51; Goldstein 1989). The cohabitation of Cerro Baúl late in the Middle Horizon by Wari and Tumilaca peoples could signify a geopolitical shift in residence related to Tiwanaku's declining eminence (e.g., Williams and Nash 2002).

The summit of Cerro Baúl, Sectors A–E, was the administrative, ritual, and social core of the settlement (Williams 2001: 70–71). These sectors have yielded some of the oldest age determinations, with calibrated radiocarbon dates at a two sigma range of AD 600–685. Occupation continued until the late 10th century, with an intermediate remodeling phase ca. AD 800 (Williams 2001: 78). Structures in these sectors are large, of well built masonry construction, and are more formal in their delimitation of space than structures found in other parts of the site. They are multiroomed and demonstrate the orthogonal cellular architecture indicative of Wari sites (e.g., Isbell and McEwan 1991) or else incorporate large, open plazas or ceremonial D-shaped structures, also typical of Wari heartland architectural formulations.

The organization of space suggests that each sector was functionally different. Sectors E, D, and C have large open plazas and structures that would suggest a combined ritual and administrative function, the architecture and material culture of Sector B suggests that ritual activities were particularly important in these sectors, and the preponderance of material culture from Sector A indicates that this area was residential and a locus of specialized artisanship (Williams 2001: 71, Williams and Nash 2002: 250–251). Sector A, on the eastern half of the summit, is one of the more intensively explored at Cerro Baúl, and is particularly important as this is where Units 7, 9, 24, and 25—from which lithic artifacts were analyzed—are located (Figure 2.3). Based on ceramic stylistic criteria, all these contexts appear to have been inhabited by Wari occupants.

Unit 9 is a complex of six rectilinear rooms that surround a central open patio. The range of artifacts recovered from each of these rooms suggests that space in Unit 9 was organized by different activities, but that overall the complex was domestic in character (Williams and Ruales 2002: 19–31, 2004: 9–20). A number of the rooms were apparently sleeping areas, while others likely served as storage areas or workspaces. Because of a density of large grinding stones and hearth features, Room F almost certainly was a domestic kitchen area. Ceramic types vary across the complex but are in keeping with what might be expected of a domestic context. Because of the large size of Unit 9, the excavators have assumed that this was an elite Wari residence.

Unit 7 is "appreciably different" from other sites in Sector A (Williams 2001: 77). It is more rustic in character and smaller, consisting of two constrained spaces. A large quantity of undecorated wares, botanical remains, and faunal materials were found in this space, as well as several large grinding stones and a significant quantity of debris from the working of local minerals and obsidian (Williams 2001: 77). Unit 7, consequently, is interpreted as the residence of craftspeople or attendants that were auxiliary to the nearby elite residences of the summit (Williams and Ruales 2002: 16).

Lithic material from only one room in Unit 24, room 24A, was analyzed. This space is fairly small, but is notable for a large number of features that cut through its floor. Most of these features were filled with botanical remains, including high numbers of pepper tree (*Schinus molle*) seeds and lithic artifacts, all of which appear to be domestic refuse. This context likely was a residence of fairly high status, and portions of this residence were converted into disposal spaces in the later phases of its occupation (Williams and Ruales 2004: 21–31).

In contrast, Unit 25 was an open patio space surrounded by a bench that had an uncertain function. Towards the western edge, there was a small recessed area approximately 3 m? that may have functioned as an *audencia*. An extremely high density of ceramic material was recovered in this excavation unit. In all, an administrative function is suggested for this space (Williams and Ruales 2004: 31–33), though the high density of ceramics in addition to the lithic evidence indicates that a substantial amount of economic activity also took place here. Unit 25 is the only context from which lithic materials were analyzed that does not appear to have been residential and may have had multiple functions, while serving primarily as a locus of administration.

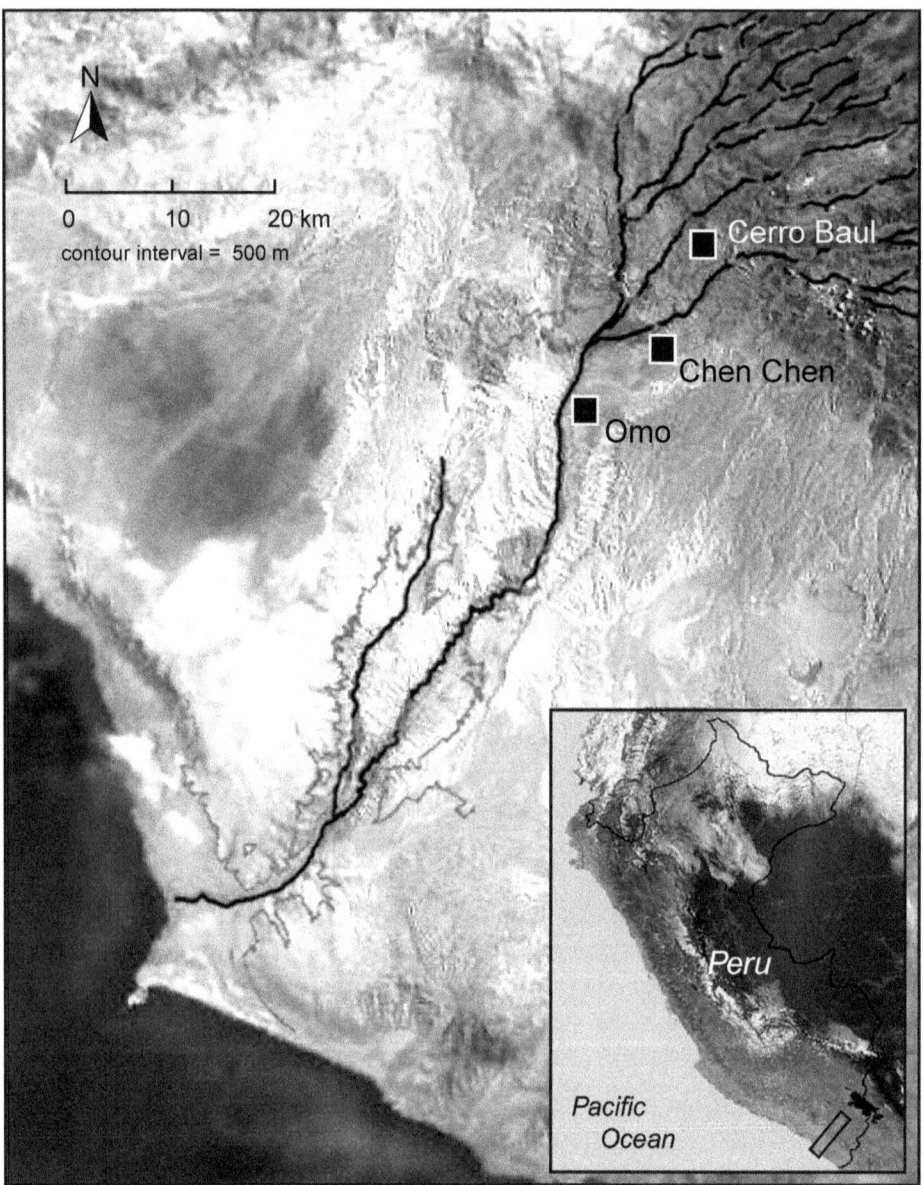

Figure 2.1: The Osmore Drainage and major archaeological sites. The location of the Osmore Drainage in southern Peru is given in the inset.

The character of the domestic contexts changes as one moves away from the summit. Structures become smaller and more ephemeral, and are frequently only indicated by terrace remnants.

Material from two units in Sector F was analyzed, Units 23 and 32 (Figure 2.4). This sector consists of a series of domestic terraces and structures that flank the access route up the northeast slope of the *cerro*. Aside from the summit itself, this is one of the more dense residential sectors. Unit 23 is one of these domestic structures, with very little material culture associated with it. That material which was found was quotidian and utilitarian in quality, and the features suggest that Unit 23 was inhabited by Tumilaca residents (Williams and Ruales 2002: 63). Unit 32 is also a domestic terrace. The overall quantity and quality of the ceramic and other artifactual materials also suggest a low status household. Throughout the stratigraphic sequence at Unit 32, excavators encountered ceramics that they attributed to the Tumilaca culture (Williams and Ruales 2004:62).

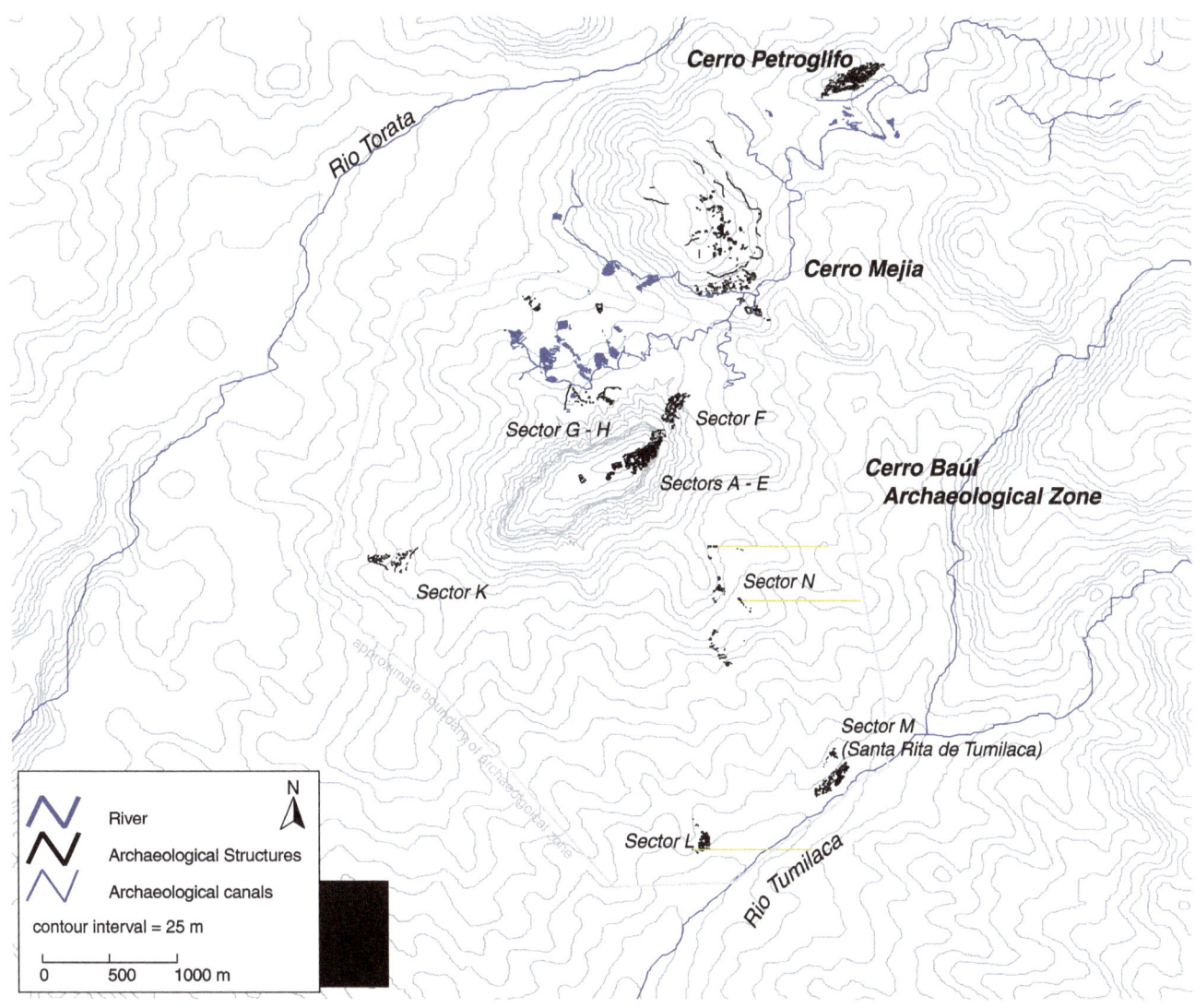

Figure 2.2: Map of the Cerro Baul Archaeological Zone, and adjacent Middle Horizon sites.

Sector H is a less densely populated area also along the north slope of Cerro Baúl (Figure 2.5). Several units have been excavated in this area over various seasons, and evidence for side by side Wari and Tumilaca occupation has been found. Unit 21 is a series of three small domestic rooms on a fairly well preserved terrace that were burned at the time of their abandonment. Botanical remains and features are well preserved, and these remains indicate a domestic function to the space. An unusual aspect of Unit 21 that is notable is a very high density of lithic materials in general, and specifically of lapidary beads and projectile points, to which I will return later. The excavators have interpreted Unit 21 as a Wari residence (Williams and Ruales 2002: 57). Unit 22, on the other hand, yielded Tumilaca style ceramics. Unit 22 had what appear to have been external, exposed terraces and sheltered domestic spaces. The overall amount of material and number of features is nominal, and it is difficult to characterize the context beyond that of a low-status Tumilaca residence (Williams and Ruales 2002: 59).

Sector L, where Units 19 and 20 are located, is one of the farthest from the summit of Cerro Baúl and sits on a Quaternary alluvial terrace just above the Tumilaca River (Figure 2.6). Sector L is a fairly tightly-nucleated settlement on several remnant terraces, and based on the material culture from several excavation units it can be said with confidence that this was almost entirely a Tumilaca community.

Unit 19 appears to have served as a domestic space dedicated to the storage, cooking, and preparation of comestibles. It is a fairly small space where large quantities of ceramic sherds and organic ash were found; sleeping and other activity space was very limited and so this context probably served almost exclusively as a type of kitchen area (Williams and Ruales 2002: 66). Similarly, Unit 20 is part

Table 2.1: Excavated units from Cerro Baúl Archaeological Zone and interpretation[1].

Sector	Unit	Location	Ethnic affiliation (inferred from ceramic types)	Function (inferred from architecture)
B	1	Baúl, summit	Wari	administrative
A	2	Baúl, summit	Wari	residential/industrial
C	3	Baúl, summit	Wari	ceremonial?
B	4	Baúl, summit	Wari	administrative
B	5	Baúl, summit	Wari	ceremonial
C	6	Baúl, summit	Wari	administrative
A	7*	Baúl, summit	Wari	residential/industrial
B	8	Baúl, summit	Wari	administrative
A	9*	Baúl, summit	Wari	residential
C	10	Baúl, summit	Wari	ceremonial
A	11	Baúl, summit	Wari?	residential?
A	12	Baúl, summit	Wari	residential
E	13	Baúl, summit	Wari?/Inka?	ceremonial
E	14	Baúl, summit	Wari?/Inka?	ceremonial
J	15	Baúl, slope	?	non-domestic
G	16	Baúl, slope	Tiwanaku/Tumilaca	residential
H	17	Baúl, slope	Tiwanaku/Tumilaca	residential
L	18	Tumilaca	Tiwanaku/Tumilaca?	mortuary
L	19*	Tumilaca	Tiwanaku/Tumilaca	residential
L	20*	Tumilaca	Tiwanaku/Tumilaca	residential
H	21*	Baúl, slope	Wari	residential
H	22*	Baúl, slope	Tiwanaku/Tumilaca	residential
F	23*	Baúl, slope	Tiwanaku/Tumilaca	residential
A	24*	Baúl, summit	Wari	residential
A	25*	Baúl, summit	Wari	adminstrative
C	26	Baúl, summit	Wari	ceremonial
N	27*	el Tenedor	Wari/Tumilaca	residential
N	28*	el Tenedor	Wari/Tumilaca	residential
K	29	P. Arrestrado	Wari	residential
K	30	P. Arrestrado	Wari	residential
K	31	P. Arrestrado	Wari	residential
F	32*	Baúl, slope	Wari	residential
	33			
	34			
I	35	La Cantera	Tiwanaku/?	ceremonial
I	36	La Cantera	Tiwanaku/?	ceremonial
I	37	La Cantera	Tiwanaku/?	ceremonial

* indicates unit from which lithic materials have been analyzed

[1] Information taken from Williams and Ruales 2002, 2004.

of a domestic complex that possibly included three other adjacent terraces. More generalized domestic refuse was found in this space—including faunal remains, botanical remains, ceramics, lithics, and a few hearth features—implying that a range of activities occurred within it. Food preparation may have been a key activity, but others were certainly also accommodated (Williams and Ruales 2002: 69).

Sector N is on the summit of a high elevation isolated from other portions of the archaeological zone by steeply incised drainages. This hill is called *Cerro Baulcito* on topographical maps, and the archaeological site has variably been referred to by this name or as *el Tenedor*. Two units were excavated in Sector N, Units 27 and 28, and several surface collections were made (Figure 2.7). Exactly who the occupants of el Tenedor were is not unequivocally clear, but the site is certainly Middle Horizon. The excavators have suggested that the site was occupied by Tumilaca residents.

Unit 27 was a small domestic space with an interior room and an exterior plaza. The density of artifacts in Unit 27 was low, but those that did appear were of a rustic and domestic quality. Unit 28 had even fewer artifacts. The terrace walls of this unit were very rustic, and it appears to have been an agricultural terrace rather than an inhabited structure. El Tenedor, thus, is a site of residential and agricultural structures that were likely used by the same Tumilaca occupants. From the size and quality of the constructions, it appears that their occupants enjoyed a marginally more affluent lifestyle than the occupants of other sectors (for example, Sectors H and F) but which did not approach the lifestyle typical on the summit of Cerro Baúl (Williams and Ruales 2004: 45–51).

Across the Cerro Baúl zone, the social landscape was comprised of both Wari and Tumilaca residents. It is not precisely clear when the Tumilaca settlement was initiated, but Williams and Nash propose a late Middle Horizon date that

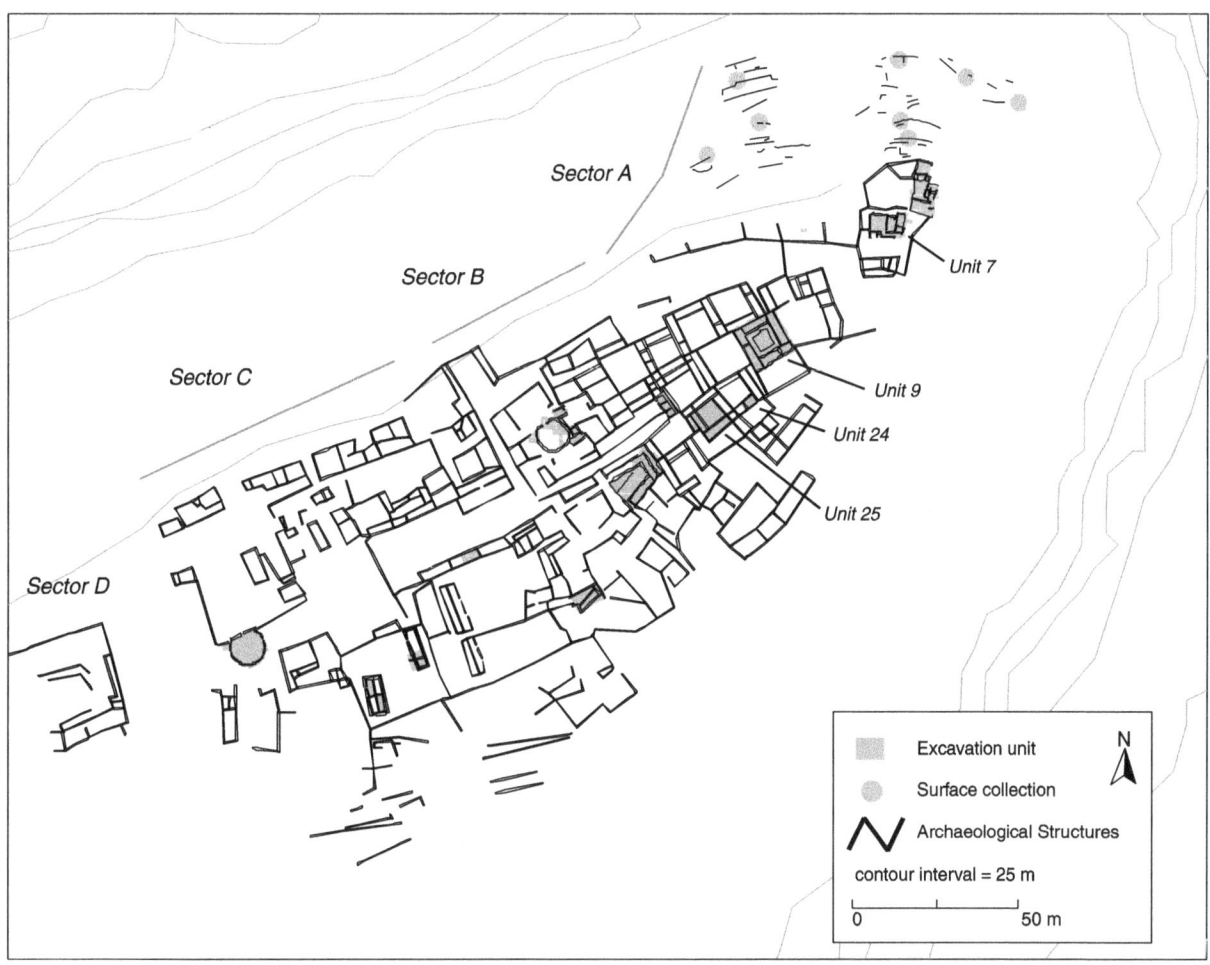

Figure 2.3: Map of Sectors A through D, Cerro Baúl Archaeological Zone.

coincides with a well-established Wari presence at Cerro Baúl and late phases of other Tiwanaku settlements in the mid-valley (2002: 248). It may coincide with a period of reconstruction and social restructuring on the summit of Cerro Baúl ca. AD 800 (Williams 2001; Williams and Nash: 2002: 259). The changes in the Moquegua Valley around AD 800, including the appearance of Tumilaca groups, may derive from incipient social balkanization or economic tensions that developed within and between the mature Wari and Tiwanaku colonies (Williams 2002: 372). In this case, the Wari and Tumilaca cohabitation of Cerro Baúl might suggest that alliances and the norms that defined social interaction had shifted away from cultural boundaries to other considerations, such as political or economic motivations.

Polity interaction in the Middle Horizon

The character of the Andean Middle Horizon (ca. AD 500–1000) Wari and Tiwanaku polities, particularly in regard to the relationship between the two as well as their relationships to other ethnic or cultural groups, is incompletely understood. This relationship has been the focus of considerable research in their respective cultural cores and territorial peripheries. The models that describe the interaction between Wari and Tiwanaku settlements focus primarily on expressions of ethnic difference and on the assumption that political tensions existed between the contemporaneous cultural groups. The particulars of this interaction are of interest not only for understanding the cultural environment of the Moquegua Valley, the only area for which there is known archaeological evidence for contemporaneous and adjacent Wari and Tiwanaku inhabitation, but also for understanding the mechanisms whereby the Wari and Tiwanaku states accommodated diverse cultural groups (and vice versa) during their expansion and subsequent periods.

Iconographic elements on Middle Horizon ceramics suggest for Wari and Tiwanaku a common ideology derived from a shared inspiration, but with some bellicose interactions (Ochatoma and Romero 2002; Isbell and Cook 2002: 297). While disagreeing on the importance of militaristic and defensive behavior, several interpretations propose that the two existed in distinct spheres of activity with minimal overlap or cultural admixture (Moseley et al. 1991, Feldman 1989, Goldstein and Owen 2001, Owen 1994). This contrasts with the increasing archaeological evidence from the upper Moquegua Valley (between approximately 2000 and

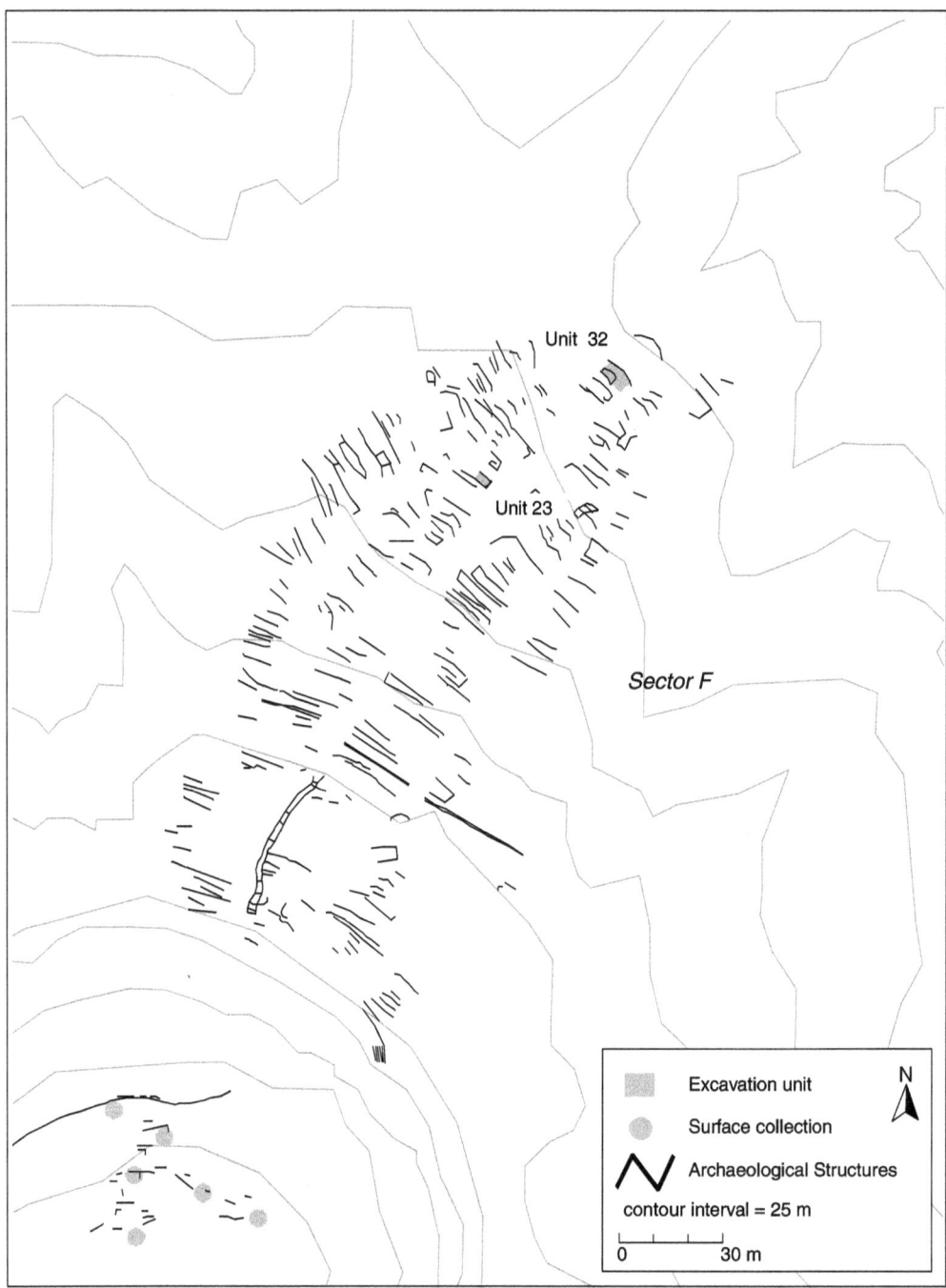

Figure 2.4: Map of Sector F, Cerro Baul Archaeological Zone.

3500 masl) that these polities did not maintain themselves in strict isolation but were in regional communication and cohabited the same valley system (Williams, Isla, and Nash 2001; Owen and Goldstein 2001; Owen 1994). The probability that dynamic interchange and historic change occurred as a result increases as this evidence accrues.

A complex constellation of stylistic and ideological similarities—and differences—confuses the origins of these two groups and hence their development in relation to one another. Tiwanaku frequently is given temporal priority as either the locus of origin for ideas that are also expressed in Wari iconography or else as an earlier crystallization of ideological constructs derived from antecedent traditions that were subsequently important to both Middle Horizon cultures. Ceramic decoration at Conchopata seemingly derived from Tiwanaku would suggest the former hypothesis, but it is associated with relatively late dates. The latter is a more

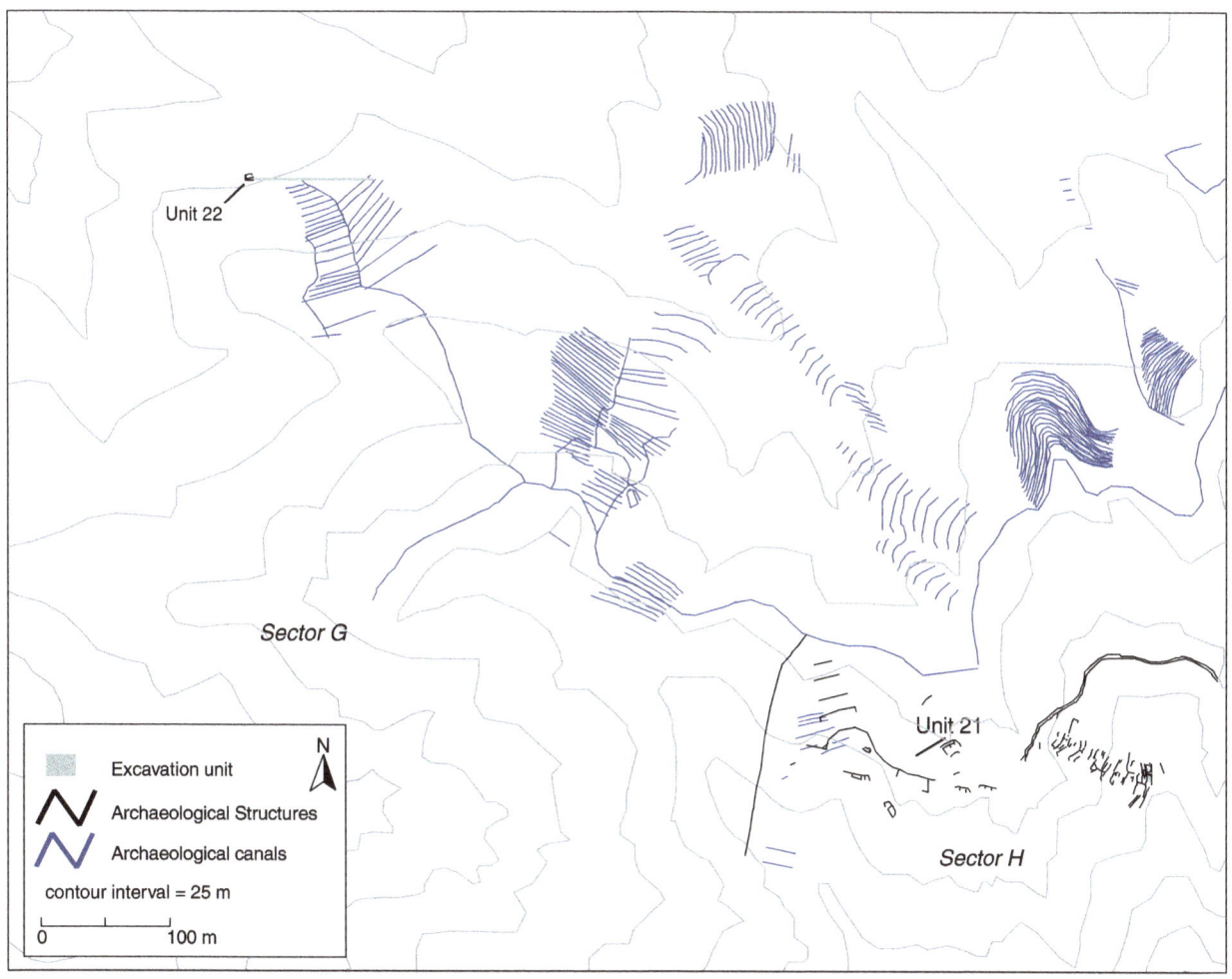

Figure 2.5: Map of Sector H, Cerro Baul Archaeological Zone.

likely scenario (Isbell and Cook 2002: 296; Ochatoma and Romero 2002) and the Wari culture certainly was the result of multiple central Peruvian cultural sequences, just as Tiwanaku developed out of altiplano cultural traditions further to the south and east. The significance of early coastal Peruvian cultures such as Nazca as well as the highland Huarpa must be carefully considered and acknowledged when considering Wari as a distinct entity with its own developmental history (Shady Solís 1988: 73).

More significant for this analysis are the mechanisms of Wari expansion—imperialistic or otherwise—and how inter-polity relationships were initiated and maintained. A significant element of Wari expansion, whether as an advertent strategy or not, was the interaction of socio-cultural elites and the development of synthetic elite styles.

The evidence of Wari expansion beyond Ayacucho is manifested at several sites, and suggests a cohesive endeavor to establish a strong presence in the north-central and south-central Peruvian sierra (Figure 2.8). Scholars disagree as to the extent that Wari expansion represents the spread of a rigid socio-political structure via "conquest and consolida-

tion," with local groups capitulating to an imperial regime—a common model of Wari culture (Schreiber 1987, see Isbell and Cook 2002: 251). Schreiber interprets the evidence that local communities in the Carhuarzo Valley were reorganized and consolidated, ca. AD 600, as reflecting an imperial agenda to coerce local labor into intensified agrarian production. The intensified production provided staple-finance support for the local administrative center of Jincamocco, as well as for Wari sites in Ayacucho (1987: 282). Other Wari centers may have been constructed to satisfy similar motives, particularly to compel the itinerant residence of local populations while they fulfilled state-oriented labor obligations in a manner comparable to that of the Incan *mit'a* tribute system (Anders 1989: 43; McEwan 1991: 117; see also Schreiber 1992). Alternative hypotheses propose that the Wari phenomenon is more indicative of a horizon of local acquiescence to exogenous technological and economic developments that spread within a package of an ideological rubric (e.g., Williams, Isla, and Nash 2001, Glowacki and Malpass 2003: 433–434). While state agendas may have been driving factors, positive local response to the cultural, economic, and technological perquisites that accompanied the more integrated socio-cultural order ensured its

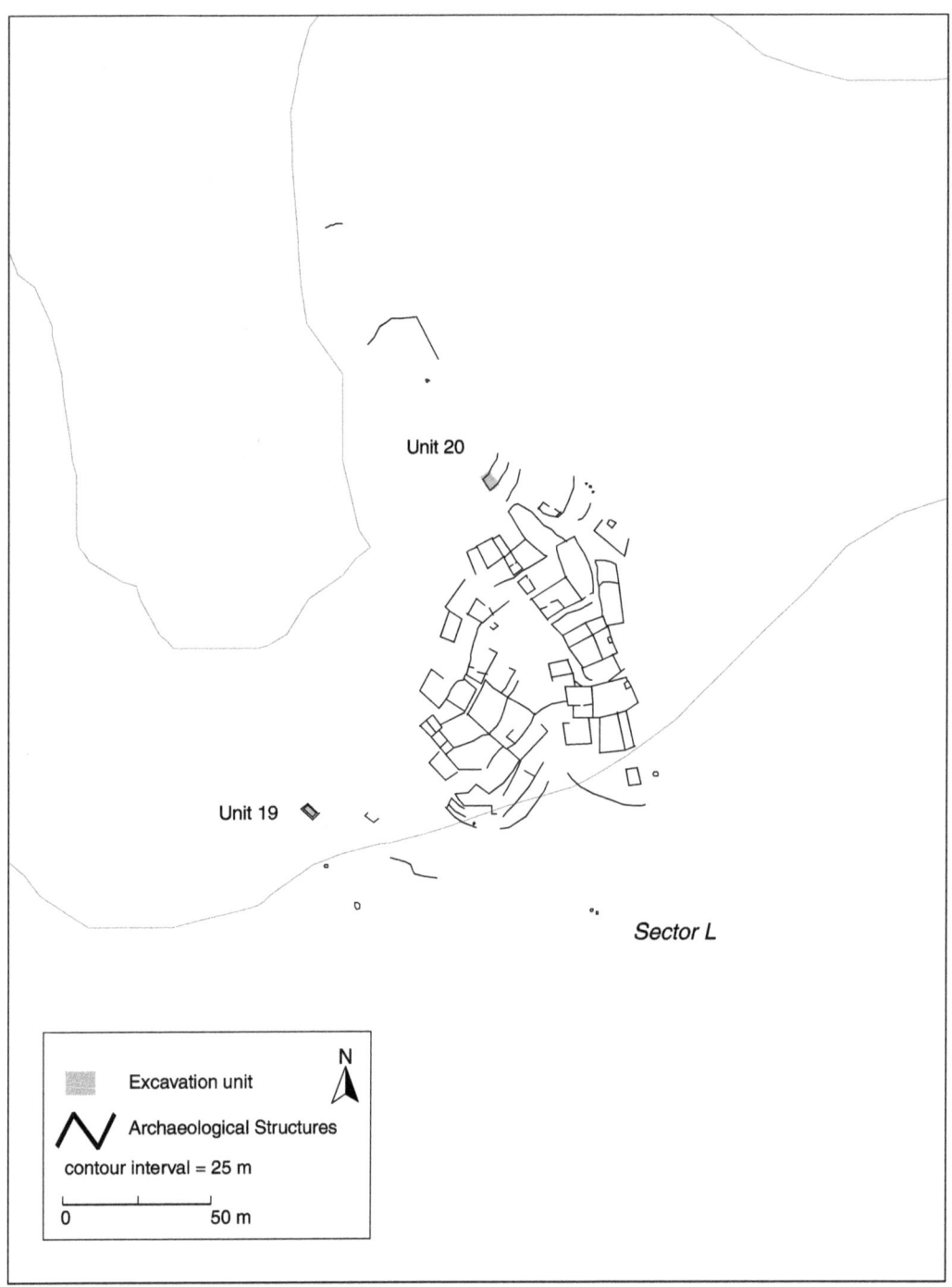

Figure 2.6: Map of Sector L, Cerro Baul Archaeological Zone.

spread and establishment. The short chronological window of the Middle Horizon 1B epoch when many Wari sites were constructed and populations established—perhaps with the exceptions of Viracochapampa and Pikillacta (Topic 1991: 161; Glowacki and McEwan 2001: 44)—supports the contention that Wari expanded out of Ayacucho and into other central Andean regions with an organized, imperialistic effort (Williams 2001: figure 11; Anders 1989: 46). The replication of the size-rank site hierarchy described for the Ayacucho Valley (Isbell and Schreiber 1978) at Wari sites in the Moquegua and Cuzco Valleys, ostensibly for the purposes of direct administrative oversight, further suggests that Wari expansion was part of a cohesive agenda that treated the problem of hierarchical interactions between local and

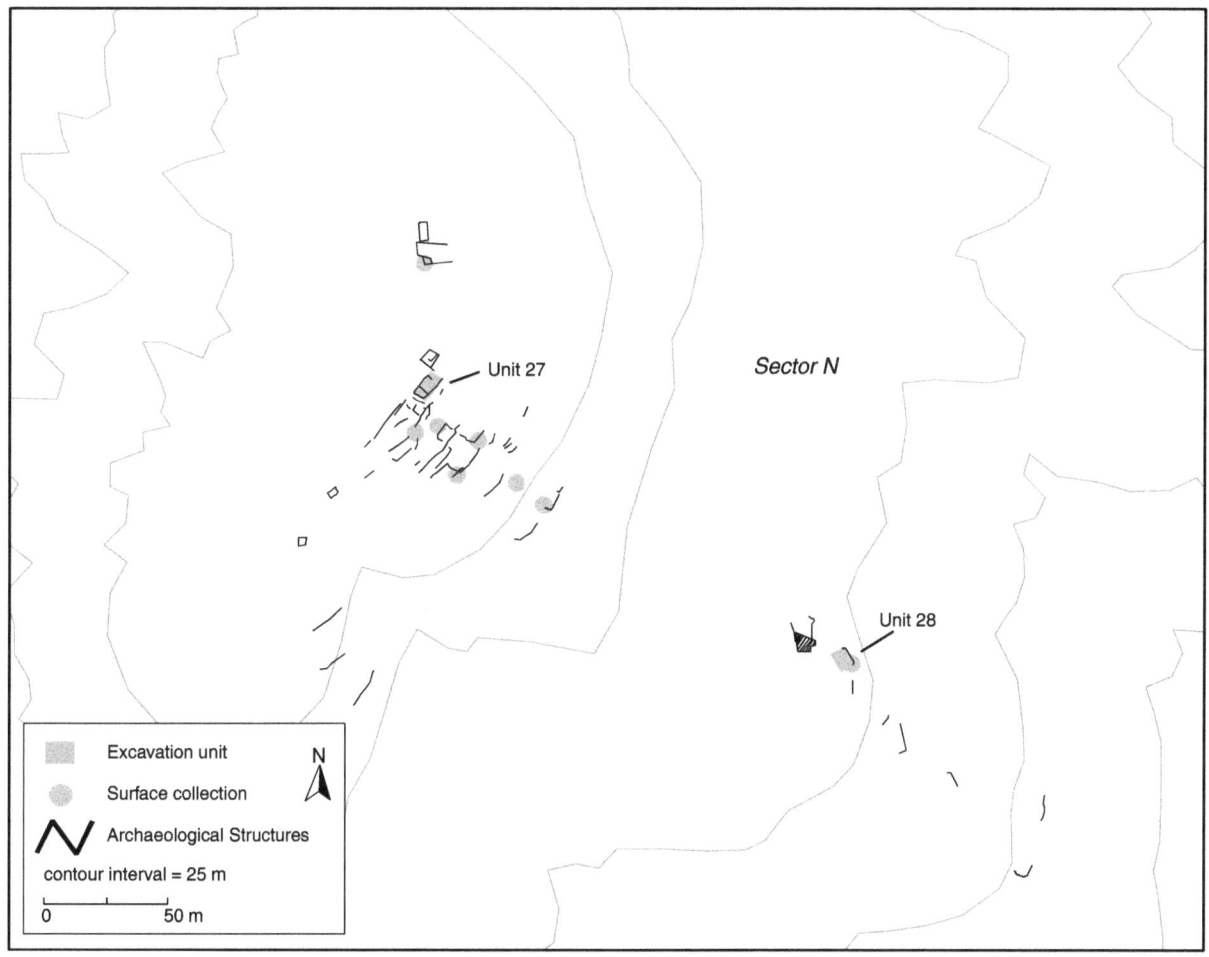

Figure 2.7: Map of Sector N, Cerro Baúl Archaeological Zone.

distant networks with a consistent approach to administering settlements (Williams and Nash 2002; Glowacki and McEwan 2001).

Despite similarities, differences among the sites indicate that the way the Wari manifested themselves was neither constant nor monolithic but could assume distinctive iterations. The organization of Cerro Baúl has several architectural likenesses to the Ayacucho sites of Huari[1] and Conchopata (Williams 2001: 70–71; Isbell and Cook 2002), inviting its characterization as a "site-unit intrusion" of Wari presence and organized state formulae into the Moquegua Valley (Feldman 1989: 76, Moseley et al. 1991: 131; Williams and Nash 2002: 245). This spatial organization is not followed at other sites, however, such as Viracochapampa, Azangaro, Pikillacta, and Jincamocco. These settlements all exhibit decidedly more rigid and standardized rectilinear-orthogonal plans that derive (but significantly depart) from the cellular-orthogonal organization seen in Ayacucho and Moquegua (Topic 1991; Anders 1989: 187; McEwan 1991, 1996: 171; Schreiber 1991). Importantly, these sites share great similarity in their organization and they may be related to a discrete class of planned settlement implemented during particular phases of Wari expansion.

The evident variability in both site organization schemes and concomitant material culture suggests that Wari expansion was not homogenous but had situational manifestations responsive to the dynamics of regionalized interactions and localized conditions. There is little to suggest that conquest and consolidation of local populations under imperial organization were, in fact, the *raison d'être* of Wari expansionism. Rather, the establishment of sites along major north-south routes of communication (Topic 1991: 162; Glowacki and McEwan 2001) and within ecotones between 2500 and 3600 masl conducive to maize cultivation on terrace agricultural systems (Schreiber 1987, 1992: 278; Williams and Nash 2002: 244, 254–256; Williams 1997) implies that Wari expansion was strongly motivated by economic concerns that sought to intensify trade relationships and agrarian production. Reorganization was an impact of the introduction of Wari settlements, but it is not certain that the reorganization was precipitated by political domination rather than new economic structures. With the influence of Wari

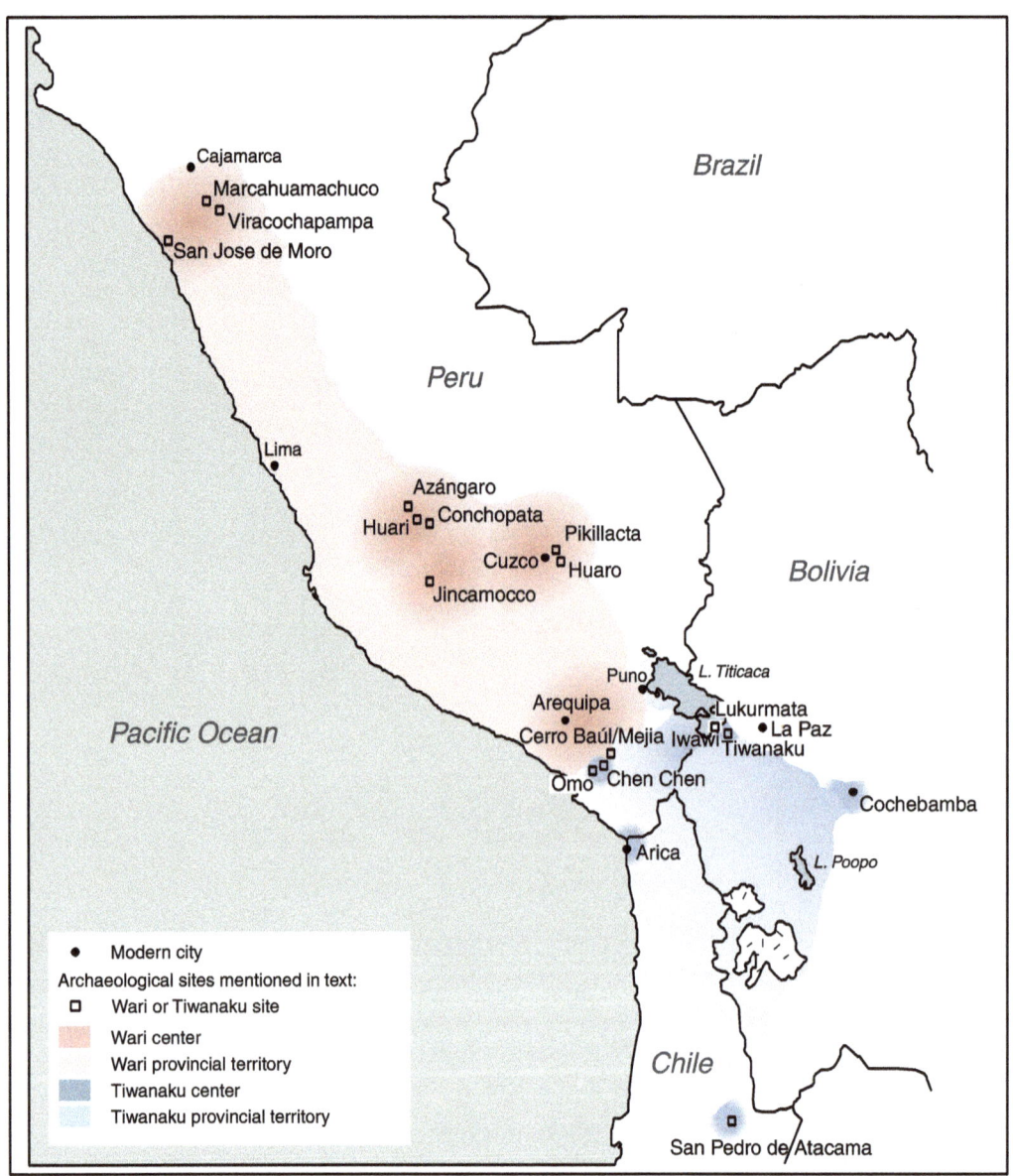

Figure 2.8: Map of the Central Andean area, showing Middle Horizon sites mentioned in the text, and proposed core and provincial territories. Modified from National Geographic source.

expansion, local groups were not truncated but appear to have participated in the introduced organization while maintaining autochthonous traits (e.g., Anders 1989). Changes that were precipitated by a Wari presence did not carry evenly across the social spectrum but rather reflect the more intense interaction of socio-cultural elites.

Schreiber indicates that a Wari presence is not strongly apparent in the quotidian aspects of Carhuarzo material culture, even at sites established after the occupation of Jincamocco, and, despite the argument for direct political control, Wari would be essentially invisible in an analysis of utilitarian materials alone (1992: 263–264). Changes in utilitarian material cultural under the influence are underemphasized, while some of the greatest differences are apparent in the material culture used by higher-status individuals.

Moreover, the presence of Wari within a region is not a certain indication of consolidation under an overriding Wari sphere of influence. Topic (1991: 161–162) proposes that an intense and mutual relationship was maintained by Wari and Huamachuco at Viracochapampa based principally on trade and economic exchange. Huamachuco maintained its autonomy prior to, during, and after the Wari culture became established at Viracochapampa and other sites within the region. Huamachuco and Wari groups not only cohabited but engaged in mutually cooperative efforts, ultimately contributing to hybridized construction styles and practices (Topic 1991: 162–163) that in turn may have served as the inspiration for the orthogonal architectural style that was to become indicative of Wari organization (Shady Solís 1988: 79; c.f. Nash 2003; Czwarno 1989 about political motivations in Wari architecture).

In most instances the greatest indicators of contact and change between Wari and regional populations are seen in classes of elite materials and/or residential contexts. Non-Wari fineware ceramics that demonstrate elements of Tiwanaku-related design were found in late Middle Horizon ritual and elite residential contexts on the summit of Cerro Baúl (Williams, Isla, and Nash 2001: 81, figures 16, 19a, 19b). Concentrations of Wari fineware ceramics from Cerro Amaru were accompanied by non-Wari decorated wares in a context interpreted as a ritual deposit (Topic 1991: 162). The preponderance of evidence from the Carhuarzo Valley for stylistic change under the influence of a Wari presence occurs as an increase in the number of fineware decorated ceramics and their stylistic elaboration (Schreiber 1992: 264). McEwan similarly notes that the Lucre and Qotakalli decorated ceramic wares in the Cuzco Valley developed along separate trajectories as an emulation of Wari decorative styles and as a continuation of local traditions, respectively (1989: 55). At Huaro, also in Cuzco, Wari face-neck jars, an anthropomorphic ritual vessel form, illustrate a combination of Wari, Tiwanaku, and Nazca stylistic elements, as well as earlier Pukara traits (Glowacki 2002: 275 - 276). The hybridization of decorated ceramic wares, many of which may have served as media for conspicuous consumption among elites, testifies to the exchange of ideas and symbolic referents among elites of diverse backgrounds during Middle Horizon rituals.

Outside the territory of direct Wari presence, in the north coast, Wari influence occurs at San José de Moro (Figure 2.8) in the form of hybridized Mochica-Wari ceramic types that innovate upon established Mochica styles by manipulating polychrome and bichrome painting, Chakipampa-style iconographic elements, and form. Importantly, the known occurrence of these hybridized ceramics is limited almost exclusively to late Mochica elite contexts, roughly contemporaneous with the Middle Horizon 1 epoch (Castillo 2000). Shady Solís has proposed that Wari culture developed as a result of exchange along regionalized elite networks and a synthesis of stylistic traits from the Nazca 9, Nieveria, Moche V, and Cajamarca III traditions that ultimately resulted in the emergence of "styles of prestige" (1988: 77). This prestige culture was strongly expressed during Wari expansion.

A rather complex expression of prestige culture appears to have occurred at Azangaro (Figure 2.8) where a dualistically organized elite hierarchy was responsible for the administration and maintenance of the site that is unequivocally Wari in its architectural organization. Indications are, however, that a remote Wari administration relied on local elites as intermediaries who implemented and managed Wari policies by establishing reciprocal exchange networks between distant and local, ethnically-differentiated communities. These elites exercised relative autonomy, expressed by the "adoption of prestigious vessel forms from other areas, eschewing Wari ones" (Anders 1989: 43). Similarly, the limited presence of Tiwanaku fineware ceramics at Cerro Baúl may indicate the participation of Tiwanaku elites in ritual feasting events and the maintenance of regional inter-ethnic ties through wealth-finance exchange (Williams, Isla, and Nash 2001: 81).

The isolationism that Tiwanaku groups in the middle Osmore Drainage purportedly maintained is problematic to this model (Goldstein 1993: 43; Goldstein and Owen 2001: 159–161). Tiwanaku, like Wari, had expansive aspects and sites with clear cultural ties to Tiwanaku were established in highland Bolivia and Peru, the Bolivian lowlands, and the Peruvian and Chilean coasts (Figure 2.8: see Stanish 2002: 177 for review). Stanish posits that imperial strategies drove the expansion of Tiwanaku from a heartland and into colonial enclaves; this expansion was not territorial but selective, spreading along node-like sites and communication routes between them (2002: 190–191). Elite ceramic styles were used as expressions of cultural affinity, where local formulations were based on Tiwanaku canons (Stanish 2002: 189).

This expansion accommodated the inclusion of diverse ethnic groups and the negotiation of new identities at both provincial Tiwanaku centers and at the site of Tiwanaku itself (Janusek 1999; Stovel 2002). Social pluralism at these sites may have conformed to the mechanics of interaction assumed for Wari sites. At Tiwanaku and Lukurmata, disparate ethnic groups were integrated into larger networks through social modes of economic production. Ethnically defined groups manufactured specialized fineware ceramics that subsequently moved through defined networks of consumers; the social position of these ethnic subgroups was promoted within elite spheres by the "strategic distribution of valued goods to enhance their own power" (Janusek 1999: 109).

The two contemporaneous Tiwanaku settlements in the Moquegua Valley (at the sites of Omo and Chen Chen, Figure 2.1) have suggested to Goldstein and Owen (2001: 161) that the Tiwanaku polity was comprised of loosely confederated ethnic groups that were markedly socially segmented and maintained separate spheres of interaction. In contrast to the situation described elsewhere, there is little indication that diverse ethnic groups became integrated into these colonies of biological and cultural Tiwanaku. This includes limited or no interaction with the Wari settlements in the upper valley.

The appearance of Qosqopa Wari ceramics in a mortuary context at Chen Chen (Williams, Isla, and Nash 2001: 81) may be the only known archaeological evidence which refutes the contention that Wari and Tiwanaku colonies existed as geographically and socially distinct entities that did not interact. Owen and Goldstein (2001: 179) play down the significance of this, noting that Qosqopa ceramics bear more stylistic affinity to late Middle Horizon styles derived from Wari traditions and that these particular ceramics may have been curated for a considerable time before being deposited in a mortuary context. Regardless, the appearance of a Wari-derived ceramic style in the context of

Chen Chen-Tiwanaku interments raises the probability that social group mixing occurred in Moquegua, at least by the time of the late Middle Horizon.

The timing of this deposit places the appearance of Qosqopa ceramics at Chen Chen roughly contemporaneous with the appearance of Tumilaca settlements in the environs of Cerro Baúl. Arguably, the derivation of new styles and related changes in settlement patterns probably indicate some form of social reformulation that initiated during the late Middle Horizon 2 epoch.

While the exact factors in the emergence of the Tumilaca culture are unclear, this group is culturally and biologically related to Tiwanaku populations. As a cultural complex it can be securely linked to earlier and contemporaneous settlements at Chen Chen and Omo. Hence Tumilaca may be related to the overall Tiwanaku complex of sites and subgroups in Moquegua, perhaps as yet another confederated ethnic subgroup. Modified settlement patterns and household composition suggest that Tumilaca is somewhat socially unique when compared to other Tiwanaku groups, although the same generalized principles of household organization—a linear arrangement with specialized activity areas—does occur at both Omo and the later Tumilaca sites (Goldstein 1993: 31; Bawden 1993: 50). The variations on the Tiwanaku theme have also been noted at post-Tiwanaku settlements in the upper Osmore Drainage, suggesting a continuous and pervasive trend of cultural development (Bawden 1993: 51). Bawden interprets the Tumilaca phase of Tiwanaku culture in Moquegua as indicative of a new form of organization that accompanied a division of social structure and space according to ideas of hierarchy and specialization. The compartmentalization of domestic space that he sees during this period reflects a similar "compartmentalization" of interpersonal roles (1993: 53–54). Importantly and despite the suggestion of social segmentation, Bawden does not describe any evidence for non-domestic architecture or spaces (e.g., for administrative or ceremonial purposes) at the type-site of Santa Rita de Tumilaca (1993: 46–47), despite several instances of probable administrative and/or ritual architecture at adjacent Cerro Baúl.

Fineware imported drinking vessels (*keros* and portrait vessels) are consistently represented at Omo-Tiwanaku sites, comprising as much as 10 % of each household's ceramic assemblage. All households, not just socially elite ones, participated to some extent in a larger Tiwanaku exchange system and ritual-beverage ceremonialism (Goldstein 1993: 31, 35). Fineware ceramics comparable to Omo blackware are conspicuously underrepresented in Tumilaca assemblages, both at the type site and from Tumilaca settlements within the Cerro Baúl Archaeological Zone, however (Bawden 1993; Williams and Ruales 2001, 2002). In contrast, Tumilaca assemblages demonstrate greater variation in decoration and form than earlier Tiwanaku ceramic phases but also an overall lower quality of execution (Bawden 1993: 46–47). Deposits of Wari and Tumilaca material culture together, in addition to spatial cohabitation, have led to the proposal that the Tumilaca may represent a synthetic culture that can claim elements from both Tiwanaku and Wari (Williams and Nash 2002: 248). The paucity of fineware ceramics associated with Tumilaca sites and the co-occurrence of Tiwanaku and Wari fineware styles in summit ritual contexts at Cerro Baúl suggests that a spatial-political shift occurred in the late Middle Horizon that displaced the locus of polity interaction and ritual hosting responsibilities to the Wari site (Williams, Isla, and Nash 2001: 81). The lack of administrative architecture at Tumilaca sites but its presence in adjacent Wari sites at Cerro Baúl could also suggest that the ritual-political focus had shifted, and Tumilaca settlements in the vicinity of Cerro Baúl may have relied on the Wari site as a civic center that hosted the interaction of players from both societies. In addition to contributing to the crystallization of the Tumilaca as a culturally and socially defined group, Wari and Tiwanaku polity interaction may have contributed to the development of a prestige culture in the Moquegua valley that pivoted on the consumption and exchange of wealth-finance commodities and interaction within class-defined social settings.

Interaction and Prestige styles

The archaeological visibility of Wari influence mainly in decorative styles may be due to several causal factors, including the requisite fine resolution of data that limits the utility of quotidian artifacts when considering abstract social and cultural processes; "material-information interaction" is less obvious and socially encoded ideas are more elusive when utilitarian materials are considered (Gero 1989: 93). On the other hand, the apparent consistency with which hybridized and established fineware ceramics appear together demonstrates that Wari influence does not mandate a complete reformulation of cultural traditions but rather allows for both innovation and continuity to occur. This synthesis happens most apparently with non-utilitarian artifact classes and most particularly with ones that have a social function within elite or ritual frameworks.

This raises the probability of regionalized inter-ethnic interaction between Wari and local populations, at least at an elite level (where elaborated artifacts make this interaction more visible) and most likely at multiple levels of socioeconomic standing. The focus on elite interactions, particularly driven by ideological and economic motivations, could have contributed to the integration of groups with strong political and economic bases. This development fostered inter-polity contact and interaction at a regional scale and also along more extensive networks (Shady Solís 1988: 75). The involvement of socio-political elites in these contexts suggests individuals of multiple ethnicities engaged each other as members of a more socially-generalized prestige culture. That is, social networks were established at the level of economic or social divisions that crossed more stylistically explicit ethnic boundaries. The social organization of many Middle Horizon sites, thus, may have followed pluralistic criteria that accommodated interaction within networks of different scales and temperaments. Participation in multiple social spheres would have the greatest impact on patterns of material procurement and distribution within a site, since material would tend to vary greatest between socio-economic classes as opposed to along ethnic or other social boundaries. The most qualitative and quantitative differences would be found, then, between elite and non-elite. While the use of non-elite material culture may resonate with assumed ethnic boundaries, differences in the mechanics of obtaining and exploiting resources across this social category would be minimal, but would be substantively dissimilar across elite and non-elite categories. Williams and Nash (2002: 261) similarly interpret some of the more labor intensive architectural constructions at Cerro Baúl and neighboring Cerro Mejia as delimiting stratified, class-differentiated social spaces. In the later Middle Horizon, thus, we begin to see the development of new social formulations and the movement of prestige items across apparent ethnic boundaries in such a way that the anticipated and perceived disjunction of artifact styles in earlier periods becomes blurred. The material culture from Cerro Baúl subsequently is not clearly organizable on the basis of ethnic styles but rather more closely adheres to categorizations of prestige:quotidian and wealth:staple commodities. In lithic materials, the division between prestige and quotidian is more difficult to elucidate, but there are apparent differences in the scale of procurement networks and material usage that reflect probable economically-organized scalar divisions within this dichotomy. The end result is that the community at Cerro Baúl appears to have been socially segmented along economic-class divisions, and these divisions functioned alongside other criteria such as ethnic identity. Economy thus served as a mechanism to integrate households with diverse cultural backgrounds into a pluralistic community and also helped define social distance between residents.

---

[1] As the name of the type site and cultures for both Wari and Tiwanaku come from indigenous Quechua and Aymara languages, respectively, there was been some question as to which orthography most accurately represents a direct phonetic transliteration. As is the current convention, in this discussion "Wari" refers to the culture while "Huari" is maintained to differentiate the type site. "Tiwanaku" refers to both the culture and as well as the type site.

Chapter 3: Analytic Methods

Excavation and Recovery Strategy

The Proyecto Arqueológico Cerro Baúl has sampled archaeological deposits during five three-month excavation seasons in 1997, 1998, 2001, 2002 and in 2004 (Williams and Isla 1998; Williams 1999; Williams and Ruales 2002, 2004). Earlier investigations, in 1989 and 1993, sampled two areas in Sector A (Unidades 1 and 2) and provided a detailed map of the site based on the surface expression of architectural remains. The lithic artifacts analyzed and discussed in this study are from collections made during the 2001 and 2002 seasons. They were analyzed in a three-month study season from June to August of 2003. All the analyzed lithic material came from excavated deposits, although several surficial collections were also made during these years. Consequently, I am confident that these artifacts originated in the spatial contexts to which they are attributed and were minimally impacted by post-depositional effects.

A similar excavation strategy was applied to each excavation unit across the various sectors in order to promote coherence among data sets. Architectonic space is the basic analytical unit for each excavation, and it is assumed that this accurately reflects the activities of the social unit—typically the household—that used and inhabited that space. The minimal sampling unit, both for the excavations of the deposits and for subsequent analyses, is one meter square (1 m^2).

Architectural remains are apparent on the surface of most site loci, either as complete constellations of walls or, at a minimum, as preserved terrace remnants. Excavation units were oriented to conform to the main axis of the structure(s) that were judgmentally selected for sampling (Williams and Ruales 2002: 6, 2004: 5). Horizontal control was achieved by positioning a grid of 1 m^2 units over the apparent architectural space, oriented along its main axis and bounded along any side by the remains of walls. The excavation unit was subdivided when breaks in cultural space were found, such as interior walls or other delimitations. Each meter grid-square received a unique number, was excavated individually, and determined the horizontal provenience of the excavated materials. The position of individual diagnostic artifacts was also occasionally recorded and point-plotted on field documents. As a result, the distribution of artifacts can be reconstructed to approximately one meter accuracy.

A consistent stratigraphic sequence has been found on the summit of Cerro Baúl during several seasons of excavation. This sequence is comprised of both natural and cultural strata whose composition and order vary little between excavation units (Table 3.1). The deposits were excavated following these natural levels, and they constituted the basic units of vertical spatial control. In instances where a single stratum exceeds 30 cm in depth, the stratum was judgmentally subdivided into levels that are 10–20 cm in depth, using criteria such as changes in color or composition whenever possible to ensure that excavation levels follow natural levels. The stratigraphic sequences for non-summit archaeological contexts are different but were treated using a similar protocol. Each artifact's three-dimensional provenience, hence, was determined by its stratigraphic position within natural levels and its horizontal position within the 1 meter grid.

This protocol for spatial control changes when an archaeological feature with a distinct quality and circumscribed extent was encountered. In this case, the artifacts' proveniences were documented relative to the spatial extent and the stratigraphic sequence of the feature rather than the general stratigraphic sequence of the excavated context.

For most deposits, a coarse screen of 0.6 cm was used to recover artifacts that were not found during the process of excavation. For features and deposits close to occupation floors, however, a finer screen of 0.1 cm was used to recover artifacts. A one-liter sediment sample from each stratum was also collected from 1 out of 5 grid squares as a column sample; one-liter samples were also taken from each grid square immediately above occupation floors and features. Macro- and microscopic lithic artifacts are frequently found in these sediment samples. They typically include small retouch flakes of local material and, more rarely, obsidian (Goldstein 2004). At Tiwanaku, Giesso has demonstrated that microlithics reveal important domestic patterns of chert and obsidian use and artifact production that are not apparent when examining only macroartifacts (Giesso 2003: 369–372). While these micro-lithics are an important category of evidence for reconstructing prehistoric economic behavior, they have yet to be systematically analyzed and provide only a provisional indication of some activity areas.

Artifact Analytic Criteria

A sample of artifacts (N=1,979) in the collection of the Museo Contisuyu formed the analysis. This collection represents one hundred percent of the lithic artifacts from twelve excavation contexts on the summit and slopes of Cerro Baúl, and includes both lithic debitage (Appendix A) and flaked lithic artifacts (Appendix B). Groundstone artifacts, while sampled, are not discussed in this analysis. The sampling strategy was not random, but rather was judgmental, and these contexts were selected in order to try to characterize the spectrum of archaeological contexts that had been excavated during previous seasons. Consequently, the range of sampled units is geographically disperse, are located in the different site sectors, and ostensibly represents the range of socio-economic and cultural variability within the Middle Horizon components of the Cerro Baúl Archaeological Zone (see Table 2.1).

The analytical criteria considered several natural and cultural features of these artifacts, including material type, categories of technological data, and descriptive morphological characteristics for both lithic debitage and implements (Appendix C). Individual raw material types were described on the basis of their petrography according to hand samples, with special attention paid to the composition of locally-available material: this is discussed in more detail below. Technological criteria included the stage and type of reduction in order to characterize the decision-making process in the production of lithic artifacts (e.g., Inizan et al. 1999; Whittaker 1994; Sliva 1997). Morphological criteria were selected to characterize the shape and edge-terminations of the overall artifact, the form of the distal and proximal portions, and metrical data for the length, width, and thickness

Table 3.1: Typical stratigraphic sequence for archaeological deposits at Cerro Baúl (from Williams and Ruales 2002, 2004)

Stratum	Stratigraphic relationship	Average thickness	Composition
Capa S	Superficial stratum that overlies archaeological deposits	c. 5–8 cm	Brown aeolian sand and silt that intermixed with light gravel, architectural rubble, disturbed archaeological materials and modern/historic cultural material
Capa A	Near-surface stratum that underlies Capa S and overlies Capa B; in many instances it is also intrusive into depressions/molds in Capa B.	variable: layered deposits c. 2–3 cm deep intrusive; pockets ≤ 8 cm	Light grey, silicious volcanic ash from the AD 1600 Huaynaputina eruption; stratum is frequently discontinues and preserved only in areas sheltered from deflation; artifacts are minimal, not in situ, and occasionally represent different time periods
Capa B	Underlies Capa S and Capa A (where extant) and overlies Capa C	c. 40–70 cm	Brown to beige sand mixed with materials from architectural rubble, including large cobbles and quantities of eroded clay-mud; artifacts are common, and become larger in size and better preserved downwards into stratum. With the exception of intrusive deposits, most are Middle Horizon. Signs of burning frequently appear in lower levels.
Capa B_2	A subdivision of Capa B when this stratum exceeds ~ 30 cm in thickness	dependent on depths of Capa B; generally ≤ 20 cm	Subdivision of Capa B with similar composition. Proportion of cobbles from architectural rubble tends to decrease as proportion of clay-mud artifacts increases; artifacts are generally larger, better preserved, and occasionally inarticulated clusters.
Capa C	Underlies Capa B and overlies Capa D	c. 3–5 cm	Varies according to context. Frequently a thin stratum of organic ash and dense artifact clusters immediately above the occupied floor. Preservationis good with frequent articulated artifact clusters and abundant botanical remains.
Capa D	Underlies Capa C and is frequently the terminal stratum	Variable; floors and related deposits are generally c. 5–7 cm	Varies according to context. Frequently the occupied floor constructed of compacted, clay-rich sediments or stone paving (which may have mud-plaster treatment). Artifacts well preserved and often *in situ*

of the artifact at its widest point. These criteria were designed specifically to focus on attributes of flaked lithic artifacts. While they were also applied to groundstone implements, they are less suited for describing this category of artifacts.

Comprehensive or well developed formal typologies have yet to be established for Middle Horizon lithic artifacts. The limited and often generalized discussion of lithic types have referred to artifacts of "Wari" or "Tiwanaku" styles: frequently, these artifacts are described only as small, triangular points with stemmed or concave bases (see Giesso 2003: 374–375, 379; Giesso 2000: Chapter 4, 320; Bencic 2000: 98; Burger, Chavéz and Chavéz: 339–343; Goldstein 1993 figure 3.7a; Seddon 1994: figures 172–174). One aim of the analysis was to work towards constructing a descriptive topology to contribute to a more convincing discussion of Middle Horizon styles. The criteria were designed to describe specifically and explicitly a large range of possible expressions each artifact could have without imposing a priori typological assumptions.

Material types used in other analyses of Middle Horizon lithics also have been somewhat generalized. Giesso lists chert, obsidian, basalt and andesite as the main types at Tiwanaku and Lukurmata in Bolivia and also specifies other volcanic and metamorphic materials that were locally available (2003, 2000); Bencic (2000) specifies quartzite, chert, quartz, sandstone, obsidian, basalt, rhyolite, and andesite as used in Iwawi, Bolivia and Conchopata, Peru; and Stone (1983) lists basalt, obsidian, and siliceous materials at Huari in Peru.

Several factors increased the complexity of raw material use at Cerro Baúl, particularly when the use of locally available material is considered. These factors include the heterogeneous geological landscape where available material is "vertically stratified by elevation" (Aldenderfer 1998: 81), the dispersed locations of the excavation units included in the analysis, and the apparent procurement strategies used in antiquity. It quickly became apparent that highly sensitive criteria were desirable to identify the wide array of raw material that was exploited and in order to resolve latent patterns in procurement strategies. Seventy three distinct material types (identified on the basis of petrographic criteria such as mineral composition, crystal development, and color) were coded for. Many of these specific materials occur infrequently, but some thirty or so material types are common. A similar variety of lithic material has been recorded at other sites in the Upper Osmore Drainage (Aldenderfer 1998: 81). The intent of such a fine resolution of data was to be able to discriminate subtle differences in the use of materials that may relate to differential procurement strategies across the analyzed contexts.

For most analyses, these material types are compressed into more general groups reflecting either their availability or mechanical characteristics in order to increase the sample size and to make interpretation more representative. Contrasts between locally available or indirectly procured raw material and the use of sedimentary, igneous, and metamorphic materials, for example, can thus be meaningfully made. The use of a diversity of materials should be carefully considered, however, and will be the subject itself of more discussion.

The analysis also focused on technological data that reflect stage and method of reduction, and possible uses of lithics. Technological criteria were based largely on Inizan et al.'s (1999) discussion of flaked lithic artifacts, as well as the analytic types established by Sliva (1997). Technological criteria describe the stage and mode of reduction that the artifact represents and any possible indications of the artifact's use. As use-wear analysis was beyond the scope of this project and laboratory conditions were insufficient for unequivocal identification in most instances, the assessments of use-wear were very conservative and err on the side of underestimation. In terms of metrical criteria, exact measurements to the millimeter were taken for lithic implements; unutilized debitage was measured along the longest axis using size-classes of 2 cm increments rather than exact measurements. In the case of debitage, weight is a more precise indicator of the size of the artifact and the relative quantity of material—of any type—that is involved in a particular strategy and flakes were individually weighed to 0.1 grams.

Remote Sensing and GIS of Lithic Environments

The word "environment" includes in its most general sense the set of physical parameters that structures the character of a setting. We must also consider those cultural and behavioral dispositions that impact how environments are perceived and which inform an archaeological group's interaction with physical parameters (the literature on this is abundant but see, e.g., Ashmore and Knapp 1999). Culture-environment interactions thus have spatial and behavioral components and it is necessary to compare and contrast spatial elements of the physical environment with spatial aspects and cultural patterns in order to elicit the import of the non-physical dispositions. In the case of Cerro Baúl lithic data, this was achieved by constructing a model through remote sensing of the physical- geological environment and through GIS by reconstructing the interaction of architectural space and densities of lithic-use activity.

Modeling the Geological Environment

Figure 3.1 is a geological map with an effective on-the-ground spatial resolution of 30 meters. The image is derived from a maximum likelihood supervised classification of remotely-sensed multispectral imagery from the Advanced Spaceborne Thermal Emission and Reflection Radiometer (ASTER) satellite. The ASTER Earth-observation satellite initiative began with the objective of providing data on land-cover classes and surficial geology and soils; the spectral ranges of the ASTER sensors were determined to discriminate important earth minerals (Table 3.2). ASTER records reflectance and thermal emission in fourteen bands of electromagnetic energy between the visible and near infra-red (VNIR), short-wave infrared (SWIR), and the thermal infrared (TIR) wavelengths (Table 3.2). Each subsystem records multiple bandwidths and collectively they resolve important reflectance and adsorption features that result from the content of iron-oxide minerals and rare-earth minerals (VNIR), phyllosilicate, carbonate, and hydrate minerals (SWIR), and feldspar and silica (TIR) in rock (Yamaguchi et al. 1998: 1062–1063; Yamaguchi et al 1999; Rowan and Mars 2003: 350–351).

The spatial resolution for the VNIR, SWIR, and TIR subsystems is 15 meters, 30 meters, and 90 meters, respectively. Compared to other multispectral systems, ASTER provides high spatial and high radiometric resolution with its fourteen bands (Yamaguchi et al 2001: 74). This accuracy allows greater ease in distinguishing surface features by more precisely assigning spectral reflectance values to specific classes of land cover, potentially avoiding mixed pixel values that are problematic with poorer spatial or radiometric resolution (Yamaguchi et al. 1998: 1062). Further, the high spatial accuracy makes ASTER imagery appropriate for attempting to resolve features on a scale that is of archaeological interest. The issue of scale is one that has hindered the use of remotely-sensed multispectral data to its fullest capacity in earlier archaeological applications. These characteristics make ASTER imagery particularly useful for the mapping of geological resources on a human scale.

Several pre-processing steps were involved in the classification. The ASTER scene was enhanced with a Principal Components Analysis (PCA) rotation to increase data variance within and between the spectral bands. The output PCA product contains decorrelated data which enhance the contrast in the spectral characteristics of individual features and reduce spectral noise by compressing the total variance of the data into fewer components that include the total variance and limit data redundancy (Lillesand and Keifer 2000: 536–539); nine PCA derived bands formed the basic dataset for the ultimate image classification. Twenty three user-specified regions of interest were used as training sites to establish spectral profiles for each of the major geological units in the vicinity of Cerro Baúl. The training sites were based on low-resolution geological maps, scale 1:100000, published by the Peruvian federal *Sector de Energía y Minas* (INGEMMET 2003), which were geo-rectified by registering them to Landsat TM scenes. The averaged spectral curves from these regions of interest were then applied to the rotated data using a maximum-likehood clustering algorithm to produce the classified image (Figure 3.1). The maximum-likelihood algorithm assigns each pixel to a class based on its proximity to the overall average digital number for the class as it is determined by the region of interest. Assuming that the region of interest accurately represents the spectral average for each geological material, each pixel will be assigned to the class average which most closely approximates its digital number.

The resulting image was groundtruthed by visiting twenty locations within and around the Cerro Baúl Archaeological Zone, taking GPS points, and recording the geological variability of these loci. These groundtruth points were selected based on the INGEMMET geological quadrants and also the output classified ASTER image and they confirm that there is accord between the two interpretations of the geological landscape. The ASTER image illustrates the geological variability in the Cerro Baúl Archaeological Zone, which is discussed in more detail in Chapter 4. Importantly, it provides a baseline from which to compare the spatial articulation of the individual excavation units with the availability of lithological resources in the immediate area. One contrast is readily apparent between the extensive intrusive igneous batholith of the Toquepala Formation and the sedimentary units of the Moquegua Formation, the latter being associated with the majority of the archaeological contexts. The Moquegua Formation is a secondary alluvial deposit of clastic material that was episodically laid down and reworked (Wörner et al. 2002, see Chapter 4), and its local lithology subsequently is very heterogeneous. Shelley proposes a direct methodology for characterizing secondary lithic deposits that includes quantification of size, round-

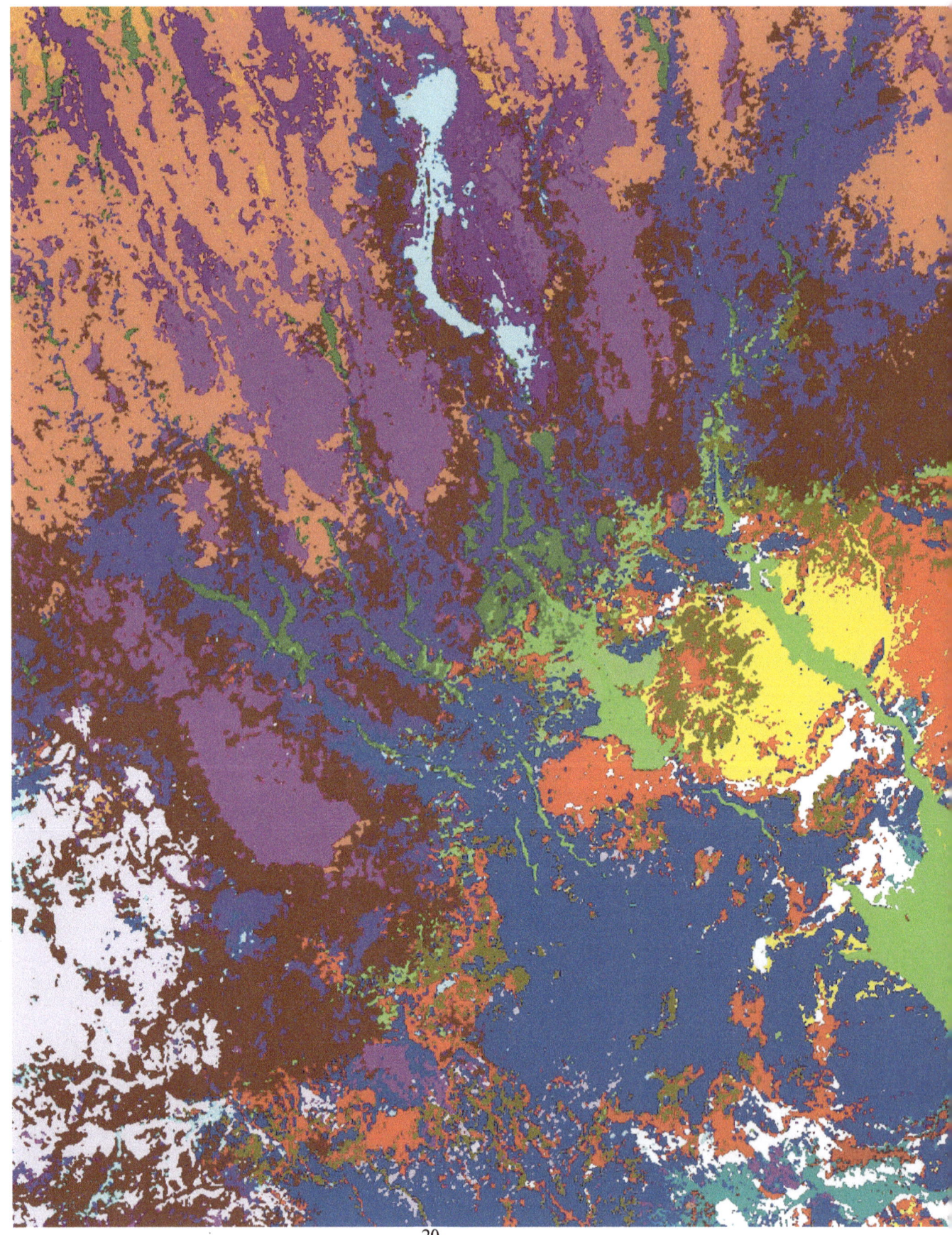

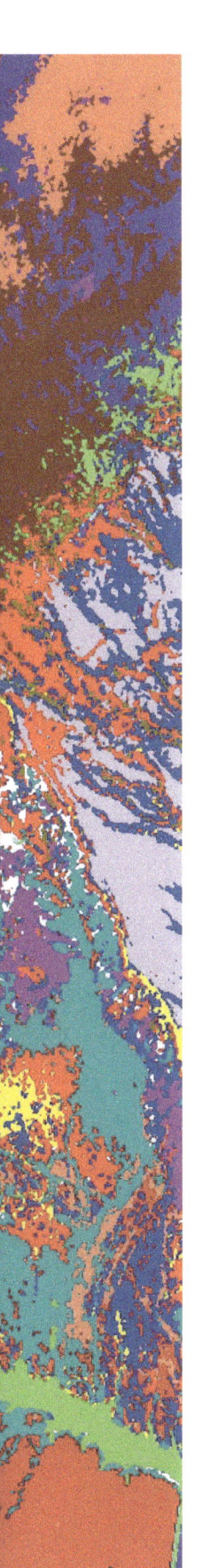

ASTER Image Classes

- Vegetation
- Vegetation, high altitude
- Southern Corp

GEOLOGICAL UNITS:

QUATERNARY

- C Baul alluvium
- C Baul colluvium
- Alluvium, C Los Angeles unit (Q-al)
- Alluvium (Q-al)
- Alluvium (Q-al)
- Alluvium (Q-al)
- Quaternary moraine deposits (Qp-m)

TERTIARY

- Barroso Formation (Tq-vba)
- Moquegua Formation (Ts-mos)
- Moquegua Formation (Ts-moi)
- Tacna Group (Ts-hu, Ts-vhu)
- Huayillas Tuff (Tms-hu)
- Jahuay Formation (Ti-ja)

CRETACEOUS/TERTIARY

- C Mejia unit (Kti-to)
- C Los Angeles unit (Kti-to)
- (Kti-gp)
- Toquepala Formation (KTi-to)
- Yarito Rhyolite (Kti-qy)
- Diorite-granodiorite (Kti-d/dg)

Figure 3.1: Lithological Map for the Upper Osmore Drainage derived from remotely-sensed ASTER data. Map was created from a Maximum-likelihood supervised classification with a post-classification Majority analysis filter.

Table 3.2: Advanced Spaceborne Thermal Emission and Reflection Radiometer (ASTER) system parameters.

Subsystem	Band number	Spectral range (μm)	Spatial resolution (m)	Principle applications
VNIR	1	0.52 – 0.60	15	Iron-oxide minerals and rare-earth minerals
	2	0.63 – 0.69		Water, vegetation moisture, cultural features
	3N	0.78 – 0.86		Healthy vegetation, cultural features
	3B	0.78 – 0.86		Vegetation and soil moisture, cultural features
SWIR	4	1.600 – 1.700	30	Phyllosillicate, carbonate, and hydrate minerals
	5	2.145 – 2.185		Mineral and rock types
	6	2.185 – 2.225		Mineral and rock types
	7	2.235 – 2.285		Mineral and rock types
	8	2.295 – 2.365		Mineral and rock types
	9	2.360 – 2.430		Soil moisture content, clays
	10	8.125 – 8.475		
	11	8.475 – 8.825		
TIR	12	8.925 – 9.275	90	Feldspars and silica content
	13	10.25 – 10.95		
	14	10.95 – 11.65		

ness, crystallinity, and homogeneity of the deposits (1993: 63–64). The criteria he describes are all factors that effect the visual characteristics of a deposit and, hence, their reflectance properties. It is this premise that makes possible the use of multispectral imagery to identify the extent of variation in secondary alluvial deposits at Cerro Baúl and to relate this variation to that seen in the archaeological assemblages. Additionally, with multispectral imagery several petrographically distinct subunits can readily be identified in the geological formations that otherwise are mapped as homogenous. For example many members of the Toquepala Formation from different volcanic events can be resolved (see Chapter 4). The spatial extent of these individual members can be pinpointed with multispectral imagery and verified by ground-truthing in order to define more precisely the location of their primary geological sources and—for some lithic materials—the location(s) from which the raw material was procured. Correlations among the classified image, published geological data, and the local geology at ground-truthing points demonstrate the effectiveness of ASTER imagery for resource mapping in the Osmore Drainage on a spatial scale that is archaeologically appropriate.

Interpolating Lithic Use Areas

The lithic analysis data were integrated into a Geographic Information System (GIS) database in order to be able to build data layers describing spatial distributions and artifact densities per meter square. GIS has the advantage of being able to juxtapose several data layers simultaneously; in this instance, I have focused on the relationship between clusters of different artifact and material types and the culturally-defined boundaries of architectural space. Layers of lithic data were integrated as ArcInfo coverages and then converted into ArcView shapefiles for display and analysis.

Density distributions are particularly useful for considering lithic debitage. Elevated quantities could reflect lithics integrated into midden or hearth deposits, recorded during excavation as features. Elevated densities—particularly of lithic artifacts in the smallest size classes—also may reflect primary reduction loci. Only a limited number of midden and hearth features were noted during excavation. Within GIS, archaeological features can be compared with artifact densities in order to describe possible spatial correlations; increased densities that correspond to these features can readily be identified and discounted. Consequently, I provisionally interpret most clusters of lithic debitage as the result of reduction activities. Finally, in special instances where social valuation is attached to a specific class of material, such as exotics, deliberate deposits of debris may be concentrated, relocated, and placed in secondary contexts that reflect neither use nor reduction loci. While this type of midden-forming behavior will impact the relative distribution of lithic artifact types across units of cultural space, it will result in specialized types of deposits that could be clearly distinguished from deposits that are economic in character (e.g., Moholy Nagy 1997). No such deposits have been excavated at Cerro Baúl. Although Giesso (2003: 363, 2000: 49) suggests a socio-symbolic and ceremonial value for obsidian as a raw material at Tiwanaku, Nash (2002) notes its ubiquity at Cerro Mejía and suggests that it had a much more quotidian economic role. Consequently, while the spatial distribution of raw material will reflect economic valuation, it probably will not reflect explicitly ritualized behavior.

ArcInfo's Inverse Distance Weight (IDW) interpolation algorithm was used to generate density grids from three data axes: x and y spatial coordinates and a z value representing the total number of lithics within a grid square for each category considered. IDW is a linear function that evaluates the significance of points in an interpolation based on an inverse relationship of distance to neighboring data points. A distance exponent of 1.5 was used to weight the value of each point and to interpolate a grid with smoothened data values. The resulting grids interpolate density values on a grid resolution of approximately 10 cm based on the number of lithic artifacts recovered from each excavation square. Discrete concentrations of activity with a spatial extension equal to or greater than one meter should be apparent as elevated densities of lithic material within or between each grid square.

Chapter 4: Geological Environment

Geographic and Geological Setting

Cerro Baúl is located in southern Peru at approximately 17° 6' S latitude and 70° 51' W longitude (8107100 N, 302300 E, UTM zone 19 south, datum WGS 84) (Figure 2.1). The Cerro Baúl Archaeological Zone is within a topographically dramatic environment at the lower edge of the upper Osmore Drainage, and it is roughly confined by the deeply incised valleys of the Rio Tumilaca and its tributaries to the southeast and by the broader valley of the Rio Torata to the northwest.

The archaeological occupation of the summit of Cerro Baúl, the site conventionally referred to by the same name, constitutes the focal core of the archaeological zone and is at an elevation 2585 masl. Other sectors of the site continue down slope to the toe of Cerro Baúl, and occupy adjacent topographic elevations such as el Tenedor/Cerro Baulito, and the remnants of relatively flat alluvial fans (*pampas*) at the base of Cerro Baúl. Sectors L and M—the archaeological sites of Santa Rita la Chica and Tumilaca la Chimba, respectively—sit on alluvial terraces immediately above the Tumilaca River at an elevation of approximately 1900 masl (Figure 2.2). The archaeological zone is thus marked by the dramatic topographic gradient of the Western Andean Escarpment that rises sharply over a short distance. Such a setting contributes to the cultural-ecological phenomenon of "verticality" proposed by Murra (1980) to explain adaptive variability in archaeological and ethnographic Andean cultures.

Wörner et al. (2002: 184) describe a geological sequence for the Western Andean Escarpment (WARP) in the Azapa region of northern Chile which is generally applicable to the geological history for the upper Osmore Drainage 150 kilometers to the northwest. Tosdal et al. (1985) relate a similar regional geological sequence for southern Peru. The WARP results from uplift and volcanism caused by the active subduction of the Farallón-Nazca plate with a rate of convergence that varies between 5–15 cm/year over the past 60 mybp. The region subsequently is both tectonically and volcanically active, with Andean uplift within the past 30–25 mybp. Prior to the Andean orogeny, continental sedimentation, andesitic volcanism, and the deposition of volcaniclastic deposits characterized the development of the WARP, with frequent fluvial reworking of deposits (Wörner et al. 2002: 184). The Cerro Baúl Archaeological Zone therefore sits along a northwest-southeast trending line that separates two geologically distinct depositional environments. To the southwest, the environment is dominated by flat sedimentary terrain and piedmont plateaus created by uplift and erosion. This sedimentary zone becomes increasingly broken and rugged towards the northeast and upwards into the WARP until it is replaced by geological units that are predominantly igneous and volcanic in nature. The terrain here is steeply inclined, broken, and quickly rises from ca. 1000 masl to over 3000 masl (INGEMMET 1979: 18).

Two geological formations and their various members figure predominantly in determining the heterogeneous geological landscape of the Cerro Baúl Archaeological Zone. These are the Moquegua Formation sandstone conglomerate and the Toquepala Formation (INGEMMET 2003a). Other geological units overlie these formations further up the WARP and contribute lithic materials from preserved remnant surfaces, as well as from erosion and redeposition. The resulting stratigraphy is an alternating, interbedded sequence of allocthonous sedimentary clastic deposits and volcanic formations (Figure 4.1).

Toquepala Group

The basal formation for this portion of the Osmore Drainage is the igneous Toquepala Group. The rocks of this group are almost exclusively volcanic. At the surface, the Toquepala Group occurs as large outcrops that were uplifted by tectonic activity. Much of the Toquepala Group has subsequently been exposed and incised by alluvial erosion made more forceful by uplift; these exposures form many of the topographic elevations that surround Cerro Baúl. The Toquepala Formation, the basal member of this Group, is variably andesitic, dacitic, and rhyolitic, and it is interbedded with constrained lenses of volcanic breccias and conglomerates (INGEMMET 1979: 23 Tosdal et al. 1985). Rhyolite dominates the lower strata of this formation, grading upwards into breccia and tuffaceous deposits and finally to andesitic strata. Conglomerates of angular volcanic clasts in tuffaceous cements are also associated with the Toquepala Formation, particularly the overlying Inogoya Formation (INGEMMET 1979: 26). These conglomerates, though, occur locally and not in important quantities in the vicinity of Cerro Baúl.

The different members of the Toquepala Formation are petrographically distinct due to factors of composition, crystal development and fracturing habit established during their formation (INGEMMET 1979: 25). Many of these differences are visible macroscopically and lithic material from each formation that has entered the archaeological record can usually be easily identified and attributed to a source outcrop. The Toquepala Formation rhyolite provides some of the more economically important lithic material in the Moquegua valley. Most of the varieties are macrocrystalline and are used minimally as material for flaked lithics; they also appear frequently as architectural material and groundstone artifacts.

Other members of the Toquepala Group are the Paralaque and Quellaveco Volcanics. The Paralaque Volcanic overlies a discordance with the Inogoya Formation and is a return to the dacitic, rhyolitic, and andesitic volcanics intercalated with pyroclastics and volcanic conglomerates as seen in the Toquepala Formation. In the Upper Osmore Drainage, the Paralaque Volcanic member is found to the north at a moderate distance from Cerro Baúl and also crops out to the southeast along the Rio Tumilaca valley (INGEMMET 1979: 28). The Quellaveco Volcanics, similarly, are highly localized occurrences of andesites, dacites, and rhyolite pyroclastics and flows that are restricted to the higher elevations above Cerro Baúl, such as in the vicinity of Cuajone (INGEMMET 1979: 30).

Moquegua Formation

The initiation of the Andean orogeny triggered the onset of continental sedimentation that deposited coarse, molasse-

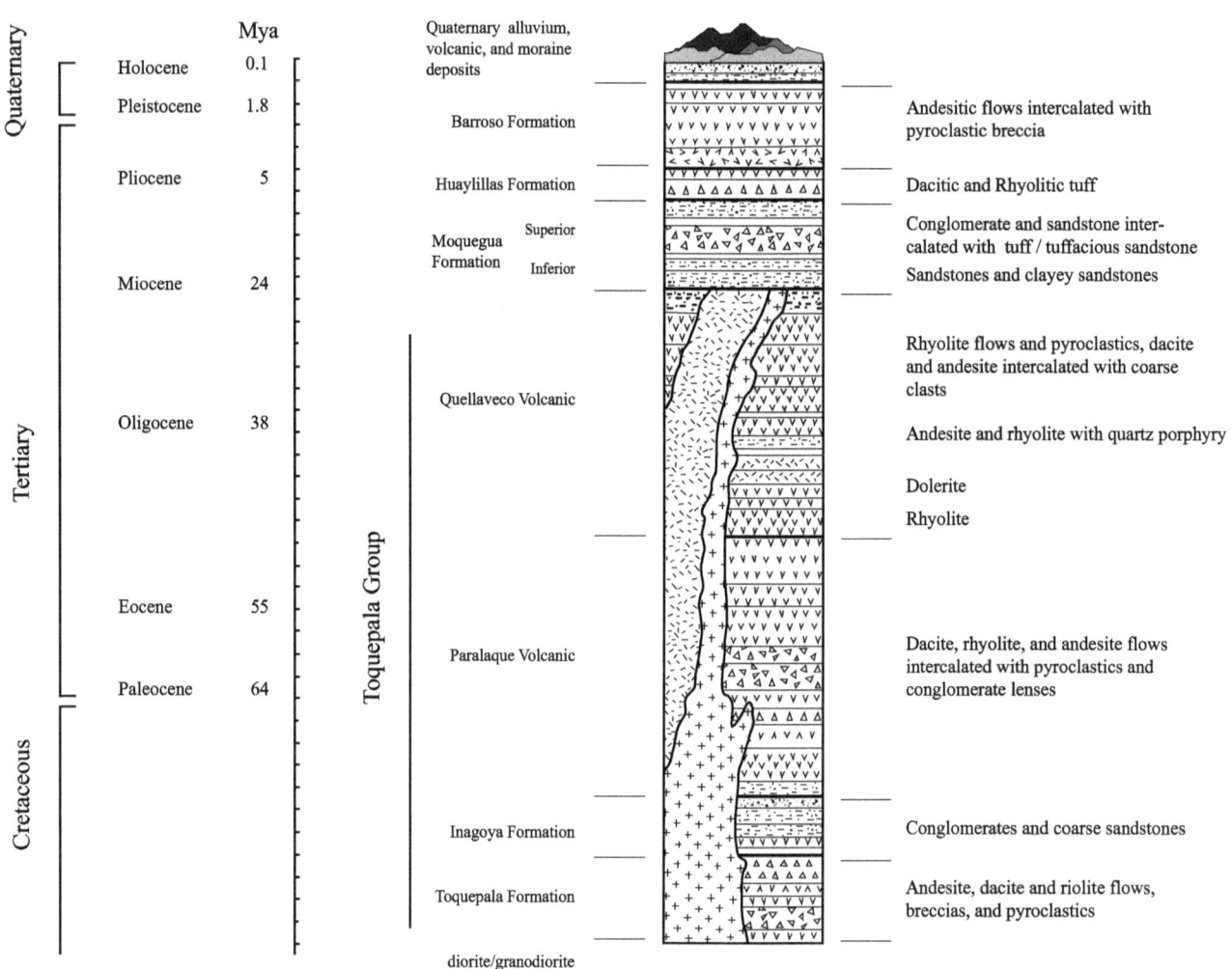

Figure 4.1: Geological column for the Upper Osmore Drainage. Modified from INGEMMET 2003 and Wörner et al. 2002

type clastic deposits along the western edge of the Andean slope in deposits that range from 400 to 1000 meters in thickness (Wörner et al. 2002: 186). The Moquegua Formation is made of these heterogeneous sedimentary deposits, and it overlies the volcanics described above with strong discordance. Both the Upper Moquegua Formation, which caps Cerro Baúl, as well as underlying early Tertiary Lower Moquegua Formation have alluvial facies and consist predominantly of large, coarse-grained alluvial fan and ephemeral-braided channel deposits. Calculations of the volumes and proposed rates of deposition as well as an east – west grading from coarse alluvium to finer lacustrine sandy-silts indicate that these clastic deposits correspond to an increase in topographic gradient along the WARP. The clastic deposits can also be linked to exposures of older, uplifted Cretaceous and Jurassic volcanic and plutonic units in the upper Western Andean Escarpment (Wörner et al. 2002: 186–187, INGEMMET 2003b). These deposits, thus, result from the transport and reworking of parent material during the uplift of the Andean slopes. Volcanism also made minor contributions to the sedimentary strata of the Moquegua Formation. The Lower Moquegua Formation is found in the lower parts of the Moquegua Valley away from Cerro Baúl and is characterized by clayey and tuffaceous sandstones, fine-grained conglomerates, and localized gypsum horizons. The Upper Moquegua Formation is exposed in the higher portions of the valley, most notably at Cerro Baúl, and is a more strongly consolidated sandy conglomerate (INGEMMET 1979: 37). Quartz, feldspar, and tuffaceous sands are all common in the Upper Moquegua Formation.

The upper members of the Upper Moquegua Formation, the *meseta* surface upon which the archaeological site of Cerro Baúl sits, are composed of angular volcaniclastic and tuffaceous sediments from a localized and somewhat minor episode (INGEMMET 1979: 36). The composition and character of these materials contrast strongly with those of the alluvially-derived sediments of the remainder of the Moquegua Formation. When these clastic materials are encountered in archaeological contexts, either as lithic artifacts or construction material, they subsequently can be readily recognized. Due to the periodicity of aggradation and incision, the secondary nature of the reworked clasts, and the variable provenance of the alluvial and volcaniclastic material, the Moquegua Formation varies quite strongly on a local basis.

Wörner et al. (2002: 187) link the uplift of the Andean slopes with increasing climatic aridity, contributing to the modern hyperaridity of the region. The Moquegua Formation conglomerate, particularly the Lower Moquegua Formation, is poorly consolidated and, in part due to conditions of hyperaridity, vegetation cover and soil formation are minimal. Soil formation is limited largely to clay infillings and minimal calcite coatings (ONERN 1976: 125). Poorly developed, shallow lithic leptosols that overlie bedrock or fragments of parent material are frequent on Andean slopes above 2000 masl and are particularly sensitive to erosion (Coppus, Imeson, and Sevink 2003: 320, 325). During periods of more humid and fluctuating, seasonal climates, dramatic increases and decreases in precipitation and runoff destabilize exposed surfaces and increase erosion and the potential for landslides and mass-wasting along the Andean slope (Trauth et al. 2003). Trauth et al. (2003) have documented episodic and increasing frequencies of erosion and landslide events during the Quaternary Period (ca. 30 kybp and ca. 5 kybp). They attribute these to climatic instability brought on by El Niño Southern Oscillations (ENSO) in conjunction with punctuated seismic events (see also Schuster et al. 1996). Keefer et al. (1998) have proposed a similar connection between the onset of ENSO and Quaternary mass wasting events along the southern Peruvian littoral. As a result, erosion and redeposition are ongoing, especially when the influences of climatic fluctuations and seismic activity are combined. Erosion occurs in much smaller volumes than during the late Tertiary Period, however, and largely impacts the reworking and secondary deposition of the poorly consolidated Tertiary alluvial deposits of the Moquegua Inferior.

Late Tertiary and Recent Volcanism

The Lower to Upper Tertiary alluvial sedimentation is overlain by several rhyolitic and andesitic volcanic rocks that formed between the end of the Miocene Epoch and into the early part of the Quaternary Period. Ignimbrites represented by the Huaylillas and Barroso Formations in the regions of Moquegua and Tacna directly overly the Moquegua Formation conglomerate. These are extensive and continue southward into northern Chile (Wörner et al 2002: 187; Tosdal 1985; INGEMMET 1979: 42). Most of these formations are thick and sheet-like and cap the underlying deposits; the Huaylillas and related ignimbrites reach 500 m in thickness in the upper Moquegua-Omate area (Thouret et al. 2002: 530). Remnants of the Huaylillas Formation are found on the summit of Cerro Baúl as large blocks (ca. 5 to 10 m in diameter) and as redeposited cobbles of less significant sizes (ca. 5 to 15 cm in dimension) along the slopes. Much smaller, weathered clasts occur in the Quaternary alluvium that mantles lower portions of the valleys. Archaeologically, lithic material from the Huaylillas Formation is present in very small amounts as unretouched lithic debitage and is found predominantly in archaeological contexts on the summit of Cerro Baúl.

Subsequent and ongoing volcanism has deposited stratigraphically higher formations in the upper elevations of the WARP above 3500 masl. These volcanics are largely andesitic or dacitic in composition and result in the formation of andesite and ignimbrite shields, lava flows, pyroclastic deposits, hydrothermally altered sediments, and tephra deposits (Wörner et al 2002: 188; Tosdal 1985; Thouret et al. 2002). In the upper Osmore Drainage, this volcanic activity is represented by the Tacna Group and the Barroso Formation. Despite this nearly continuous activity, there is little suggestion of direct and important impacts from volcanism on archaeological occupations. An exception to this is the severe Huaynaputina eruptive event in AD 1600 that deposited pumice, ignimbrites and lava flows locally and vitric-ash and lapilli regionally (Thouret et al. 2002; Thouret et al. 1997). At the site of Cerro Baúl, intact deposits of vitric ash from the Huaynaputina event provide a *terminus ante quem* for the prehistoric occupations and indicate the onset of historic deposits (Williams and Ruales 2001, 2002).

The Spatial Interaction of Geology and Archaeological Occupation

As a result of the interbedded sedimentary and volcanic deposits as well as the geologically active environment that has caused erosion, incision, and redeposition, the geology that underlies a particular point within the Cerro Baúl Archaeological Zone will be different than that found at other loci. The depositional mechanics are similar but the material composition and, in the case of sediments, the parent material varies. The composition of these heterogeneous units guaranteed that suitable lithic material was immediately available within clastic deposits, but it also contributed to a high degree of variability in the available range of raw material types. Over thirty minor varieties of local lithic material in the archaeological deposits were identified on the basis of petrographic criteria such as mineral composition, grain size, and associated color and texture. This diversity is an important factor when considering patterns of raw material procurement and use among the various archaeological sectors. The archaeological sectors are underlain by dissimilar geological units (Figure 3.1). Consequently, the specific materials that were exploited by archaeological materials were differentially available to the inhabitants of each unit.

The spectral variance of deposits in fact reflects compositional differences. There is important variation in the surface reflectance of these deposits, resulting in their differential classification, and in some instances the raw material can be linked to formations of parent material further up in the Andean escarpment. Of particular interest is the apparent high variability of deposits on the slopes and on the summit of Cerro Baúl (Figure 3.1). In addition, the extension of remnant Moquegua Formation (red) at the summit of Cerro Baúl and an isolated occurrence of igneous material (apple-green) at the western extreme of the mesa were both successfully mapped by spectral matching. The spectral variation is due largely to a stratum of conglomerate composed of volcanic clasts and tuffaceous rock that covers the summit of the mesa and which was exploited during the Middle Horizon for both architectural and lithic materials. Two classes of material were resolved on the mesa's slopes:

colluvial deposits (tan) and alluvial deposits (yellow). While much of the alluvial deposits are due primarily to the reworking of Moquegua Formation alluvium during the Quaternary, the colluvium is due to the erosion of the consolidated and resistant upper strata of Moquegua Formation conglomerates and sandstones. Soil formations can be differentiated due to different spectral characteristics, such as texture and clay content (Kooistra et al. 2003), and the identifiable difference in Cerro Baúl slope deposits may indicate similar compositional differences due to the ages of Tertiary deposits and the lithology of the parent sources for the secondary clastic material.

Spectral mapping reveals how the geologic landscape interacts with the archaeological sectors. Sectors A–C, on the summit of Cerro Baúl, are directly underlain by a conglomerate of angular, volcaniclastic material. Sector F is associated with different areas of the Moquegua Formation that are characterized by a conglomerate of rounded, mixed clasts. Sectors H and G are in geologically heterogeneous settings with an assortment of pixel classes, as is Sector N. Interestingly, a number of pixels classified as volcanic are in the vicinity of Sector N, indicating a more strongly volcanic composition. Sectors L and M, finally, sit on the alluvial terraces above the Tumilaca River. The variable geology of these deposits had a direct relationship with the diversity and quality of the lithic material that was utilized in each archaeological household.

Chapter 5: Lithic Material Use and Procurement Strategies

When the variety of lithic raw materials from which both flaked and ground implements were fashioned at Cerro Baúl is considered, a clear dichotomy can be drawn between local material that is geographically proximate and exotic material whose geological source is geographically distant. This dichotomy between a generalized suite of local material and exotic obsidian matches a similarly differentiated pattern of lithic procurement at other Middle Horizon Wari and Tiwanaku sites (Stone 1983; Giesso 2000; Nash 2002; Bencic 2000). This dichotomy of source—whether a material is either local or non-local—can be reformulated so as to consider each class as the result of the social mechanisms that are involved in the acquisition and transport of material prior to its ultimate use and deposition. The distances involved in transport, the relative quantities of material types, and the technological attributes of artifacts from each category suggest that raw material use can be organized into opposed strategies of direct procurement and indirect procurement. The latter occurred through extended exchange networks. This approach is "consumer-oriented" and evaluates the origin point and final attributes of each class of raw material at the site as a means of elucidating the social modes involved in material distribution (McAnany 1989: 332-333). At Cerro Baúl, there is a clear contrast between directly-procured local materials and obsidian—the primary indirectly-procured commodity that carried specific social and symbolic import in addition to its economic valuation (e.g., Giesso 2000:363, table 9.6).

There are significant gradations, however, in the distances over which both local and non-local materials were transported, and these differences ostensibly correspond to finer-scale variations in the mechanisms for direct and indirect procurement. A few geological sources of obsidian are represented at Cerro Baúl (Burger, Chávez, and Chávez 2000) and, as will be the focus of more discussion below, material available locally within the Upper Osmore drainage was available at differing spatial scales. These materials share technological characteristics with immediately available material and are classed as directly procured. "Direct" and "indirect", then, should not be construed as binary oppositions between strategies that involve single-individual and multiple-individual efforts, but more accurately reflect differing scales of intra-community and inter-community social networks of which material procurement and distribution is one aspect.

Material use can thus be used as a proxy for social networks—it indicates the spatial extension of interpersonal relationships and social interaction involved in procurement and movement of raw resources. When this stance is taken, no clear divisions are apparent between Wari and Tumilaca social groups. Rather, apparent status and "topographical" social hierarchies (i.e., marked by differences in summit and slope occupations) more clearly characterize the variable sizes of the social networks represented in the use of material from each archaeological context.

Local Material

As described briefly in Chapter 3, a considerable variety of lithic material was locally available to the occupants of Cerro Baúl and every indication suggests that this variety was thoroughly exploited during the fabrication of lithic artifacts. This variety is due to the considerable geological diversity and activity of the Upper Osmore Drainage, where sedimentary formations transition to volcanic ones in a tectonically active setting that also provides localized environments for the formation of unique materials, such as hydrothermal and metamorphic minerals (see Chapter 4). Variations in temperature, pressure, and rates of cooling result in different formation environments for volcanic and igneous materials and particularly have an effect on the extent of crystal formation in each material. Figure 5.1 shows seven geological hand samples representative of archaeologically-occurring material which were collected from the primary geological sources. While the composition of this material is felsic and generally similar, there are important petrographic differences in grain size, texture, and color, such that each type of igneous material can be readily identified macroscopically (Figure 5.1). In several instances, natural clasts of material as well as archaeological artifacts can be linked to their primary geological sources—usually to members within the Toquepala Formation—based on the same criteria. The task of differentiating lithic material that occurs within sedimentary environments is somewhat more difficult due to the transported and secondary nature of these deposits. However, the different compositions are expressed in the spectral characteristics of these formations, so that some attributions to geological occurrences can be made, although these are less irrefutable.

Once the raw material used archaeologically was organized into exclusive categories based on petrographic criteria, the specific geological sources that were exploited were identifiable. Meaningful differences in the specific suite of material that occurs in each context were then analyzed.

In addition to exotic obsidian, twenty-four types of locally available material occurred frequently in the twelve analyzed contexts. Table 5.1 gives the percentage of lithic raw materials from each of these units. These percentages are based on the total number (n) of debitage and waste-products per unit, and they do not consider the amount of material occurring as implements. As such, the data do not represent the overall diversity of raw material types that was exploited for fashioning artifacts, but they do characterize the diversity of material which was actively reduced in each residence. Moreover, these data do not indicate the volume of material that was exploited, but rather they reflect the relative diversity of material used by each household. The volume (m^3) of each excavated context was different, and so the effect of sampling area was normalized by comparing the frequency with which a material was found in a unit to the percentages of other material in the same unit.

Several of these categories represent generalized classes of materials that could be further differentiated. "Porphyritic rhyolite," for example, is actually an amalgamation of several varieties of rhyolite with different textures and crystal development which are compressed here for the purposes of analysis. Regardless of slight variations in color and texture, different types of porphyritic rhyolite co-occur in the vicinity of most contexts, and are easily available. Consequently, compressing these varieties into one analytical class does not substantively impact cultural patterns of procurement and use. While this and similar types of material vir-

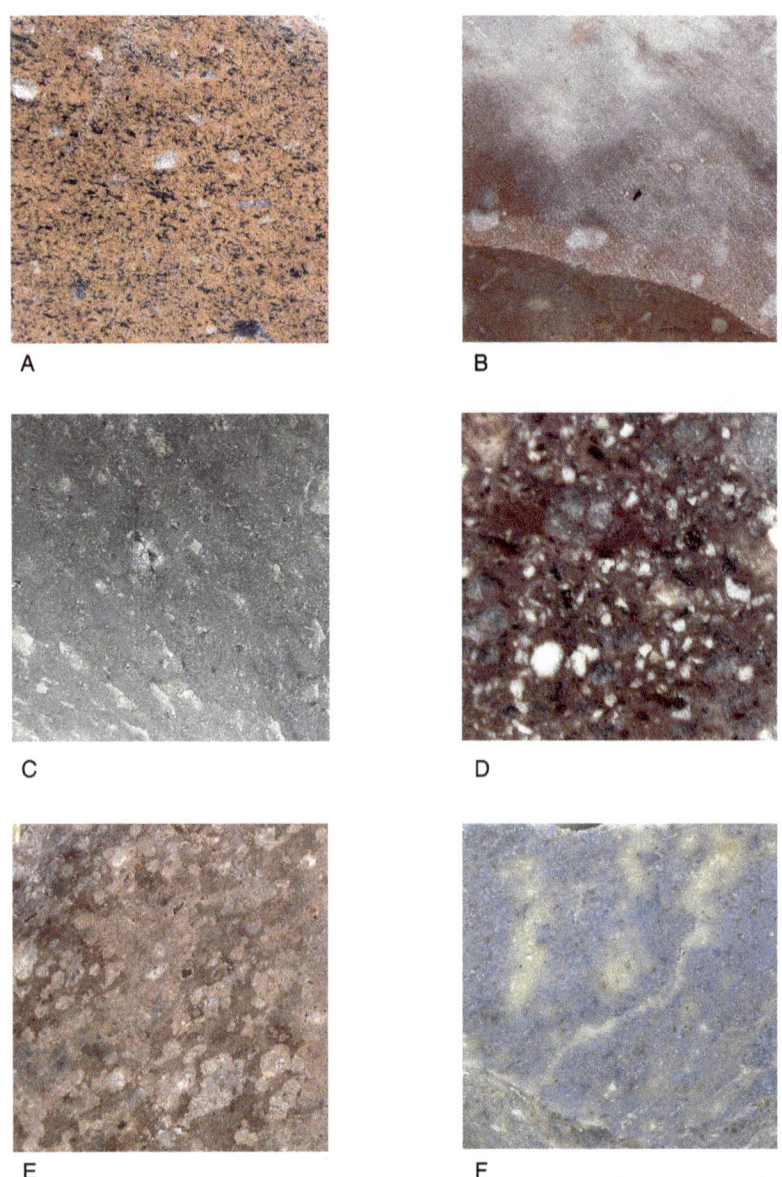

Figure 5.1: Geological hand samples of local material that was exploited archaeologically at Cerro Baul. A) Dacite (code 141), B) fine-grained rhyolite (code 151), C) rhyolite (code 152), D) Los Angeles rhyolite (code 154), E) Cerro Baul rhyolite (code 155), F) sodalite (?, code 412, primarily a sumptuary material). Bar represents one cm.

tually reach ubiquity—varieties of rhyolite and chert are found in almost every context—other lithic material is notably limited to a few of the archaeological contexts and only occur in specific geological environments. The most significant patterns of cultural behavior can be gleaned from these raw material types.

In Table 5.1, the excavation contexts are ordered left to right by their Euclidean distance from Unit 9, which, as the largest and most elaborate domestic context, is assumed to have been something of a social and economic focus of the Wari settlement. Unit 24 is the closest while Unit 20 is the farthest removed. As the distance from Unit 9 increases, the variety of lithic material that is found in each context decreases. In each general category, there are two plateaus in the variety of material used: those units on the summit of Cerro Baúl (Units 9, 24, 25, and 7) used the greatest variety of material while the remainder used considerably less. Units 28, 22, 19, and 20 were particularly conservative in their use of raw material types. Unit 21 is a glaring exception to this general trend of decrease with distance, with a very rich variety of material types that approaches the wide variety seen in excavation contexts from the summit. These relationships are given graphically in Figure 5.2, which

Table 5.1: Percentage of raw material types that were found in each excavation context as lithic debitage. The percentages were calculated from the total weight (g) of debitage in each context.

material	un9 (n=688)	un24 (n=116)	un25 (n=198)	un7 (n=84)	un23 (n=69)	un32 (n=40)	un21 (n=138)	un27 (n=78)	un28 (n=3)	un22 (n=2)	un19 (n=19)	un20 (n=18)
igneous												
obsidian	0.84	3.26	0.83	0.04	0.56	0.30	0.04	0.06				
dacite	3.80	3.25	9.06	2.22			1.86	7.07				
rhyolite, nfs	0.72			0.71			4.03				3.72	12.12
rhyolite, fine-grained	5.59	7.53	14.15	0.52	42.24	62.93	13.57	1.17			2.34	52.34
rhyolite, porphyritic	63.95	24.33	49.74	73.37	53.03	13.11	53.98	13.73			39.13	27.48
rhyolite, Los Angeles	3.01	12.01	1.05	0.63								
rhyolite, Cerro Baul	10.55	1.22	20.91		3.42		17.46	36.57	53.87		48.92	4.51
andesite, Barrosos	1.25						3.43	40.81	46.13			
diorite, gran-diorite	0.37											
sedimentary												
cryptocrystalline silicate, nfs	0.95		0.05	3.04		0.38						
chert, nfs	2.18	4.66	0.63	4.40	0.31	3.62	3.90	0.08			5.89	3.54
chert, pink - red	0.19	1.84	0.07		0.01	0.23						
chert, white opaque	0.87	20.15	0.06	1.32	0.09	5.35	0.55	0.25				
chert, translucent yellow	0.22			0.13								
chert/jasper	0.03											
chert, dark grey - black	0.16	0.06	0.03	0.17			0.01					
chalcedony	0.28	0.02		6.25			0.06	0.25				
agate	0.01						0.28					
chert, fine-grained brown	0.74		0.04				0.01					
gypsum		0.08										
metamorphic and mineral												
metamorphic		19.77					0.21					
mineral, nfs	0.35	0.44	0.04	1.01								
copper mineral	2.65	1.37	0.79	5.22	0.34	12.17	0.46	0.02				
quartz	0.02		1.97				1.92	0.15		100		
"onyx"	1.25		0.60	0.97								

show the decrease in diversity with distance from Unit 9. Many of the minor varieties of material disappear from the left- and right-hand margins of the graph, being replaced by greater proportions of local "staple" lithic raw materials with distance from the core of the site.

The issue of material diversity is more complex, and is dependent on the overall variability or richness of a population and the relative abundance/evenness of the possible types within a population (Kintigh 1989; Ringrose 1993: 280; Popper 1988: 67; Jones and Leonard 1989: 2). The variables of richness and evenness combine to indicate what could be a wealth-differentiated model of lithic resource at Cerro Baúl, where certain domestic units enjoyed a rich range of material types. Those households farther from the summit utilized a poorer assemblage of material types, but each material type that was exploited is more evenly represented. For example, while Unit 9 has a variety of raw material, the percent frequencies for several classes (e.g., "agate" and "chert/jasper") are quite low, suggesting an overall very rich but heterogeneous use of material in this context. In contrast, the distribution of material abundance in Unit 20 is fairly even, as each constituent has a more equal role in the assemblage. This suggests a relatively poor material assemblage for units with low diversity, and perhaps a more limited or generalized use of material (Jones and Leonard 1989: 2). Neither of these measures of richness or diversity based on the raw number of material types present will be resistant to the great difference in sample sizes (Kintigh 1989: 26), and rigorous indices of diversity most likely cannot be calculated for units 28 and 22 because of their small sample size (n=3 and n=2, respectively). Popper states, however, that a sample as small as n≥10 is sufficient to calculate meaningful measures of diversity using a Shannon-Weaver index (1988: 69), where the diversity, H, is given as:

$$H = -\sum_{i=1}^{k} p_i \log(p_i)$$

and evenness, J, is given as:

$$J = \frac{H}{\log(k)} = Hmax$$

when p_i equals the proportion of the ith category (obtained by dividing the frequency of a type by the total number n in a sample), k is the number of categories represented in a sample, and H_{max} is the maximum possible diversity for k categories (Kintigh 1989: figure 4.5, Popper 1988: 69).

The diversity indices for lithic debitage are given in Table 5.2. The four units on the summit of Cerro Baúl as well as Unit 21 have the greatest variety (k) of lithic material types, with between 15 and 20 different types of material represented in each. Raw counts of variety, however, are not sufficient to assess the diversity of material use as it does not consider issues such as the richness of material use. The calculated index for diversity more accurately represents the

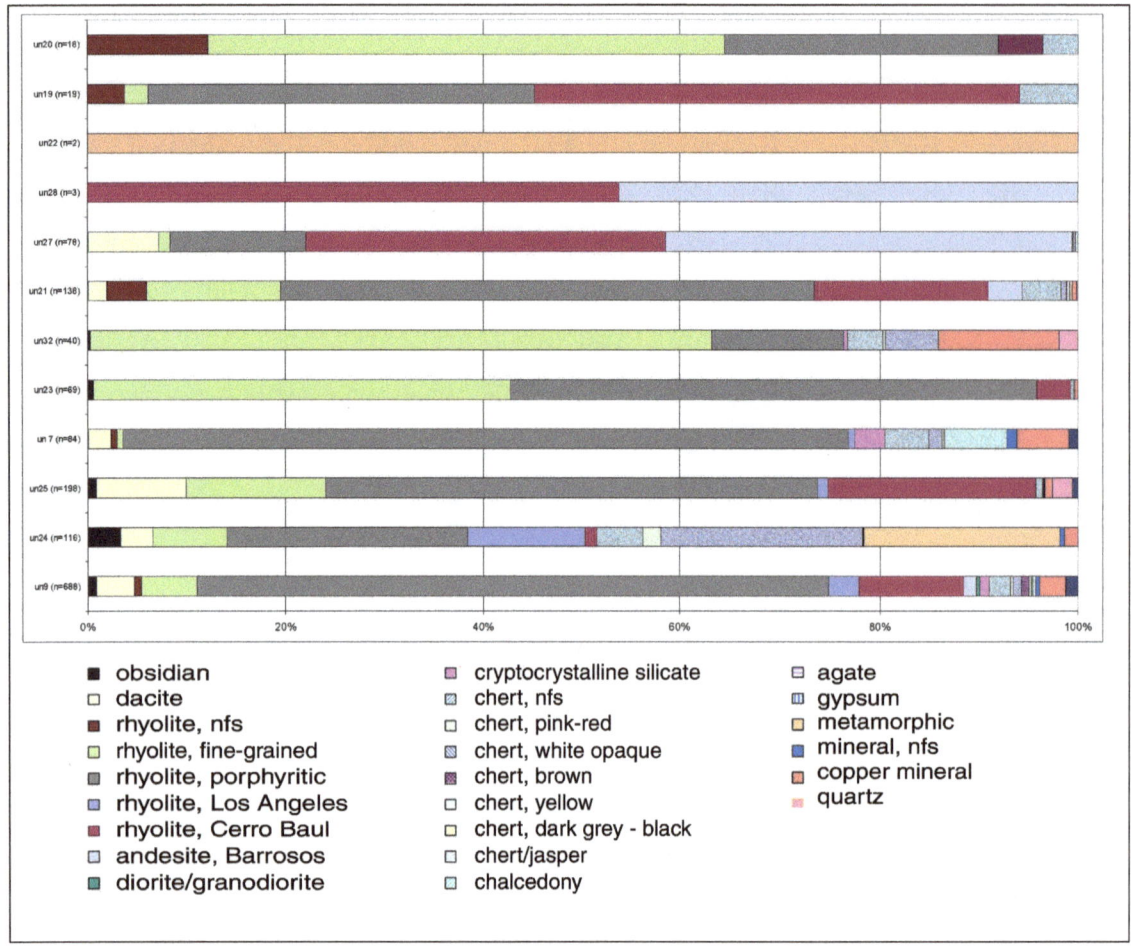

Figure 5.2: Bar-graph of the raw material variety that was exploited in each archaeological context. The data are the same as those presented in Table 5.1

relationship between the variety of material used and the proportional abundance of each type. The resulting diversity indices for the units, given as H, in large part replicate the pattern of high variety in these contexts, with the exception of Unit 7. Units 9, 24, 25, and 21 all have indices above .600, indicating a greater diversity of material in these units than in the other analyzed samples. Importantly, Units 23, 32, 19, and 20 all have relatively quite low indices for material diversity, and the sample for Unit 7, despite its geographic location, is within this range of values. Relative to the material in other nearby contexts, the activities that occurred in Unit 7 used a less diverse suite of raw material types. The range of material that was used is just as varied as in other contexts—including proportions of minerals and sedimentary material—but this variability is depressed by a much higher percentage of porphyritic rhyolite (73.37 %) than is found in any other context. This emphasis on porphyritic rhyolite which was largely used for expedient reduction may reinforce the proposed interpretation of Unit 7 as a utility area for many of the other summit households (Williams and Ruales 2001: 10–13, 2002: 16, see pp 8). A higher diversity of material also has been documented for Unit 27, whose value (.599) falls short of those for the summit contexts but exceeds those from the other units. The residents of this context ostensibly enjoyed access to a wider variety of material than many of their other non-summit contexts did.

The indices for evenness, J, in concert with the data in Table 5.1 provide a basis for evaluating economically-differentiated patterns of material use across the contexts. There is a negative correlation, though neither strong nor very significant, between the diversity and evenness of the raw material types across the units. Generally speaking, as diversity (H) decreases, evenness (J) increases (Table 5.2). Those assemblages which are less diverse have fewer material types, but the proportions for each type are distributed more equitably. In the diverse assemblages, the relative amounts of raw materials are much more disproportionate, and the proportion(s) of one or two raw material type(s) may outweigh all the others by a factor of ten or greater. As noted above with the indices for diversity, there are exceptions to this pattern

Table 5.2: Indices for diversity and evenness for lithic debitage within each excavation unit.

Diversity indices	Un 9	Un 24	Un 25	Un 7	Un 23	Un 32	Un 21	Un 27	Un 28	Un 22	Un 19	Un 20
n	688	116	198	84	69	40	138	78	3	2	19	18
k	23	15	16	15	8	9	16	10	2	1	5	5
H_{max}	1.362	1.176	1.204	1.176	.903	.954	1.204	1	.301	na	.699	.699
H	.758	.878	.624	.499	.386	.530	.632	.599	.300	na	.474	.524
J	.557	.747	.518	.424	.427	.556	.525	.559	.997	na	.678	.749

yet the general trend holds. From Table 5.1, it is clear that these trends in diversity and evenness across the units have much to do with inputs from raw material that is either exotic or which is regionally available but is not present in the immediate vicinity of the archaeological units. This includes obsidian as the only true exotic, rhyolite from Cerro Los Angeles, andesite, the diorite-granodiorite group, many of the sedimentary silicates, and all of the minerals and metamorphic materials. These raw materials are most abundant in the units with the greatest diversity and least evenness, yet they comprise only small proportions in most instances. Additionally, these raw material types can be linked to finished objects with specialized functions such as grinding implements (e.g., diorite-granodiorite and Los Angeles rhyolite) or sumptuary goods and beads (the finished products manufactured from the class of minerals). These items themselves occur in limited quantities relative to the socio-economic privilege of each household. Increased diversity and decreased evenness can be attributed to participation in extended (though still relatively local in extent) procurement networks and which were aimed at material types associated with particular functions. We can assume that some order of economic valuation was attached to these raw materials, perhaps because of mechanical properties or perceived attributes within a social environment that made them desirable for a given function. The relative abundance and diversity of these materials in one context as opposed to another speaks to the ability of the residents of the first household to procure a desired material, particularly if this entailed participating in a procurement network that extended beyond the individual residence. The relative dearth of these same materials in other households implies that these residents were less able to secure these raw materials through the same mechanisms.

Importantly, the gradual decline in the diversity of materials and the concurrent increase in evenness suggest that exacting, draconian policies did not regulate the procurement and distribution of raw materials and perhaps even the finished artifacts. There are no sharp breaks in the quantity or type of material that would imply an absolute restriction on a household's ability to use a class of material. Instead, a variety of material was found in both Wari and Tumilaca contexts, and the actual amount of material appears to correspond to proxies for the presumed economic status of the household. A similar pattern of raw material consumption, including presumed sumptuary materials, has been found at neighboring Cerro Mejia, suggesting that many of the different types of production were generally distributed and only varied from household to household in the intensity with which they took place (Nash 2002). Units 22, 19, and 20 are possible exceptions, and the latter two appear to have utilized only raw material that was available in immediate proximity to these structures and which had minimal social or economic value.

The distance over which raw material was transported before reaching the respective households is one proxy that can be used for evaluating economic status. Domestic units in a socially and economically commanding position can access a more geographically dispersed and diverse suite of resources. With their economic and presumably social status, they can manage to requisition materials from larger procurement networks and compensate through economic, social, or political collateral for the greater energy involved.

Networks and Minimum Convex Polygons

With a careful eye towards the differentiated raw material types exploited in the particular contexts and the moderately-high resolution geological data derived from the ASTER classification, we can interpret with greater sensitivity the availability and use of localized resources around Cerro Baúl and approximate transport distances for the particular suite of raw material recovered in each context. By comparing both the variability of local materials that were used as well as the geographic dispersal of these materials' sources, quantifiable and qualitative differences in the spatial dimension of a household's acquisition network become clear. In this respect, material serves as a proxy for the social mechanisms of procurement, fabrication, and ultimately use and it can be seen that some archaeological contexts participated in more extensive networks than others.

To arrive at this index of comparison, I use the concept of the "minimum convex polygon" to determine the local resource areas, vis-à-vis lithic artifacts, exploited by each household. The minimum convex polygon is a method derived from behavioral ecology for estimating a population's home range area. It is based on the premise that all available point observations of an animal's location, including points of resource exploitation, can be used to delineate a ranging territory as a polygon with all inner angles ≤ 180° that surrounds a nucleated home area which is more habitually frequented than the ranging territory (Samuel and Green 1988: 1067; Gamble and Steele 1999: 399). Though it derives from studies of ecological biology, Gamble and Steele have demonstrated its utility for archaeological populations where the geological sources of raw materials that occur at a site can be used to establish the vertices of a polygon that enclose the home range territory, while the site itself serves as the core home area (1999: 400). The intensity and repetition of activity are, of course, important factors in evaluating the extension and weight of the point observations, for a locus that is visited rarely or only once would represent a minimal contribution to the ranging behavior when compared with loci that are habitually frequented; any locus that exceeds an "equal-use pattern" can be significant in terms of defining the home range polygon, with the most heavily used locus representing the site (Samuel and Green 1988: 1067).

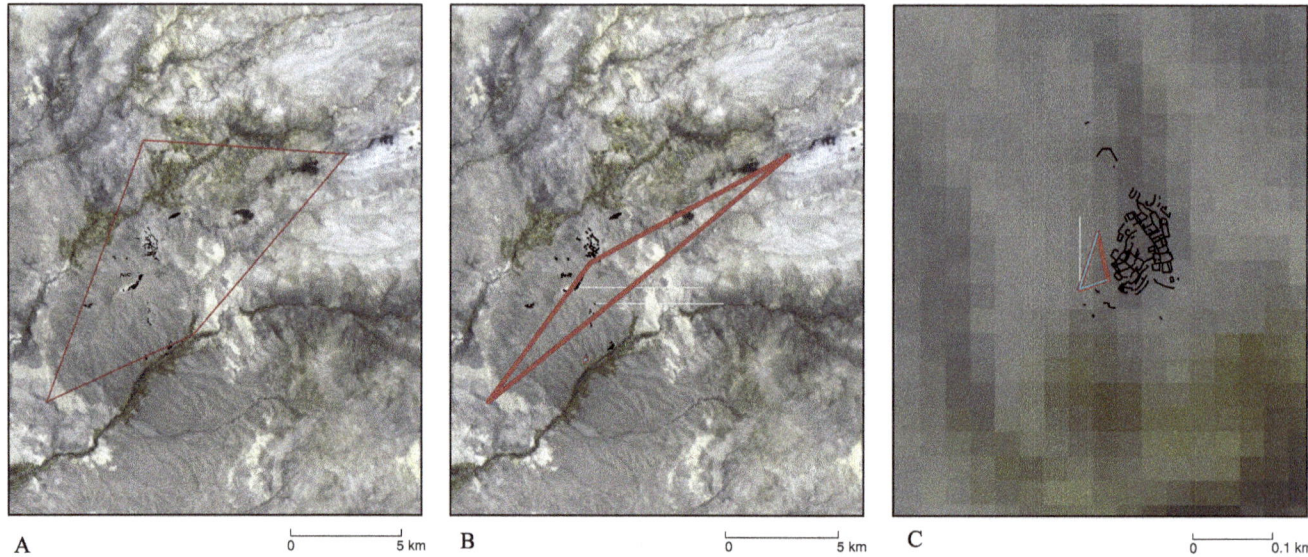

Figure 5.3: Minimum convex polygons for sample excavation units, A) Unit 9; B) Unit 24; and C) Unit 19. The architecture is represented by the black vector layer, and the vectors are displayed against an ASTER two-band composite with a pixel resolution of 30 m. The areas for these and other polygons are given in Table 5.3.

Of course, there are several caveats relevant to applying such a model to a site as socially and economically complex as Cerro Baúl. Certainly the concept of a home range territory as it derives from animal or even hominid ecology cannot be applied in a literal manner. It cannot be considered as a measure of the direct involvement of a home area/household population for, without doubt, various other mechanisms existed that provided for transport and indirect procurement of materials, even at a local scale. That is, for complexly integrated communities—both sedentary and mobile—the process of obtaining and using resources will entail some degree of extra-household relationships.

The minimum convex polygon does obtain, however, as a comparative measure of the scale of networks that introduced resources into a given context. While it is likely not a suitable predictor for the movements of individuals within a community like Cerro Baúl, it is a suitable proxy for the relative extension of the intra-community social and economic interactions involved in resource use, and thus it is constructive to think of the minimum convex polygon not as an ecological ranging area but as the extent of networks that radiate out from the individual 'home area' or residence. In this regard, polygons representing procurement networks have benefits over absolute spatial measures, such as cost-path analyses, since it provides a relative measure for comparing household strategies and is not constrained by the need to identify the particular agents and nodes involved in procurement and redistribution. Subsequently, the minimum convex polygon serves as a measure of the scale of human resources that contributed to the economy of a household rather than a register of individual behavior.

Raw material diversity can be converted into an estimate of network areas by using the materials' sources as vertices for that residence's minimum convex polygon, with the residence itself at the center of the polygon (Figure 5.3). The geological sources are linked to the household with a simplistic model of material acquisition, where a series of vectors radiate from the residence as the central hub outward to the closest primary location where the resources occur; the outermost points are then connected to define the minimum convex polygon. Each polygon defines the maximum spatial extent over which local materials (i.e., ones in all probability procured by members of the Cerro Baúl community) were transported from the source to their use-context, defining the local resource universe for each household[2].

As with the indices for diversity and evenness, there are marked scalar differences in the polygon's areas that reinforce the privileged economic status of the residents on the summit of Cerro Baúl and along its slopes (Table 5.3). The resource area represented with each minimum convex polygon decreases as distance from Unit 9 (again taken as the standard summit residence) increases.

In part, the polygons' areas depend on the diversity of resources, as a greater variety will result in more vertices and subsequently more area. More significantly, though, area is a factor of distance and the polygons emphasize the ability of the household to extend itself beyond its immediate residence to procure resources from across the community and the upper valley region. Many of the lithic resources that were utilized are available in geological deposits in the immediate vicinity of the households, and much of the diversity in material use across the site can be explained by the fact that the residences sit on geologically distinct deposits. The fundamental approach across the site is a "doorstep" strategy to material acquisition, where the underlying geology yielded suitable flaking material for the

Table 5.3: Euclidean distance between each excavation unit and Unit 9 at the summit of Cerro Baúl, and the resource area for each context estimated from the Minimum Convex Polygons.

	Un 9	Un 24	Un 25	Un 7	Un 23	Un 32	Un 21	Un 27	Un 28	Un 22	Un 19	Un 20
Distance (m)	00	22	32	61	362	472	604	1037	1190	1273	2738	2630
Resource area (sq km)	49.81	12.11	37.78	37.78	2.39	1.29	7.94	5.73	.4	-	.1	.1

Table 5.4: Pearson's r correlations for resource area, distance, and diversity indices from Tables 5.2 and 5.3.

	Resource area (km^2)	Residential area (m^2)	Distance (m)	Variety (k)	Diversity (H)	Evenness (J)
Resource area (km^2)	1	.744 *	-.609	.835 *	.449	-.424
Residential area (m^2)	.744 *	1	-.483	.731 *	.642	-.056
Distance (m)	-.609	-.483	1	-.696	-.410	.463

* correlations are significant at a 0.01 level

bulk of domestic activities and minimal effort was made to secure higher quality material found at farther distances. The polygons reveal, though, that some households' "doorstep" resource spheres were considerably more extensive than others and included accessing raw material as far as five kilometers away. In the case of Units 9 and 20, the most extensive minimum convex polygon is some 500 times larger in area than the smallest (Table 5.3). By implication, these households could take advantage of the greater human energy required to procure and move distant materials, and the larger polygons speak towards these residence's enhanced social stature. The materials that were transported greater distances are also those that are assumed to have had an elevated economic value and were used for specific industrial applications or sumptuary functions (such as granodiorite, Los Angeles-area rhyolite, and minerals) as described above. Thus, those households with a larger resource area also had an elevated economic status, not only because they could call in more distant resources but they did so to acquire raw materials with more socio-economic value.

There are strong correlations between the trends in resource area size and other indicators of the socio-economic status of archaeological residences (Table 5.4). The diversity indices from Table 5.2 all have strong correlations with the size of the resource areas. The Pearson's r coefficient between the resource area and the number of material types (K) is the strongest, which is intuitively reasonable since it reinforces the fact that residences with the greatest variety of resources acquired resources from the most dispersed locations. There is also a moderately positive correlation between the size of the resource area and the index for diversity (H) that is countered by a moderately negative correlation with the index for evenness (J), indicating that the residences with the largest resource area were utilizing a wide variety of raw materials in unevenly-distributed proportions. As discussed above, this is due to the presence of sumptuary and other specialized materials in significant but relatively small proportions in some contexts but entirely absent from those residences with small resource areas. The resource area, then, appears to be strongly linked to the economic status of the household and is even a determinate factor.

To corroborate this contention, resource area can be compared to the area (in meters square) of each residence, based on the premise that a residence's size and elaboration—other factors including family structure being constant—can also serve as an index of economic status (e.g., Blanton 1994: 112). Household size, as with local resource area, has strong correlations to the indices for variety and diversity, but does not appear to be significantly linked to evenness. If we take this to mean that the physical size of a structure reflects economic status, then the residents of the larger structures were accessing and utilizing more diverse resources from across a greater area, again reinforcing their economic privilege. Table 5.4, finally, shows the strong negative correlations among these indices and the Euclidian distance that separates each context from the summit of Cerro Baúl (again, using Unit 9 as the point of measurement). As the distance increases, there is a corresponding decrease in the size of the local resource areas, the size of the residence, and the indices for variety and diversity of material; in contrast, evenness has a moderate correlation with distance.

This completes the picture of how resources were used across the site of Cerro Baúl where there are important economic differences even at a local scale. Several factors suggest that to live on the summit of Cerro Baúl was to participate in an economically privileged lifestyle. Here, the greatest diversity of material was brought and utilized from the most dispersed of locally available sources. This variety also suggests that the residents could afford to use particular raw materials at their discretion, while less privileged ones were constricted to the spatially-limited doorstep strategy of material acquisition. For all practical purposes, these local materials were all directly procured, in that they stayed within intra-community networks and were not imported via external relationships. Regardless, the differences in resource area and diversity suggest that certain households, namely those on the summit of Cerro Baúl, were able to compensate for or command more human energy while procuring local resources and their method of direct procurement included extra-household effort. Less economically affluent residences, in contrast, depended on direct procurement in the most literal sense.

Indirect Procurement of Non-local Obsidian

The use of exotic obsidian at Cerro Baúl adhered to similar trends of economic difference as did local material, even though it was indirectly acquired through long-distance networks. The technological characteristics of debitage and artifacts strongly suggest that obsidian was indirectly acquired through long-distance networks, and consequently as a material it can be used as a proxy to represent the social interaction and economic status acted out during exchange relationships that went beyond the single community.

McAnany (1989: 333, 335) describes several characteristics of finished lithic artifacts that identify indirect versus direct procurement strategies from the perspective of the consumer, such as would be the case for the Wari and Tumilaca residences at Cerro Baúl. Key among these are low raw-material variability, indicating the use of a limited number of sources during repeated exchange events within established networks, and artifacts with relatively complex and late-stage technological attributes in the consumer assemblage. While the specific technological attributes are more complex, the range of technological types will be narrower as many stages of reduction—especially the initial ones—will be absent or underrepresented. Lithic materials procured as reduced and finished artifacts will be accompanied by small-sized debitage, which represent terminal stages of reduction, edge refurbishing, and/or recycling (McAnany 1989: 333). The entire sample of obsidian recovered from these contexts (n=282) corresponds well with the criteria anticipated by McAnany's model and it can be stated with confidence that obsidian was introduced into these contexts after having been reduced elsewhere. While the possibility that obsidian was reduced elsewhere at the site cannot yet be negated absolutely, the correspondence with the indirect procurement model and the contrast with local material make it clear that obsidian was involved in a different technological mode of production. Indirect procurement, subsequently, is the most parsimonious explanation for obsidian arriving at Cerro Baúl in this state.

Geological Sources and Archaeological Occurrences

Geochemical sourcing of a sample of archaeological obsidian collected from the surface of Cerro Baúl (n=89) as well as from the nearby site of Omo (n=8) indicates that most obsidian in Moquegua comes from distant geological sources and was distributed along Wari networks. Alca, Andahuaylas, and Quispisisa were the three most commonly represented, and these sources have been tied to exclusive use by nearby Wari sites during the Middle Horizon (Burger, Chavéz, and Chavéz 2000; Burger and Glascock 2000a: 267; Burger and Glascock 2000b: 295; Jennings and Glascock 2002: 112; Brooks, Glascock, and Giesso 1997). Obsidian from Chivay/Cotallalli was also present in Moquegua—predominantly at Omo, but most obsidian at Omo can still be attributed to Wari sources—but in small portions, while it comprises as much as 90% of the obsidian at Tiwanaku itself (Giesso 2000: 204). For Cerro Baúl, 79% of the obsidian sourced originated at Alca. The other Wari sources included material from Andahuaylas (8%), and "Andahuaylas-like" obsidian (1%), and Quispisisa (8%); the Tiwanaku sources at Chivay/Cotallalli were underrepresented and only account for 3% of the obsidian at Cerro Baúl (Burger, Chavéz, and Chavéz 2000: table 6; 1% is, I assume, lost to rounding error).

As there are geographically more proximate sources of obsidian with known economic value, the dominance of more distant sources and the under representation of Tiwanaku sources at Cerro Baúl suggests that political and cultural motives figured prominently in obsidian distribution networks. In the case of Quispisisa obsidian, linked to Wari heartland sites in Ayachucho, material was transported over 800 km from its geological occurrence to Wari and non-Wari sites in both northern and southern Peru (Burger, Chavéz, and Chavéz 2000: 267). The Alca source is considerably closer to Cerro Baúl (ca. 300 km); while this proximity relative to other Wari sources accounts for its predominance, Alca still is much farther from Cerro Baúl than Chivay or other underexploited sources. Burger et al. (2000: 334–337) point to the increase of distant Quispisisa and Alca obsidian at Cerro Baúl as heralding the establishment of state involvement in the procurement and distribution of obsidian between the source and consumer locus. Many of the geological sources are large and spread out with several exposures of economically viable material, however. In such a situation, a politically sponsored censure on the procurement and use of obsidian may have been difficult if not impossible to accomplish (e.g., Jennings and Glascock 2002: 115).

In archaeological contexts, however, the character of obsidian is somewhat different and it is largely spatially circumscribed. Giesso notes the highest percentages of obsidian artifacts in "ceremonial" and "non-elite residential" contexts within the core of Tiwanaku (2000: table 9.6), and interprets this to reveal both a social and ceremonial value inherent in obsidian as a material and also the control over its distribution by elite interests (Giesso 2003: 363). In Middle Horizon Wari sites, obsidian frequently occurs as a class of bifacial preform with technologically distinctive attributes (e.g., Bencic 2000: figure 17; Castillo 2000: figures 8b, 12; Owen and Goldstein 2001: figure 11; Burger, Chavéz, and Chavéz 2000: 337; see Chapter 6). Deposits of stylistically identical obsidian points were recovered as cached items as well as scattered grave furniture within Moche V elite mortuary contexts at San José de Moro in the North Coast Jequetepeque Valley. Castillo interprets these bifaces as reflecting dedicatory and ritual activities where each point was an offering (Castillo 2000: 149–150). The stylistic and technological regularity of these artifacts as well as geo-chemical attributions to the Quispisisa source ostensibly controlled by Wari settlements suggests that these bifaces, perhaps with significant symbolic overtones, were a standard medium for inter-group exchange between local populations and Wari emissaries in northern Peru (Burger, Chavéz, and Chavéz 2000: 337; Burger and Glascock 2000a: 267). The prevalence of obsidian artifacts in elite contexts at Wari sites as well as San Jose de Moro implies that this material was particularly important as an exchange commodity at the level of elite interaction (Castillo 2000: 149). State involvement,

Table 5.5: Comparison of the five percent trimmed-mean statistics for obsidian and local materials, in weight in grams.

	Obsidian		Local material
	debitage	implements	debitage
N	138	112	987
μ (g)	0.4	1.2	5.4
σ (g)	0.4	1.6	8.2
Variance	0.2	2.4	67.4
95% confidence level			
upper	.46	1.50	6.76
lower	.31	.92	4.06
One sample statistics			
t	10.60	–	21.11
df	137		986

Table 5.6: Observed versus expected frequencies for cortex morphology based on χ^2 analysis.

	Obsidian		Local Material	
	O	E	O	E
No clear morphology	0	3.98	31	27.02
Platform and dorsal	0	5.51	43	37.48
Platform and partial dorsal	0	5.13	40	34.87
Platform, no dorsal	0	10.65	83	72.35
No platform, dorsal	0	5.39	42	36.61
No platform, partial dorsal	2	15.01	115	102.02
No platform, no dorsal	102	63.89	396	434.11
Platform missing, dorsal	0	3.85	30	26.15
Platform missing, partial dorsal	3	10.01	75	68.10
Platform missing, no dorsal	54	37.59	239	255.41

if any, took place as formalized networks of transport and distribution.

Nash suggests that obsidian entered into more quotidian behavioral spheres as well. She notes that obsidian "was available to every occupant of the settlement," at Cerro Mejia, adjacent to Cerro Baúl, and infers that it figured prominently in food-preparation activities as well as reflecting elite status and ritual engagements (2002: 108–109). Ubiquity testifies to the integration of Wari communities in Moquegua within larger economic networks. But, as presence-absence, ubiquity does not reveal the internal economic dynamics of the community vis-à-vis the ability of the individual residences to participate in these networks.

While obsidian debitage and implements are not strictly limited to elite contexts, they are most frequent on the summit of Cerro Baúl where the residences exhibit other evidence of social and economic privilege. As with particular types of local material, the relative amounts of obsidian decrease with distance away from the summit residences. Obsidian's economic value and desirability as a raw material may be directly linked to symbolic associations evocative of its ritual import (Giesso 2000: 49) but social order and political structure also played a role in its distribution. As it may not have been possible to monopolize geological sources of obsidian, sponsorship or centralized organization likely took place precisely during the process of producing obsidian artifacts and disseminating them to more distant sites, and obsidian from relatively few of these sources was integrated into large scale distribution networks. Upon reaching the site at the receiving end of these networks obsidian would have been imbued with economic and social significance as an indirectly procured commodity.

Technological Attributes of Obsidian

Obsidian can be distinguished from local materials at Cerro Baúl since, based on the suite of technological characteristics that were analyzed, it appears to have been treated differently and subject to a different mode of reduction. While some specific elements differ, in spirit these technological attributes fulfill many of the criteria described by McAnany (1989: 333–334), cementing the notion that obsidian was indirectly procured.

Six technological characteristics were recorded for lithic debitage that distinguish patterns of obsidian use from those of local material; some of these criteria also single out obsidian implements as being qualitatively and quantitatively different from other tools. These attributes are the morphology of each flake's platform and margins and the related attribute of the technology involved in flake production (e.g., whether hard hammer, soft hammer, or pressure-flaking was involved), flake size (recorded as size classes in 2 cm increments) and related weight (in grams), and the extent and location of cortical surfaces. The latter three attributes speak towards the extent to which obsidian was reduced prior to being deposited in these contexts, while the former set of three attributes document the specific modes of reduction that occurred in the excavated deposits. Together these data reveal that obsidian was largely reduced elsewhere and that, once within these contexts, primarily late and technologically specialized types of reduction—stages of reduction that are linked with shaping and retouching implements—occurred.

True to the model anticipated for indirectly procured material, obsidian debitage (n=161) is predominantly small; over 83 % of this material measures under 2 cm in its maximum dimension. The proportion of obsidian in larger size categories drops off quickly, in contrast to material that is available locally. Weight, as a function of an object's three dimensions and mass, provides a more accurate index of the size of obsidian debitage for comparison with other obsidian artifacts as well as artifacts of local material. Table 5.5 presents summary statistics for the weights of flaked local material and obsidian debitage with extreme values removed to provide a 5 % trimmed mean. Obsidian debitage is considerably smaller than debitage from local material, with a mean of 0.4 grams versus 5.4 grams: 95 % of the obsidian debitage lies within 0.3–0.46 grams, while local debitage is heavier by over a power of ten, with 95 % of this material weighing between 4.0–6.76 grams. The values for variance demonstrate the close clustering of obsidian flakes at very low weights, while the values for local material are affected by a wide range of highly variable flake weights.

Importantly, the range of weights for obsidian implements also substantially outweighs that of obsidian debitage (Table 5.5). The mean weight for obsidian implements (1.2 grams), while remarkably small, still lies outside of the 95 % confidence bracket for obsidian debitage, as does the lower end of the 95 % confidence range for the implements itself at a value of 0.92 grams. This not only reflects the fact that obsidian debitage overall is very small, but the lack

Table 5.7: Observed versus expected frequencies for flake technological attributes based on χ^2 analysis.

	Obsidian		Local Material	
	O	E	O	E
Decortification flake	0	.69	6	5.31
Reduction flake, nfs*	31	33.77	2	2.65
Shatter	30	27.99	212	214.01
Hard hammer flake	54	88.94	715	680.06
Soft hammer flake	5	1.85	11	14.15
Pressure flake	3	0.81	4	6.19
Biface reduction flake	16	3.82	17	29.18
Retouch flake	19	2.20	0	16.80
Microdebitage	1	0.35	2	2.65
Core rejuvenation flake	2	0.46	2	3.54

* "Not further specified"

of a significant quantity of obsidian debris that is equal to or greater in size than the implements suggests that the obsidian artifacts were not produced on site from primary flakes. During the initial reduction, flakes are removed from a core that are large enough to serve as blanks or preforms for implements; larger flakes will subsequently be deposited as fragments or rejects. Table 5.5 indicates that this is not the case, but that obsidian debitage consistently falls below the weight range predicted for implements. This discrepancy implies that such small debitage was produced in late stages of reducing larger forms, i.e., implements or preforms themselves in the absence of cores and raw nodules of material. Lending weight to this assumption, only one obsidian core was found among the entire sample of obsidian artifacts from all contexts (n=250), and this single core fragment was small and exhausted. Further, obsidian debitage is well below the size ranges for local material, where primary reduction did occur.

In addition to the small size of this debitage, most obsidian lacks cortical surfaces. In fact, no obsidian implement was recorded with remnant cortical surfaces, and only about 3 % of the flakes had any cortical surfaces preserved. Since cortex, the weathered natural exterior of lithic material, is gradually removed as reduction progresses, partial or complete cortical surfaces (and the lack there of) on the dorsal side and platform of a flake can serve as a relative measure of how early or late an individual flake falls within the reduction sequence (Toth 1987: 771, 1985). Complete cortical surfaces on the platform and dorsal side of flakes indicates primary reduction and the initial removal from a natural cobble, while the complete absence of cortical surfaces indicates a late stage of reduction. Toth outlines six such relative stages, with decreasing relationships between platform and dorsal cortical surfaces. In the first three relative stages of reduction, cortex will be present on the platform but will be reduced from the dorsal surface, while in the latter three it will be absent from the platform and also gradually absent from the dorsal surface (Toth 1987: 771). These relative measures were used, with additional categories to account for incomplete flakes with missing platforms. Cortex was recorded as present or absent from both platform and dorsal surfaces, and if present the relative amount (either complete or partial) was also noted. Given the cortex morphology on any particular flake, that flake can be placed within a relative sequence of reduction. A flake with complete platform and dorsal cortex represents primary reduction stages, while a flake that entirely lacks cortical surfaces represents the latest reduction stages.

Cortical platforms were completely missing from the sample of obsidian flakes, and late stages of reduction are represented by the predominantly cortex-free debitage (Figure 5.4a). Together, complete flakes with no cortex whatsoever and partially complete flakes with no cortex represent 96.89 % of the obsidian debitage, as compared to 58 % of the local material represented in the same two categories. Table 5.6 presents the values calculated for chi-squared analysis given as:

$$\chi^2 = \sum \frac{(Oi-Ei)^2}{Ei}$$

where Oi gives the observed number of cases for a given category i and Ei gives the expected value for the i category given the total population proportions (see Drennan 1996: 188–189). The χ^2 value for these relationships is 92.43 with 19 degrees of freedom. This translates to an inordinately high probability that the differences in these two populations (obsidian and local material) are not attributable to sampling, but rather reflect substantive differences in the populations themselves. The χ^2 values from both Tables 5.7 and 5.8 are problematic due to a large number of empty cells and low expected values. Consequently, the significance of these probabilities is decreased but it still illustrates the point that obsidian and local material where reduced in two different modes.

More striking is the discrepancy between observed values and expected values, however. These discrepancies between observed and expected frequencies when obsidian debitage and local material are compared reveal the different reduction strategies in which they were involved, as seen in Tables 5.7 and 5.8. During initial stages of reduction, represented by cortex morphology, the observed values for obsidian are consistently lower than the expected values. In contrast, the observed values for flakes with no dorsal cortex (both complete and incomplete) are substantially higher.

With local material the trend is the opposite, however. The observed values for the earlier stages of reduction are higher than the expected values, whereas those for the latest stages of reduction represented by no dorsal cortex are lower than expected. Not only does χ^2 suggest that these two samples are qualitatively different, it also emphasizes the mismatch between the two where obsidian was disproportionately involved in late stages of reduction during which cortex was absent.

As mentioned above, a high proportion of small, late-stage reduction flakes could signify the final working or retouching of pre-fashioned implements and preforms. Whether or not this occurred can only be argued by examining the flakes themselves according to technological criteria that will ascertain the modes of reduction that were involved. These criteria are based on metrical and morphological attributes of the flakes and reveal the mechanics that were involved in flake removal in order to characterize the type and stage of reduction (Sliva 1997, Inizan et al. 1999; Whitakker 1994). Contrary to a criterion anticipated by McAnany's model for indirect procurement, obsidian deb-

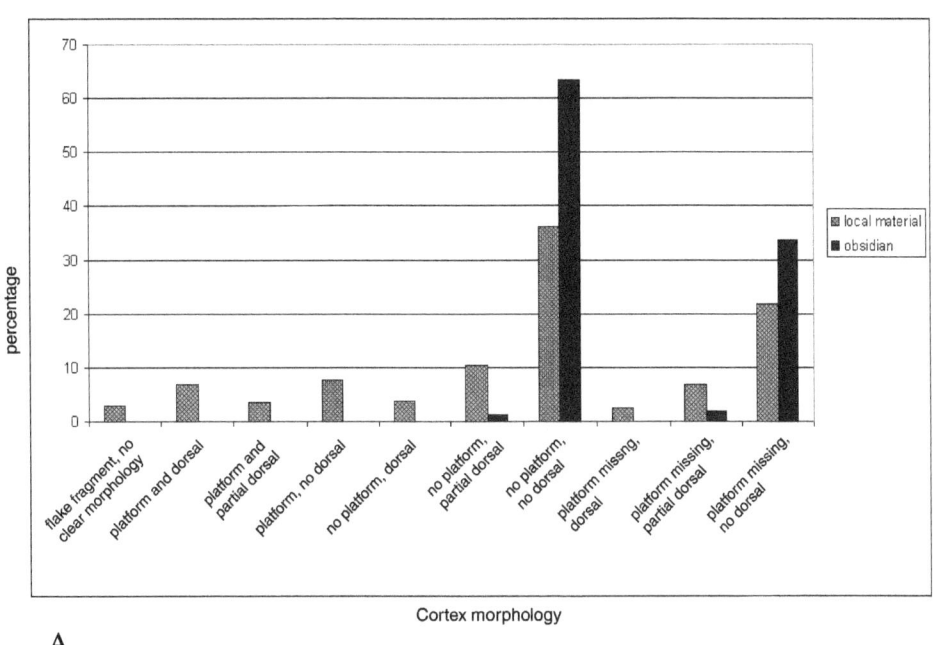

A

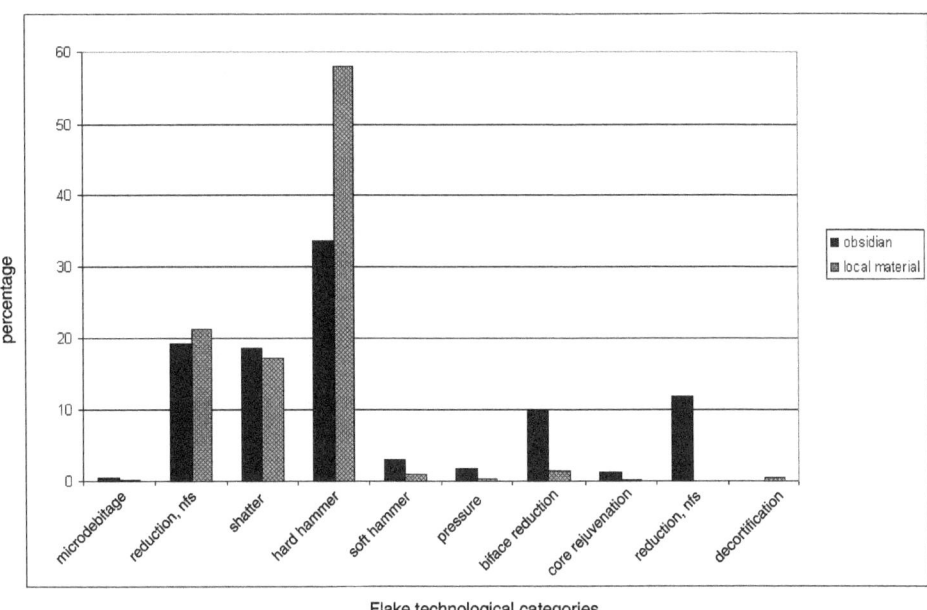

B

Figure 5.4: Histograms of obsidian and local-material debitage based on the percentage of flakes represented in each class. A) precentage of cortex represented by each flake, and B) Technological types represented by each flake.

itage shows a wider range of technological attributes than the directly-procured local material, since this latter class was not used to make the same types of artifacts as obsidian was (Figure 5.4b). In keeping with her model, however, there are greater proportions of obsidian flakes with technologically more complex attributes. Specifically, a greater percentage of flakes suggest terminal reduction stages and edge refurbishing, such as bifacial reduction and retouch.

37

Table 5.8: Densities of exotic and local raw material per cubic meter in each excavation unit. The values for local material exclude implements, to avoid skewing from oversized artifacts that are statistical outliers.

Excavation Unit:	Un 9	Un 24	Un 25	Un 7	Un 23	Un 32	Un 21	Un 27	Un 28	Un 22	Un 19	Un 20	total
m^3	190.4	12.6	67.5	22.5	6.0	17.5	6.0	7.7	4.8	4.2	18.0	12.0	369.2
Obsidian debitage													
(g/ unit)	47.4	15.4	20.4	0.2	4.5	0.8	0.6	0.6					89.9
(g/m^3)	0.3	1.2	0.3	0.01	0.8	0.05	0.1	0.08					
Obsidian implements													
(g/ unit)	123.5	52.4	13.6	4.5	0.7	0.6	2.3	0					197.6
(g/m^3)	.6	4.2	.2	.2	.1	.03	.4	0					
All obsidian													
(g/ unit)	170.9	67.8	34.0	4.7	5.2	1.4	2.9	0.6					287.5
(g/m^3)	0.9	5.4	0.5	0.2	0.9	0.08	0.5	0.08					
Local material													
(g/ unit)	34142.9	3513	17946.9	8874.9	2372.9	593.4	2873.6	2334.1	33.2	1120	587.1	476.4	74868.4
(g/m^3)	179.3	278.8	265.9	394.4	395.5	33.9	478.9	305.1	6.9	266.7	32.6	39.7	

These stages of reduction are more equitably represented in obsidian debitage, whereas local material is dominated by technologically simpler flake forms from initial reduction stages. Chi square analysis, again, is useful for evaluating the proportions of technological types within and across these two populations, although—as was the case above—the contrast between observed and expected values is perhaps more revealing than is the actual χ^2 statistics (Table 5.7). When comparing technological attributes, the χ^2 value for obsidian versus local material again is inordinately high— $\chi^2 = 229.81$ with 19 degrees of freedom. The difference between observed and expected values for obsidian shows a heavier emphasis on later, technologically more complex stages of reduction. Observed values for soft hammer reduction, pressure flaking, bifacial reduction, retouching, and microdebitage are all considerably higher than expected values for obsidian, whereas for local material these values are all lower than expected. Overall obsidian is underrepresented less complex stages of reduction while local material is more strongly represented.

As with flake size and cortex, the technological attributes of obsidian flakes indicate that they derive from later stages of artifacts that are partially if not already entirely shaped. These factors combine with the other metrical and morphological criteria outlined at the beginning of this section to show that obsidian use clearly differed from that of other material at Cerro Baúl. Prentiss (1998) has shown that flake size, completeness, and morphology dependently can be used to isolate divergent reduction strategies and even early versus late stages within a sequence when represented in different populations (c.f., Rozen and Sullivan 1989).

A principal components analysis of the six similar variables coded for in this analysis clearly isolates obsidian as being technologically distinct from dacite and the numerous varieties of chert and rhyolite, the other three main classes of material from which similar implements were flaked (Figure 5.5). All four classes of material load heavily in Component 1, with similar values. While the local materials have Component one values between .960–.973, obsidian rates somewhat lower and loads into Component 1 at .926. In Component 2, obsidian shares a relatively close relationship with chert (similarly used predominantly for fashioning bifaces), but with values of .359 and .157 respectively it is still substantially isolated. Similar treatments of local material are not supported by the components analysis, which clusters dacite and rhyolite closely together.

Certain technological classes such as core rejuvenation flakes and shatter as well as partially cortical flakes are not completely absent from the population of obsidian debitage. These suggest a limited level of reduction occurred that was not exclusive to refurbishing finished tools, but may have involved partially reduced cores. Overall, the primary stages of reduction are "divorced spatially" from the context of obsidian use at Cerro Baúl: this, in concert with the low geological material variability and formalized morphology of obsidian implements, makes indirect procurement and the "institutionalized separation between the place of production and the subsequent place(s) of consumption" the most parsimonious mode of obsidian procurement (McAnany 1989: 341).

The Domestic Contexts of Obsidian Use

An "institutionalized separation" also implies an institutionalized system of artifact production, transport, and redistribution through, if not centralized, at least established and repeated network connections. The amount of material that is moved and consumed via these established networks thus stands as an indicator of the relative intensity with which households participated in a network. As with the local scale of material procurement and use, the consumption of obsidian across Cerro Baúl indicates that not all households participated in these networks equitably. Instead, the nucleated pattern of resource diversity and economic status is reinforced by the intensity of each household's use of obsidian. Importantly, this exotic material is present in all contexts except for those that are most distant from the summit of Cerro Baúl. Moreover, the apparent ethnicity of a household—either Wari or Tumilaca—appears not to be ans operative variable that determines the scale of obsidian consumption.

Obsidian is ubiquitous in those contexts near the center of the site (Table 5.8), but the amounts of both debitage and implements decrease dramatically with distance from Unit 9, just as was seen with the diversity indices. The density of material is given as grams per cubic meter per excavation unit, and the values for obsidian debitage, implements, and all locally available material are given in Table 5.8. In

Table 5.9: Coefficients for the correlations between the Euclidean distance from Unit 9 and the average density of raw material per cubic meter in each excavation unit.

	Distance	Obsidian debitage (g/m^3)	Obsidian implements (g/m^3)	All obsidian (g/m^3)	Local material (g/m^3)
Kendall's Tau					
T	1.000	-.286	-.618	-.785	-.273
sign.		.322	.034	.001	.217
Spearman's R					
r_s	1.000	-.476	-.731	-.920	-.392
sign.		.233	.040	.000	.208

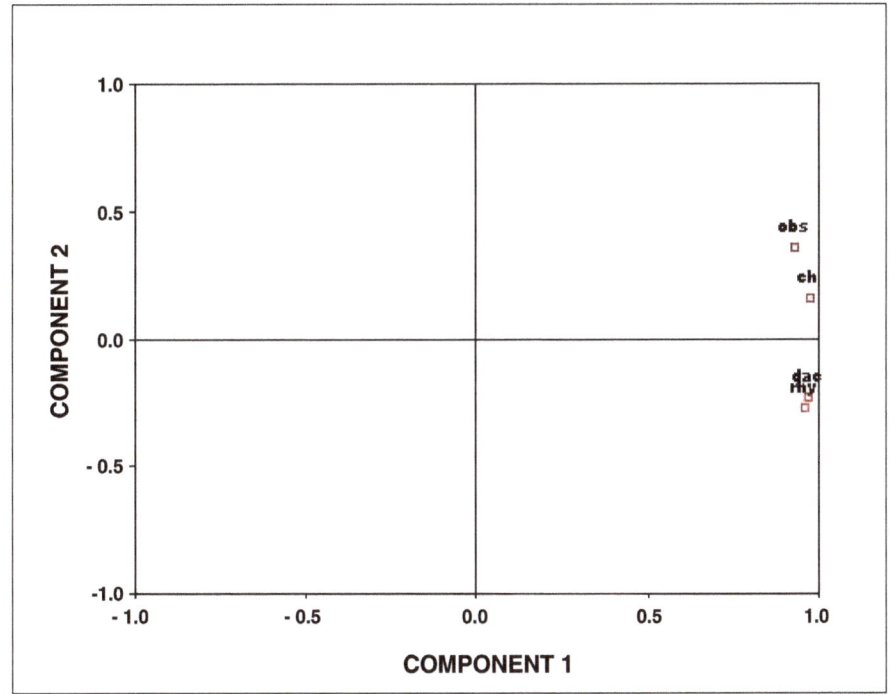

Figure 5.5: Principal components plot of material types based on the data from lithic debitage in all analyzed contexts

absolute amounts (grams per unit) there is a striking trend in the amount of obsidian that was controlled and consumed by each context. Unit 9 clearly leads this trend, suggesting that this household participated most directly in the "institutionalized" networks of obsidian consumption that linked Cerro Baúl to other Wari sites near Alca and further to the north. The other contexts adjacent to Unit 9 also would have participated intensively in these economically-based exchange relationships that were socially-realized. There is a strong negative correlation between the quantity of obsidian consumed by a household and their distance from Unit 9, however. Interaction may have decreased with distance across the site or, at the very least, the socio-economic profile of the community changed dramatically between the summit and non-summit residences (Table 5.9). The picture of material use changes substantially when the volume of lithic material per volume of excavated context is normalized for (as grams per cubic meter), yet there is still a significant negative correlation. Spearman's r for the amount of obsidian per cubic meter (both implements and debitage) versus distance is -.920 (prob. < .0001). There is only a moderate direct correlation, however, between the volume of debitage and the volume of implements per unit, however, as well as a moderately negative correlation in the volume of debitage per unit against distance from the summit. This underscores a disconnected relationship between debitage production and tool use, where many contexts had relatively greater quantities of obsidian debitage despite a relative lack of tools. Unit 23, in particular, stands out as a locus where the volume of obsidian represented by implements does not mirror the density of debitage per square meter, though it does replicate proportionately the density of local material per square meter relative to other contexts. This suggests an asymmetrical relationship in the intensity

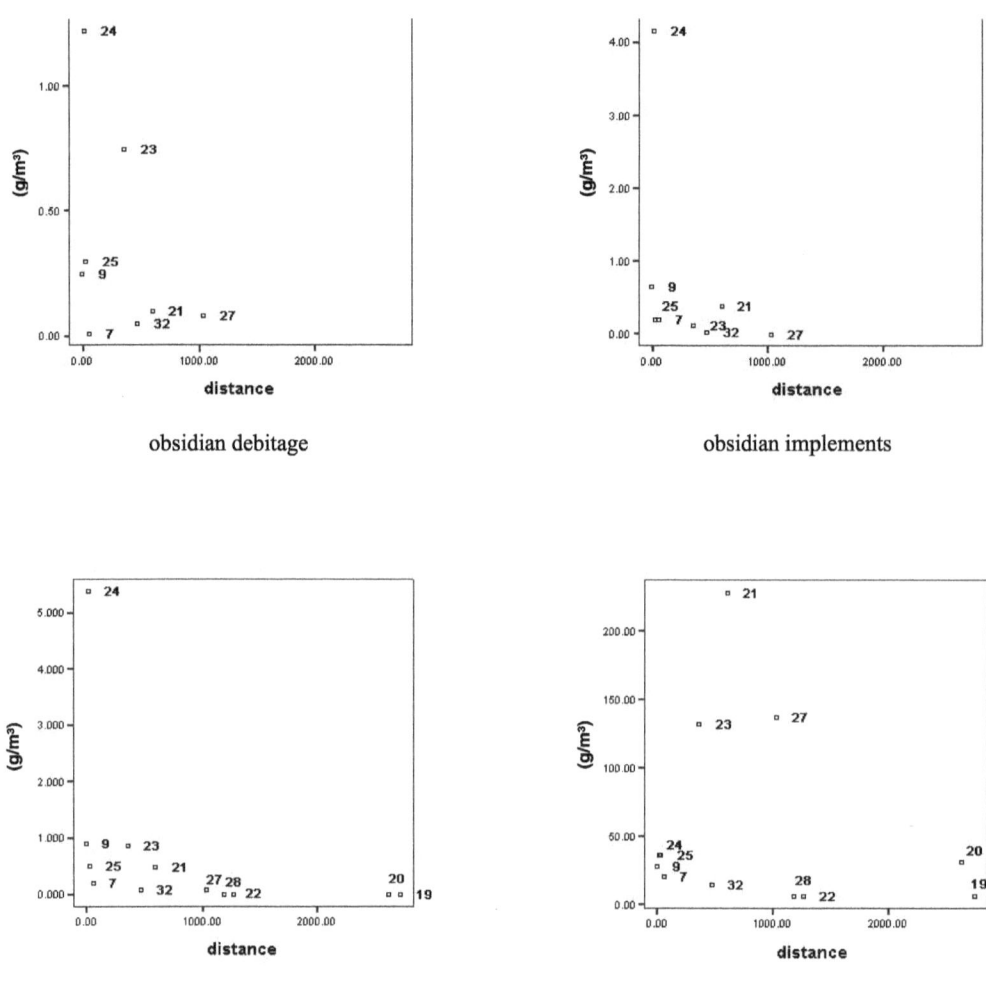

Figure 5.6: Scatterplots of density of raw material (measured in grams per cubic meter) in each excavation unit versus distance from the center of the site (measured in meters from Unit 9).

of obsidian use relative to other material categories, including obsidian tools (Figure 5.6). The decrease in obsidian use over distance, in most all other respects has a negative, nearly linear relationship (Figures 5.6).

Figure 5.6 may reveal some of the social dynamics of economic interaction at Cerro Baúl and the articulation of extra-household relationships within the community overall. These plots demonstrate the relationship between distance and the overall consumption of obsidian per household. These units can be roughly clustered into four groups based on the correlation between how far removed the residence is from the center of the site and the amount of obsidian that was used. These groups are: Units 7, 9, 25, and 24 (which, because of the high quantity of obsidian in one feature consistently acts as an outlier); Units 32, 21, and 23; Units 27, 28, 22; and Units 20 and 19. As distance increases, there is little economic interaction with the center, as embodied by the group of four contexts on the summit and economic differentiation subsequently has a radial or concentric pattern across the site.

We can presume, also, that these economic differences probably reflect social distances. Each group may define intra-community clusters with a concordant increases and decreases in social interactions between the households (Peterson and Drennan 2005: 6). Less obsidian implies that these households participated to a lesser degree in the established, long distance networks of obsidian procurement. Further, if we assume an institutionalized organization for indirect procurement, it also speaks to a lower intensity of involvement in intra-community relationships through which these resources were distributed among consumers.

Economic differentiation at Cerro Baúl is most responsive to inclusion/exclusion within a sub-community over distance, rather than the apparent ethnic affinity of each household. In this sense, neighborhood-like groups based on the proximity of one residence to others were important units of social and economic interaction. For many of the sectors of Cerro Baúl, these neighborhood groupings would include multi-ethnic clusters of households with similar economic bases despite other apparent cultural differences.

---

[2] (The scale of these networks would change if other resources, such as agricultural products and ceramic materials, are considered. I feel confident, however, that while the exact spatial extent may be greater or lesser, the relative ordering among residential contexts will be similar to that seen when lithic materials are evaluated.)

Chapter 6: Artifact Densities

Defining Artifact Clusters

The distribution of flaked lithic debitage shows variable patterns in each context, suggesting in some instances areas spatially circumscribed behavior. These peaks in the densities of lithic artifacts are likely attributed to specialized activity areas, as these densities of artifacts correspond with clusters of other artifact types suggesting a coherent activity that engaged these variable media. Some clusters, however, can be linked to midden deposits. In other cases, however, dense clusters of lithics are not apparent, and a generalized distribution best characterizes the deposition of lithic debitage. The lack of discrete densities can be related to a few causal factors (Table 5.8). Several of the units that have low volumes of lithic debitage overall (such that recurrent activities are not expressed) also tend to be residences that are smaller in extent (so that spatial variation in the frequency of activity is not reinforced). Alternatively, due to cultural preferences either there was no tendency towards defined areas or cleaning and maintenance were more frequent.

Figures 6.1 and 6.2 show the densities of lithic material for each residential context based on a count of debitage per square meter. The number of obsidian and local material flakes for each square meter were tallied. Grid cell values were then interpolated based on these quantities, using ArcInfo's Inverse Distance Weighting algorithm, to model densities values for 10 cm^2 cells across the surface of the room. While these data were effectively sampled at one meter resolution and the 0.1 meter modeled resolution is primarily a fiction of interpolation, a smaller cell size is desirable so that the sampled population more accurately represents the scale of archaeological phenomena targeted for inference (Kvamme 1990: 372). This modeling had two objectives. The first objective was to compare the distribution of locally available material across space to evaluate denser concentrations suggestive of activity areas. Second, the distribution of local material was compared with exotic obsidian to reveal spatial patterns that suggest differential deposition, and which might indicate different emic perceptions in the use and cultural content of these materials. The distribution of local and exotic material could not be compared in Units 7, 19, 20, 21 and 28 because of an insufficient number of data points (≤ 3) for obsidian. There were also an insufficient number of data points to interpolate the distribution of local material in Unit 28.

Opinions differ as to the validity and rigorousness of visual interpretations of artifact distributions. Berry et al. emphatically state their "admonition that visual inspection and subjective assessment may be inadequate approaches to [the] spatial analysis" of artifact associations (1983: 552). Their criticism stems largely from the lack of reproducibility inherent in visual assessment which considers the locations of individual point-plotted artifacts. In the approach taken here, the problem of reproducibility is circumvented by the use of specific interpolation algorithms for cell values for each meter square from each residential context. It is the resulting grid which is afterward subject to "visual inspection"—although the methods I use here lack much of the statistic rigor that their proposed approach possesses.

Dacey suggests a much more manageable method for comparing the distance between pairs of cases within artifact classes based on the mean frequency and variance among a set of cells for an intrasite area (1973: 321–322). Values are compiled for individual cells of a constant size based on the frequency of the artifact class within each cell. These cells create a "numerical summary" of the mapped distributions by comparing the relative frequencies of the artifact across the constant cells (Dacey 1973: 321). While Dacey's method is meant to compress the data for artifacts which are individually plotted, the same effect can be achieved by simply using non-point excavation proveniences such as grid locations in a rasterized distribution. The index of artifact distributions is calculated as the quotient of the variance and the mean of the artifact frequencies. Those values more closely approaching 1, or unity between the mean and variance, reflect more homogenous distributions whereas values diverging from unity indicate statistical, spatial loading. While this is a rougher measure and lacks some of the statistical sophistication of other indices, it can be modified to the frequency/m^2 values used here, since point-data on individual artifact locations are not available for Cerro Baúl. Other common methods for analysing spatial variation, such as nearest-neighbor statistics, are precluded by their requirement of coordinate pairs for artifacts, so that they can not be applied to cell values (e.g., Whallon 1974; Pinder et al. 1979; Kintigh 1990).

The organization and analysis of frequencies as raster data, rather than as vectorized points, has several advantages. Data-smoothing is necessary for many varieties of spatial interpretations, especially those relying on contouring of artifact densities, and fortunately the data smoothing inherent in compiling cell values has a negligible effect on the overall patterning of distributions (Whallon 1984: 245). It is, however, always important to consider the issues of scaling that are involved in representing spatial data. Finally, the use of a rasterized grid format for data presentation and analysis ensures spatial consistency and thus integrity between the observed artifact frequency values between locations; the raster grid acts as a constantly organized background against which the individual cell values—in this instance artifact frequencies—can be evaluated with confidence as a single sample variable (Kvamme 1990: 371–372).

The use of a raster format within a geographic information system allows several factors of spatial association to be evaluated simultaneously, including coincidence, proximity, dependence, and heterogeneity, in order to investigate the causal factors of non-homogenous clustered distributions (Goodchild 1996: 243–244). The variables of these factors determine the differential loading of phenomena across space and help us characterize the causal elements, as well as enabling us to identify the discontinuous phenomena in the first place. Importantly, these interpolated data do not represent true distributions, but rather they present model distributions based on true grid-cell values. The operative element in this approach is, in fact, data smoothing in order to create a dimensional model of the homogeneity and heterogeneity of artifact frequencies in such a way that it represents evenness and concentration. The approach taken here

Table 6.1: Density indices for each excavation unit based on the mean and variance of debitage frequencies per square meter. Asymmetrical distributions are given as higher values of σ^2 / μ.

Excavation Unit:	Un 7	Un 9	Un 19	Un 20	Un 21	Un 22	Un 23	Un 24	Un 25	Un 27	Un 28	Un 32
Local material												
mean	9.67	36.43	2.0	3.6	12.55	1.00	6.29	10.55	22.22	10.14	na	8.0
variance	47.25	782.26	9.0	8.3	68.67	2.00	15.91	55.27	277.94	32.14	na	38.5
σ^2 / μ	4.88	21.47	4.5	2.31	5.47	2.0	2.53	5.24	12.51	3.17		4.81
Obsidian												
mean		14.67					2.5	4.5	7.0	2.0		1.5
variance		279.07					12.5	6.7	70.0	4.0		4.5
σ^2 / μ		19.02					5.0	1.49	10.0	2.0		3.0

to identify discontinuous distributions of lithic materials has much in common with the basic premises outlined by Whallon (1984: 245), though it focuses on one type of material (debitage) and does not compare two or more classes of artifact as is frequently common in archaeological spatial analyses. Where sufficient data points were available, comparison between types of material was an important aspect of this analysis.

Possible Activity Areas at Cerro Baúl

The quotients for debitage distributions, expressed as σ^2 / μ, are presented in Table 6.1. The excavation units that diverge most strongly from unity, when considering both local material and obsidian, are located on the summit of Cerro Baúl, Units 9 and 25. None of the distributions approach perfect unity, although the distributions found with several are more heavily loaded than in other contexts. These include Units 7, 21, 24A, and 32 whose quotients exceed 4.8. Defined concentrations, possibly indicative of activity areas, are evident graphically in the distributions of lithics in Units 9, 25, and 7 (Figures 6.1 and 6.2). In other contexts, such as Unit 24A and Unit 21, the dense clustering of artifacts can be linked to midden deposits. By virtue of these interpolations, we can explore the spatial relationships between artifact densities and other features in order to infer plausible causal behaviors.

Unit 9 has one of the more complex and interesting distributions of lithic debitage (Figure 6.1a). Locally available material clusters strongly in rooms 9F, 9D, and in an adjacent corner of patio 9B. In contrast, densities are very low in rooms 9C and 9E. Combustion features within room 9F and even 9G fall within the distribution of both local and exotic lithic debitage but do not match the denser areas of the distribution. The paucity of lithic artifacts within these features contrasts with that seen in Unit 7 and suggests a different cleaning behavior. During excavation, Unit 9 was characterized as an elite residence, and a considerable quantity of prestige goods (fine ceramics, copper-alloy artifacts, obsidian, and mineral and shell beads) were recovered from the various rooms. Room 9F, in particular, was notable because of a large quantity of grinding stones (*manos* and *batanes*), large storage vessels, and faunal remains including bones and even high quantities of preserved guinea pig excrement. Room 9F was most probably a domestic kitchen area, where moderate quantities of comestibles were prepared for consumption within Unit 9. Similarly, large quantities of preserved botanical remains were found near the floor in room 9G (Williams and Ruales 2004: 14–20). Local lithic materials figured prominently in the quotidian economic activities of Unit 9, particularly by providing cutting and milling artifacts as well as serving as large working surfaces in room 9F. The higher densities of local debitage within room 9F suggest that expedient reduction and edge refurbishing occurred in close association with the area of their use and that this space was one of dense and redundant activity.

The distribution of obsidian debitage partially overlaps that of local material. Significantly it is confined to limited clusters in spatially discrete architectural contexts, especially room 9D and to a lesser extent room 9C. Unlike in other spatial contexts, the distribution of obsidian debitage does not coincide with features. The character of the artifacts in rooms 9D and 9C is also distinct from that of the artifacts in 9F and does not specify food preparation but is more general in nature (Williams and Ruales 2004, 2002). Obsidian debitage reaches its highest density in room 9D (approximately 4 flakes per m?), a room that also had the highest frequency of copper alloy artifacts, similar sumptuary items, and pointed bone implements resembling weaving tools (Williams and Ruales 2004: 13). Unlike other settings, features such as hearths and groundstone implements were absent from this context. The spatial separation in local material and obsidian reduction imply that obsidian was used in Unit 9 for purposes other than food preparation (cf. Nash 2002: 108–109), and that it was linked with other spatially-confined economic activities indicative of a high-status setting. In this high-status context obsidian was exploited in different spheres than local material. Complementary to its ethnohistorically documented ideological content (Giesso 2000: 49), it may have applied to a different system of social valuation. The prestige status of obsidian seen at other Middle Horizon sites certainly had parallels at Cerro Baúl, likely because of the place of obsidian in elite exchange networks.

The distribution of material in Unit 24A, both local and exotic, almost overlaps entirely (Figure 6.1b). Much of the occupation level in room 24A was the upper surface of midden deposits, and the majority of the lithic material was found in secondary contexts within these deposits (Williams and Ruales 2004: 21–24). The very dense concentrations of debitage especially in the southern corner of the unit can thus be attributed to maintenance and cleaning behavior in the rest of the residential area. Unit 24, totaling four rooms, was excavated in its entirety but only the lithic artifacts from room 24A have been analyzed. Once the material from the rest of this unit, outside this single room, is analyzed, more divergent patterns in the use and reduction of obsidian and expedient materials may become apparent.

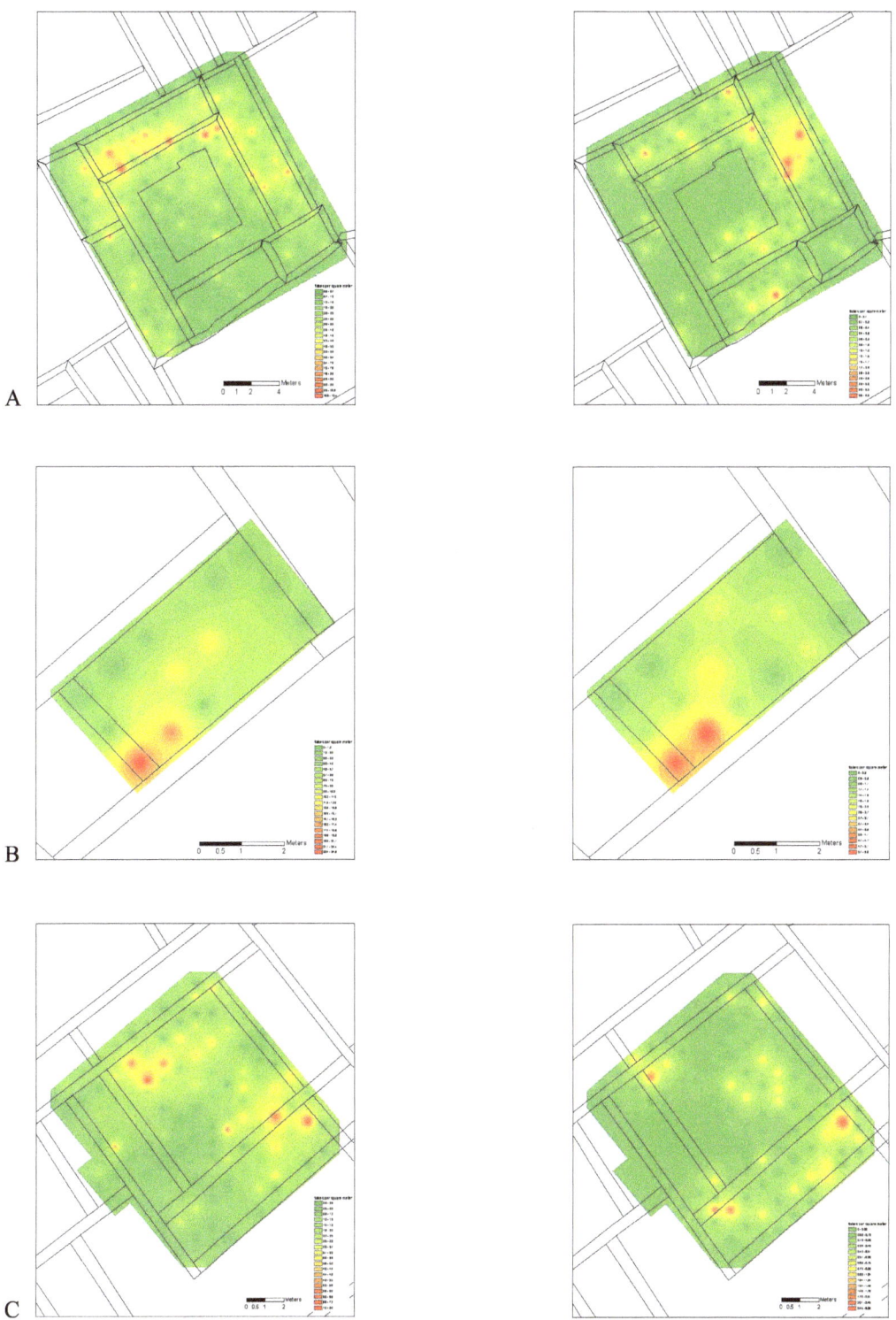

Figure 6.1: Density grids of local (left) and obsidian (right) debitage per square meter. A: Unidad 9, B: Unidad 24A, C: Unidad 25. Data are classed at natural breaks (Jenks) using 20 classes for local material and 15 for obsidian.

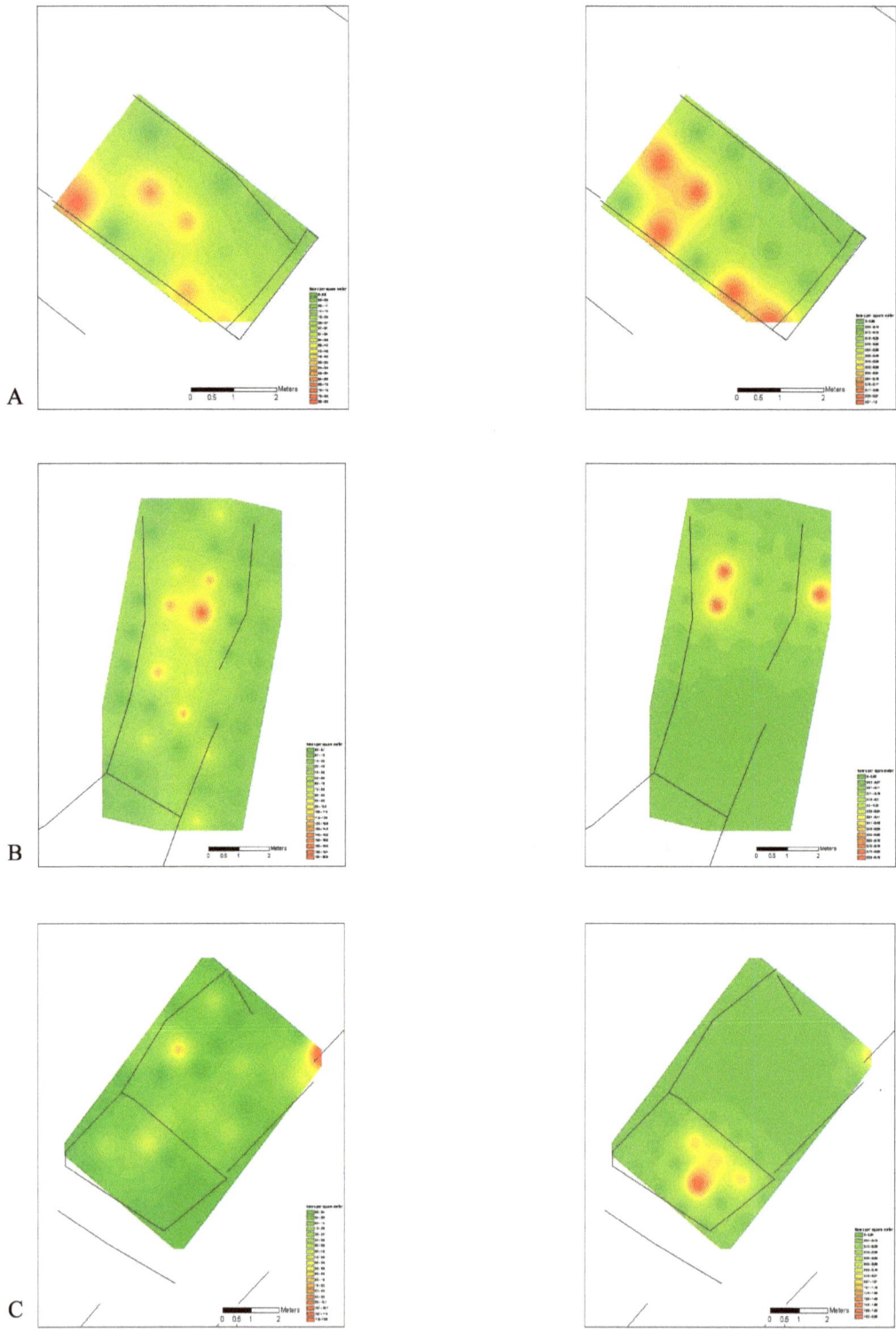

Figure 6.1 (continued): Density grids of local (left) and obsidian (right) debitage per square meter. A: Unidad 23, B: Unidad 32, C: Unidad 27. Data are classed at natural breaks (Jenks) using 20 classes for local material and 15 for obsidian.

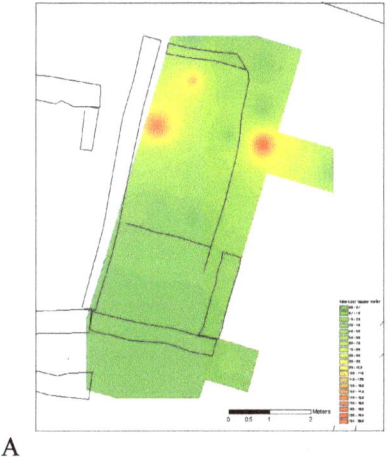
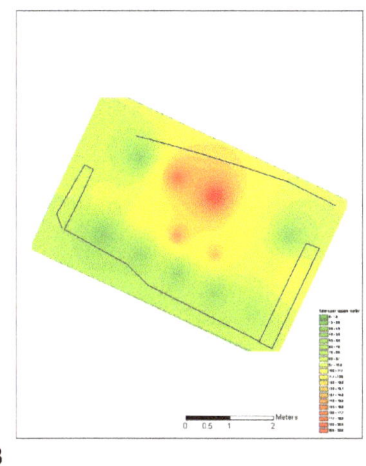
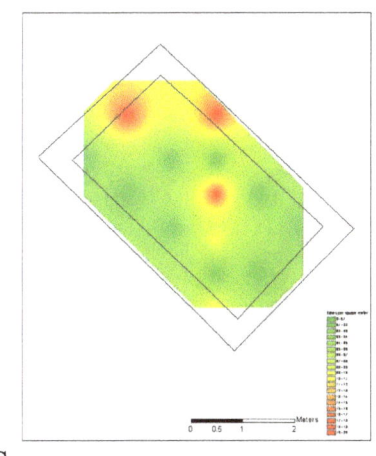
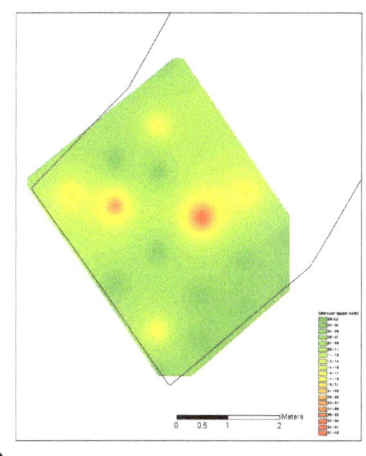

Figure 6.2: Density grids of local material debitage per square meter. Because of low quantites of obsidian (n= < 3), only local material is represented. A: Unidad 7, B: Unidad 21, C: Unidad 19, D: Unidad 20. Data are classed at natural breaks (Jenks) using 20 classes.

The distribution patterns in Unit 25 more closely reproduces those seen in Unit 9, in that the densities do not correlate with features but rather indicate the loci of lithic reduction and probable use. In this context lithic distribution overall is more generalized, but clusters in two broad and dispersed clusters of debitage in the interior eastern and northwestern corners of the patio (Figure 6.1c). The low-density pattern of obsidian debitage overlays the distribution of local material, and the two material classes are not spatially segregated as in Unit 9, but debitage overall is confined to these two areas.

Units 7 and 21 both have dense clusters of lithic debitage suggestive of defined activity areas (Figures 6.2a, b). In each of these contexts, the densest clusters of lithic debitage are spatially associated with midden deposits, but are not limited to them; rather, clusters extend beyond their boundaries. Unit 7, like room 9F has been characterized as a locus of food preparation and other domestic activities (Williams and Ruales 2001: 13). The peak densities of lithic debitage in this unit (up to 20 flakes per m^2) correspond with archaeological features (Figure 6.2a). The pit features of room F predominantly show evidence of burning, while one—larger and deeper—had a significant quantity of Pepper Tree seeds (*Shinus molle*) suggesting a function as a storage area. In room G, the western wall of the two-meter excavated space was occupied by an elevated but low grinding surface, with several large milling stones nearby (Williams and Ruales 2002: 10–12). The debitage cluster in Unit 7 corresponds to but extends beyond these features. There is no density that goes with the milling surface. Reduction activity may have taken place close to this feature, with waste material deliberately deposited within it, or else the activities that created the feature and the lithic reduction were closely related.

Unit 21 (Figure 6.2b) has a very high density of lithic debitage (as many as 21 flakes per m^2) centered within the room. The peak density is adjacent to, but does not overlap, Feature 2, a domestic refuse pit (Williams and Ruales 2002: 40). During excavation, it was also noted that much of the subfloor matrix was refuse that had secondarily been deposited. The spatial articulation between these deposits and high densities of debitage imply an association between the production of debitage and storing other waste materials, probably as cleaning/maintenance.

Unit 21 is exceptional overall for the high quantity of local lithic material and particularly bifacially flaked points which were recovered in this context. Unit 21 has the highest density index for debitage material, with an average value of approximately 479 grams of lithic material per cubic meter (Table 5.8). Despite this high value, however, obsidian debitage was limited to a single flake, and there were only a moderate number of obsidian implements (all projectile points). The anomalous quantity of projectile points and the high density of debitage suggest that Unit 21 was actively engaged in producing flaked lithic implements, possibly these very points. Occupational, as well as spatial, specialization is indicated for this household. The relationship between deposits of garbage and dense concentrations of debitage in both Unit 7 and 21 may reflect a consistent attitude towards spatial organization in these economically very active Wari households where waste and dangerous materials were confined to similar activity areas and methods of disposal.

Units 23 and 32, in contrast to the summit occupations, both have very generalized distributions with no clear activity areas defined by the distribution of debitage (Figures 6.1d, e). Obsidian is slightly more circumscribed in Unit 23, but still falls within the distribution of debitage overall. Unlike the domestic spaces described above, both of these contexts consist of only one interior room: presumably there may have been outdoor space articulated with these residences reserved for economic activity, as described for other Middle Horizon sites (Nash 2002; Bawden 1993; Goldstein 1993; Bermann 1994). The lack of clear patterning may be due to the small size of these two residences. In contrast with the generalized space in small residences, spatial specialization may have been a luxury afforded by much larger summit households with multiple living-spaces that also enjoyed a more elaborate material culture. The role of elite etiquette and the reproduction of social classes through an expressive use of material culture (e.g., Couture and Sampeck 2003) also may account for the separation in material use on the summit, as opposed to the overlap perceptible in the residences on the slope. The differential patterns seem to correlate to class structure—reproduced in summit occupations and relative residence size—rather than to behavior that is delineated along other social divisions.

Although the low density of material makes it difficult to ascertain, no clear activity areas within most Tumilaca residences are represented in the lithic distributions, such as in Units 19 and 20 (Figures 6.2c, d). Rather, lithic distributions are low-density and generalized within these contexts, similar to that seen in Unit 23 and 32. This may correspond to Bawden's notion (1993) that Tumilaca households consciously maintained discrete activity areas. I reject the hypothesis, however, that the low volume of material is due solely to circumscribed activity areas or site maintenance behaviors, which infers that the majority of lithic material would be found outside the excavated area. Aside from this possible factor, a lower volume of material culture was found in these units and these artifacts are of a more rustic quality. These units, affiliated with the Tumilaca culture, are also the furthest from the elite summit contexts of Cerro Baúl, and are also removed from those Tumilaca contexts at the site of el Tenedor. Consequently they appear to have been peripheral to the community at Cerro Baúl and this may be reflected in the minimalist material that was found there.

Two contexts were excavated at el Tenedor, Unit 27 and Unit 28. No spatial data can be described for Unit 28 because of an insufficient number of objects. The archaeological material from Unit 27 is more substantial, however, and is described both in Table 6.1 and in Figure 6.2f. Two rooms that defined three spaces were excavated in Unit 27, making this one of the few multi-roomed contexts found off the summit of Cerro Baúl. A low density of debitage was distributed across the floor but also clustered in the eastern corner of the second room. Unit 27 has one of the lower indices for debitage distribution, despite the concentrated hot-spot and there appears not to have been a confined space for reduction activities. Obsidian is visually clustered in the southernmost room—it appears to be somewhat spatially segregated and not as dispersed as in other contexts—but in terms of this material Unit 27 also has one of the lower indices.

The definition of activity areas at Cerro Baúl depends in large part on the size and spatial complexity of the domestic structure, as well as the economic activity which occurred there. Discrete patterns of spatial differentiation are most recognizable in Unit 9, where the complexity of this multi-room structure allows for different types of functional space to be segregated and consequently to be apparent in the archaeological materials. In contrast, both Units 7 and 21 were rather small, but circumscribed artifact densities are notable in these contexts largely because of the intensity of economic activity which occurred. An interesting pattern in the spatially complex structure of Unit 9 is the separation of locally available material from obsidian debitage, implying that the two classes of material were engaged in different types of economic activity, and there is a slight suggestion of similar differentiation for other units.

Chapter 7: Lithic Tools

Bifacial Implements

Bifacial lithic implements at Cerro Baúl can be grouped into two very general classes. The first includes informal, expedient tools with mixed and somewhat irregular morphologies. Artifacts in this group are primarily made of local material, but the class also includes one known implement of obsidian (Figure 7.1). Within the second class, there are several varieties of formalized, bifacially flaked points. The latter is by far more common than the expedient tools. Within this group there are several subtypes with different forms and dimensions, suggesting that established types existed for a wide variety of bifacial artifacts with conventional functions.

The repetition and distribution of types is obviously an important issue, whether these types became established through the reproduction of standardized templates in formalized systems (such as has been suggested in the previous section for obsidian distribution) or through the customary production of types within a shared social context. Following Gero (1989), we can assume that, relative to other classes of flaked lithics, more symbolic and social content will be encoded in bifacial artifacts by the greater energy investiture and premeditation that is embodied in their complex reduction sequence. The difficult issue is not deciding to analyze bifacial artifacts because of their inherent social content. Rather, the difficulty is in ascertaining the character of the social content that is encoded and, most immediately of concern, ascertaining the different functional and stylistic types within which meaning was contained. A considerable body of literature has been devoted to separating out these complexities of typology as they pertain to issues of style, functionality, and personal and social expression that are encased in the formal variation of artifacts, and also as they differ from mechanical or economic considerations (e.g., Wobst 1977; Weissner 1983; Shennan 1989; DeBoer 1990; David and Kramer 2001: Chapter 7; Dobres 1995; Sheets 1975; Meltzer 1981). Given the intricacy of the social and economic dynamics at Cerro Baúl and the contemporaneous Wari and Tumilaca/Tiwanaku sites in the Moquegua Valley, a closer examination of point typologies and their social ramifications would be highly productive. The scale of an analyzed sample necessary for a comprehensive analysis is greater than the database presented here, but nonetheless some inferences can be made about the significance of morphological types based on the data available from these twelve units.

Biface types are mentioned in most discussions of Middle Horizon lithic artifacts, usually as specific forms attributed either to Wari (Pineda Rivera 1978; Nash 2002 123–124, Bencic 2000: figure 17; Castillo 2000: figures 8b, 12; Owen and Goldstein 2001: figure 11; Moseley et al. 1991: 135) or Tiwanaku culture groups (Bencic 2000: 98–99, figures 4, 5; Goldstein 1993: figure 3.7a; Seddon 1994: figures 172–174; Giesso 2003: 378, figures 15.12–15.14; Burger, Chavéz, and Chavéz 2000: 326–327, figures 12, 13; Couture 2003: figure 8.31). It is my opinion that—despite the potential contributions of a rigorous typological analysis to discussions of social identity and economic interplay—only cursory attention has been devoted to establishing formal typologies for Middle Horizon bifaces. The characteristics most often cited while referring to biface types are the morphologies of the proximal end, either "stemmed" or "concave," and the relative size, either "small" or "large," of the individual biface when compared to the entire population. Different combinations of these attributes are intuitively related to Wari and Tiwanaku technological complexes, such that small stemmed points, frequently of chert or chalcedony are a typical part of Tiwanaku assemblages while larger, concave implements are frequently related to Wari. Rivera Pineda describes several types of small, silicate points with concave or stemmed bases at the site of Huari (1978: 590–592). Burger, Chavéz, and Chavéz note that larger convex-sided points with concave or straight bases are associated with Wari sites but rare for Tiwanaku, while the smaller stemmed points already mentioned are ubiquitous in many periods at Tiwanaku but do not appear in Peru until Wari expansion and may represent a generalized Middle Horizon type (2000: 326). Despite these attributions, the lack of certainty and the ambiguity within these casual typologies—which Burger *et alia* themselves lament—are problematic for careful discussions of cultural interaction during the Middle Horizon and particularly for understanding the dynamics of a community as complex as Cerro Baúl, with both Wari and Tumilaca inhabitants. This vagueness highlights the need for reproducible and prescribed typologies for Middle Horizon materials, and I offer some initial contributions towards establishing such a descriptive typology based on the materials at Cerro Baúl.

This discussion focuses primarily on the "procedural modes" involved in fabricating bifacial artifacts, where production behavior is manifested in a hierarchical sequence of decisions that determine the artifact's ultimate morphology, rather than the potential communicative content of the style (Rouse 1960); many theoretical models of artifact type and style would see this as an artificial and unproductive separation to make, but it is necessary for the level at which I will discuss bifacial tools. Moreover, an analysis based on procedural modes circumvents the debate over whether or not classificatory categories reproduce emic or etic perceptions, since the different expressions of attributes are the result of decisions made during the reduction sequence and at some level these attributes will be appropriate to both analysis and archaeological behavior (Read 1974: 222).

The utility of a basic morphological typology is helped by the fact that Cerro Baúl was likely a single component site (Williams and Ruales 2002, 2004) and during its occupation the factors that limited the availability of both local and exotic material were behavioral. The issues that complicate morphological types as culture and time markers elsewhere, such as tool refurbishing, recycling, and refitting, should not be problematic for this assemblage (Hurst Thomas 1986). I recognize that the cosmopolitan character of Cerro Baúl, while it offers the opportunity to examine a wide suite of morphological types, ultimately may compound the difficulty of ascribing types to any cultural group.

The Cerro Baúl bifaces were initially described not by type but by a series of attributes, any combination of which established the complete morphology of the artifact and any repetition of attribute sets would constitute, at one analytical level or another, a type. These attributes include metric

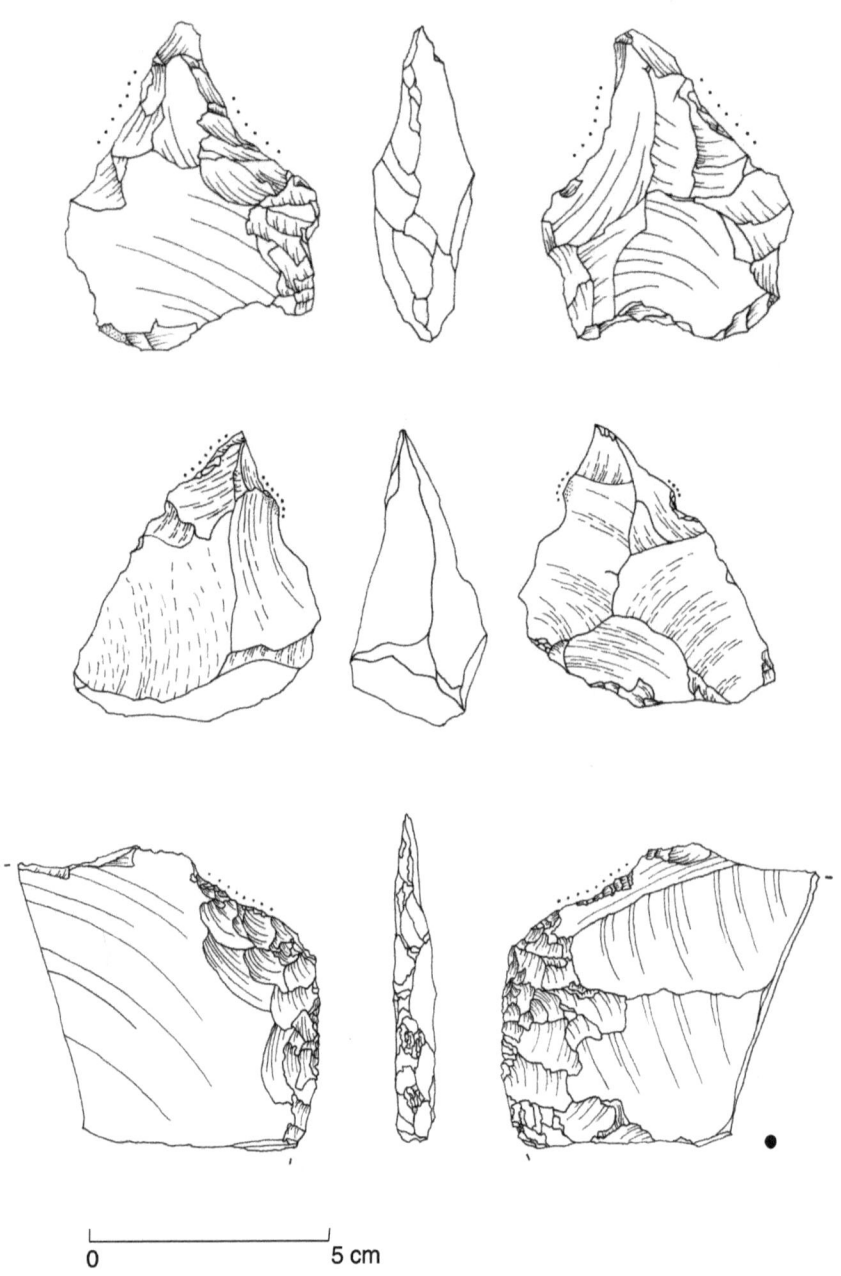

Figure 7.1: Expedient bifaces at Cerro Baul. The bottom is obsidian, and all show heavy use wear on margins. Reproduced at 75 %.

dimensions for length, width, thickness, and weight, nominal categories to describe the shape of proximal, midsection, and distal portions, and nominal categories to describe flake-scar patterns and margins as outlined by Sliva (1997) and Inizan et al. (1999). A sample of the complete artifacts was drawn following Addington (1986). While not minimizing analytical bias as completely as would entirely metric data, a wider range of variables can be more efficiently coded and analyzed with nominal categories, many more than were in fact observed in the Cerro Baúl assemblage.

Further, an attribute-based analysis documents "multiple dimensions of variability that are potentially significant," allowing greater flexibility for using these data in future syntheses to address a range of theoretical questions to which typological classifications are not suited (Clay 1976: 304). This includes, in the present case, contributing towards a typological classification itself. As I alluded to above, a comprehensive and conclusive typology is beyond the limits of this work: given the potential benefits of an established typology, it is an endeavor which future work

Table 7.1: Contingency table of nominal morphological data observed on bifacial implements.

Body shape	Basal shape									
	fragmentary	concave	straight	convex	stemmed	eared	bifurcate	basal notched	asymmetrical	∑
fragmentary	25	1	4	1						31
incurvate	1	2				1				4
parallel	2									2
straight	5	32	7	1	18		2	5	2	72
excurvate	7	27	10	3						47
ovate	1									1
irregular	1		2						2	5
∑	42	62	23	5	18	1	2	5	6	162

Table 7.2: Observed versus expected frequencies for the major bifacial morphological attributes based in χ^2 analysis.

Body shape	Basal shape							
	concave	straight	convex	stemmed	bifurcate	basal notched	asymmetrical	∑
straight								
O	32	7	1	18	2	5	2	67
E	36.9	10.6	2.5	11.3	1.3	3.1	1.6	
excurvate								
O	27	10	3	0	0	0	0	40
E	22.1	6.4	1.5	6.7	0.8	1.9	0.7	
∑	59	17	4	18	2	5	2	107

should address. This discussion will make some provisional contributions, nonetheless, to the general understanding of Middle Horizon bifacial implements and the possible relationship of types to the Wari and Tiwanaku cultures.

Biface Morphological Types

The population of bifacial artifacts (N=162) includes a variety of probable function types, including expedient bifacial implements and discoidal tools (Figure 7.1), that presumably constitute a different category of object from the more regularly formed bifacial points. In addition to size, the defining morphological criteria for bifacial artifacts are the shapes of the proximal/basal portion and the overall shape of the artifact's "body" (i.e., its midsection); distal, or tip, morphology also is important but tends largely to be a product of the latter criterion. In the spirit of identifying "attribute clusters" as discussed by Cowgill (1982: 36–37), Table 7.1 provides the frequencies of various combinations of attribute variables for basal and body morphology of Cerro Baúl bifaces.

Asymmetrical clustering of attribute variables in and of itself may be sufficient to establish rudimentary types:

> ...one may find that certain combinations of values of different variables occur much oftener than would be expected if the frequencies of the combinations of variable values were simply what one would expect from randomly combining the different values of the different variables. If so, then the objects that share such an unexpectedly frequent combination of values can usefully be labeled a type, and the combination itself can be called...an attribute cluster (Cowgill 1982: 37)

Table 7.1 shows that attribute combinations are not symmetrically distributed across all the possible combinations of variables that occur for bifaces at Cerro Baúl (to say nothing of all the possible morphological variability for bifaces in general). Rather, while there are 24 observed combinations of basal and midsection morphology, seven attribute clusters have a frequency of n ≥ 5, suggesting the repetition of established types. Further, the variety of infrequent and singular biface morphologies, those occurring with a frequency ≤ 2, appear outside the attribute clusters. These rarer expressions point out that the Cerro Baúl assemblage has a relatively high degree of "typability" but, like most, is not perfectly "typable," and includes a selection of "transitional" or "deviant" artifact forms (Cowgill 1982: 34–35).

These data can be further reduced in order to facilitate the elucidation of morphological types. For the sake of inferring morphological types, fragmentary bifaces—those artifacts missing portions of their mid- and/or basal sections and in comparison to complete bifaces are non-diagnostic—pragmatically can be disregarded. Additionally, expedient implements with irregular and asymmetrical morphologies (e.g., Figure 7.1) and which belong to a different reduction strategy and possibly economic activity than those represented by formalized points can momentarily be set aside.

The relationships between variables for the resulting population of bifaces (n=107) are given in Table 7.2 (compressed biface variables), along with the expected values for each attribute cluster calculated from the cell totals as for a ?? analysis (see Chapter 5). Notably, the cell values are not equally distributed across the possible attribute combinations but rather they load unevenly in a few attribute clusters, as described by Cowgill (1982). The most frequent attribute clusters are represented by those points with 1) concave bases and straight sides (that form small, triangular bodies, Figure 7.2), 2) concave bases and excurvate sides

Figure 7.2: Bifaces that fit the provisional type A, with triangular bodies and concave bases. Reproduced at 75 %.

(Figure 7.3), 3) straight bases and straight sides (Figure 7.4), 4) straight bases and excurvate sides (that form lanceolate bodies, Figure 7.5), 5) convex bases and excurvate sides (Figure 7.6), 6) stemmed bases and straight sides (Figure 7.7), and, somewhat surprisingly, 7) basal-notched points with straight sides (Figure 7.9). This last is most likely a slight modification on the sixth type, allowing, perhaps, for personal innovation in the specific mode of production since all instances of basal-notched points occur in a single context. In addition, there are a number of bifaces with irregu-

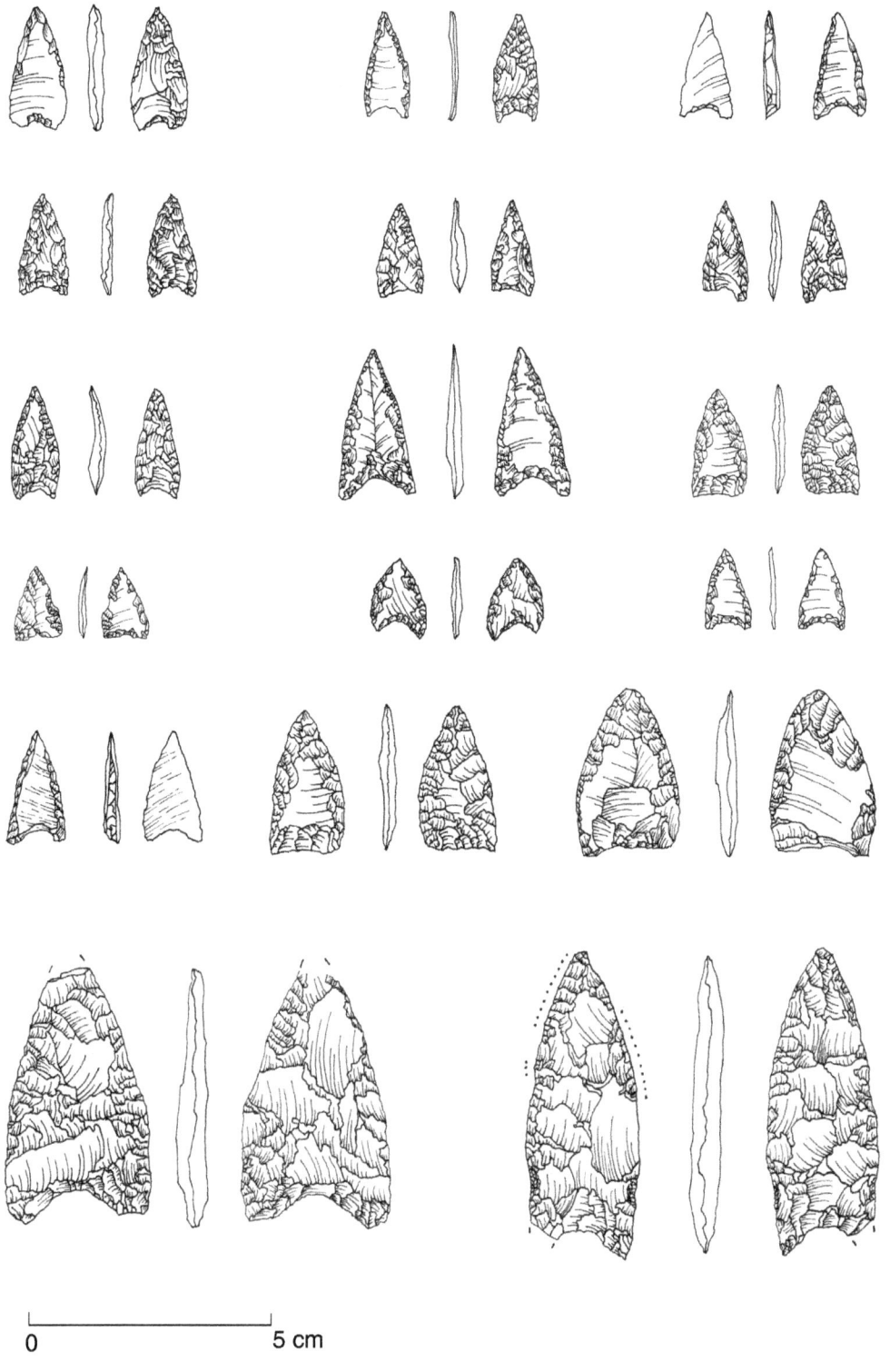

Figure 7.3: Bifaces that fit the provisional type B, with lanceolate bodies and concave bases. Reproduced at 75 %.

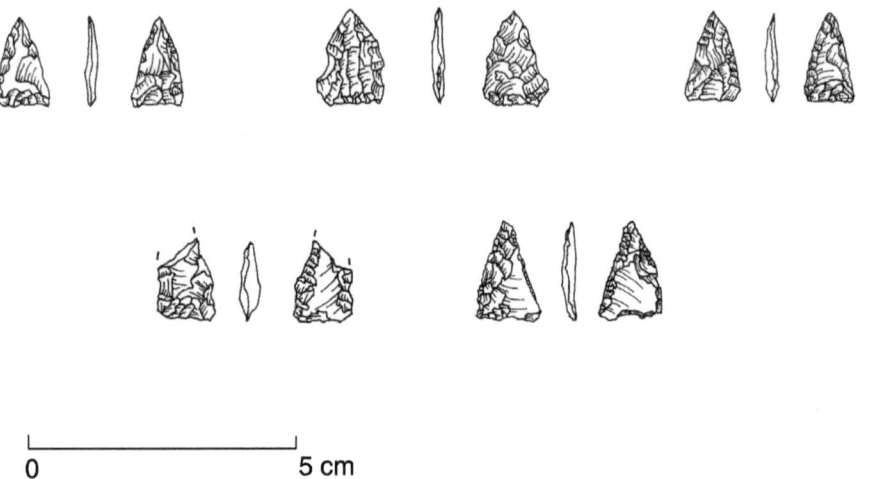

Figure 7.4: Bifaces that fit the provisional type C, with straight, triangular bodies and straight bases. Reproduced at 75 %.

lar forms, suggesting that they are preforms that could be finished with any of the above combinations of attributes (Figure 7.8). The first, second, fourth, and fifth of these provisional types have the same morphology as that described in the limited literature on Middle Horizon lithics as being either typically 'Wari' or 'Tiwanaku,' but it is clear that there are a substantial number of other attribute combinations that are repeated even in a relatively small sample of n=107 cases.

Referring again to Table 7.2, attribute clusters 2, 4, 5, 6, and 7 as described above have observed frequencies that are higher than the expected frequencies for their cells assuming symmetry across the possible attribute combinations. The observed and expected values for attribute cluster 1 are also close, though the number of observed cases is less frequent than would be expected. For Table 7.2, $\chi^2 = 23.61$, $p \leq .0375$ and the distribution of attribute clusters most likely is not an artifact of unknown bias but rather reflects real patterns in the overall assemblage. As with the χ^2 statistics for debitage, there are problems of low expected cell values and while this χ^2 statistic likely reflects true patterns of morphological types, the strength of this relationship is reduced. This statistic is relevant, however, for the purposes of exploring the variability of types.

This distribution of attribute clusters thus likely represents, to some degree, real morphological types that were deliberately selected for at Cerro Baúl. Clearly some types were more important than others; those attribute clusters that occur more frequently than expected represent morphologies that were repeatedly created and used while other types were infrequent. Consequently, a provisional range of morphological types can be defined as in Table 7.3, with Types A, B, C, D, and G as the most important, major morphologies which constitute approximately 88 % of the bifacial points assignable to any specific type.

Size has also been cited as an operative factor in descriptions of Middle Horizon points. Metrical dimensions of length, width, and thickness (as well as weight) were measured for the bifacial points from Cerro Baúl, and these implements have a fairly well-defined range between 30–60 mm in length by 10–35 mm in width (Table 7.4). Overall, bifacial points are remarkably small, reinforcing the popular suggestion that most Middle Horizon points were primarily for projectiles (e.g., Giesso 2000, 2003; Burger, Chavéz, and Chavéz 2000; c.f. Nash 2002). Unfortunately, size cannot be used to discriminate between typological categories, as all bifacial points, regardless of their morphology, occupy a similar size range. While size cannot be used across categories, there are consistent relationships between length and width within the typological categories (Figure 7.10). Table 7.4 also demonstrates that there is a group of biface types that are very regular in their manufacture, and subsequently in their dimensions, and also a group of types that are considerably more irregular. Considering both length and width, types A, G, and I all have relatively very small indices of variance and very close upper and lower values for the 95 % confidence intervals. The lack of variability in width for these three types is remarkable, as they all measure within less than a centimeter of each other. Of course, there are issues with sample size, but Type I (straight-sided, bifurcated points) is remarkable because, despite the small sample size (n=5), this rarer form of point demonstrates remarkable consistency. Type G (straight-sided, stemmed points) is also interesting, as this Type corresponds to that most frequently referred to as "Tiwanaku" style and it continues to demonstrate a regularity and consistency of form that has been noted elsewhere. These two artifact types have the tightest relationship of length versus width, followed closely by Type A (Figure 7.10). The other categories of points show considerably looser relationships between length and width (Table 7.4, Figure 7.10), and there is more irregularity in their form.

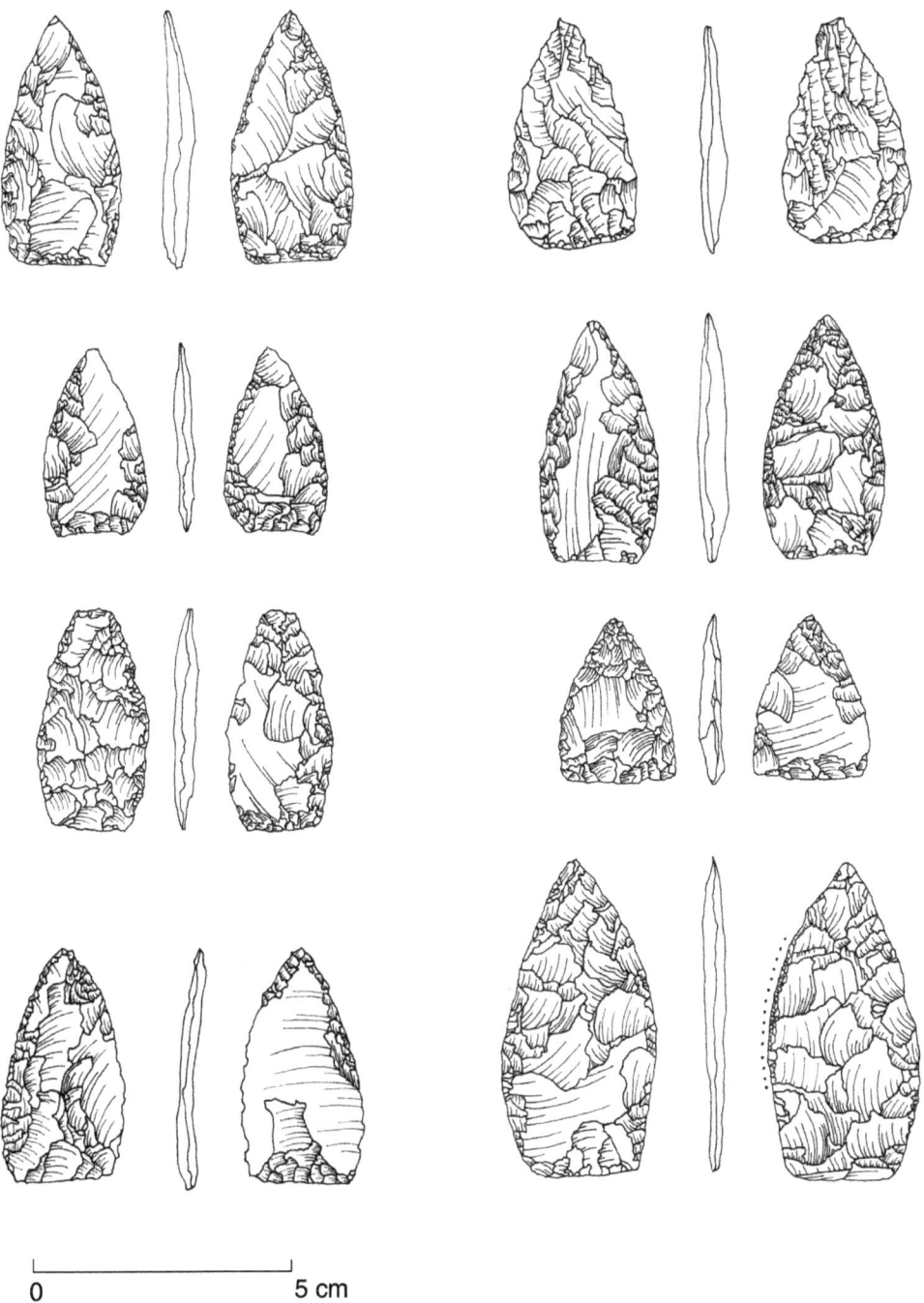

Figure 7.5: Bifaces that fit the provisional type D, with lanceolate bodies and straight bases. Reproduced at 75 %.

Interestingly, concave- and flat-based, excurvate forms are frequently associated with Wari and quite a number of these points were made of obsidian. The diversity in dimensions may reflect a variety of causal factors, issues which should be pursued further. In part, this may be related to raw material, as points of a valued material may be more intensively curated and reworked. Basic relationships between the provisional types outlined here and the raw materials from which points were fabricated are given in Table 7.5. Obsidian and chert are by far the preferred materials, but those points made from local materials share similar morphological attributes to foreign materials, suggesting—to some

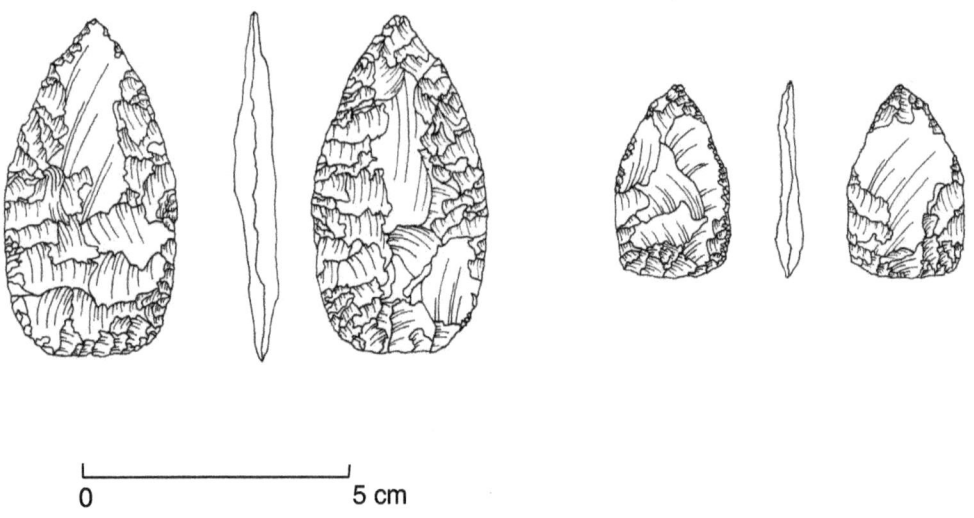

Figure 7.6: Bifaces that fit the provisional type F, with excurvate and convex bases. Reproduced at 75 %.

extent—a local participation in cultural templates recognized over a greater area. Notable are the few instances of bifaces flaked from locally available fine-grained rhyolite that were produced following a similar reduction strategy as bifaces made of exotic obsidian. Of the main point types that have been described, obsidian appears to have been preferred for most of the forms, while 66 % of the stemmed points were fashioned from chert. As has been suggested elsewhere (Burger, Chavéz, and Chavéz 2000; Giesso 2000; see Chapter 5), the choice of material was likely related to whether or not obsidian as a commodity was state controlled and distributed through administered networks. Subsequently, the discrepancy in raw material gives an added dimension to the definition of Middle Horizon points, and the relevance of material, including the probability that prefabricated and standardized bifaces were imported from exotic locales, is an important element for comprehensive understanding Middle Horizon artifact typologies.

Point morphology, size, and material are all attributes which can contribute to the successful definition of a Middle Horizon bifacial point typology. The attribute clusters discussed here are summarized in Table 7.6, to synthesize a provisional, unimaginatively-named typology which will, I hope, be subject to further refinement and application at other Middle Horizon sites. Among the principal issues which should be explored is how well this (or for that matter any) typology withstands a comparison of point distribution versus other cultural markers.

Biface Types and Domestic Contexts

Despite the continued debate over the significance and interplay of style and function and their relation to typology, diagnostic artifact forms are routinely used as cultural indicators, usually without prejudice and frequently with complications. Particular approaches to artifact production or the decorative elements with which they were embellished become analytical indicators of preferential modes of behavior employed by the fabricator, who presumably shared these preferences with affines or social intimates within a larger cultural system. The use and production of types is understood to express an affinity to a group—that is often social in nature—either as a deliberate expression of identity (e.g., Wobst 1977, Weissner 1983) or as a matter of even more salient "economic rationality" (Sahlins 1976: 171). These types are part of a setting of cultural elements—"trait inventories" that include abstract behavioral criteria and formal material culture—which establish overt cohesion within hierarchical subsets of discretely and continuously defined social order (Barth 1998: 12–13; Eidheim 1998). It has been suggested that Andean households played a fundamental role in the formulation of behavior and the reproduction of cultural elements (Bermann 1994: 21–23) by grounding "behavioral conventions...in the common ideational fabric of their society" (Bawden 1993: 42). As the main context of production in a non-industrial setting, households serve as the primary locus by which economic activity is organized and from which interaction with other levels of social organization extends outwards. Social linkages should be seen primarily within households and then within sets of related households. At the most general, extra-household level, the individual interacts with the community overall as the largest scale of immediate social network.

Using biface styles alone (even with an established typology) to define such scales of social networks is questionable, but it is one place to begin exploring social interaction. The distribution of biface types, however, indicates that the social environment at Cerro Baúl was considerably more complex than can be defined merely by a dichotomy between Wari and Tumilaca residents. Rather, as with other

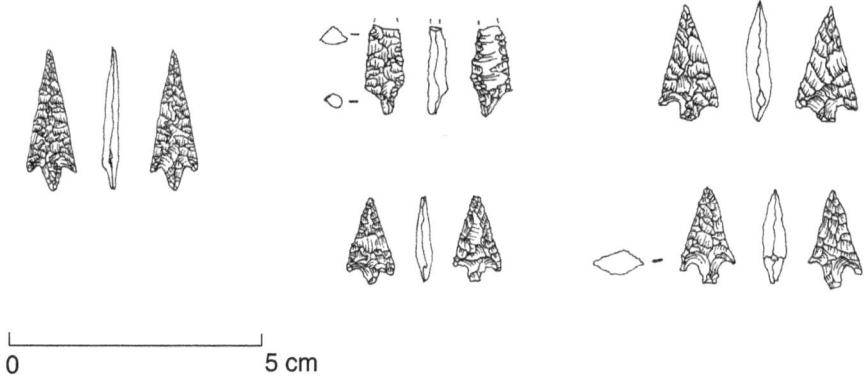

Figure 7.7: Bifaces that fit the provisional type G, the "Tiwanaku" type, with triangular bodies and stemmed bases. Reproduced at 75 %.

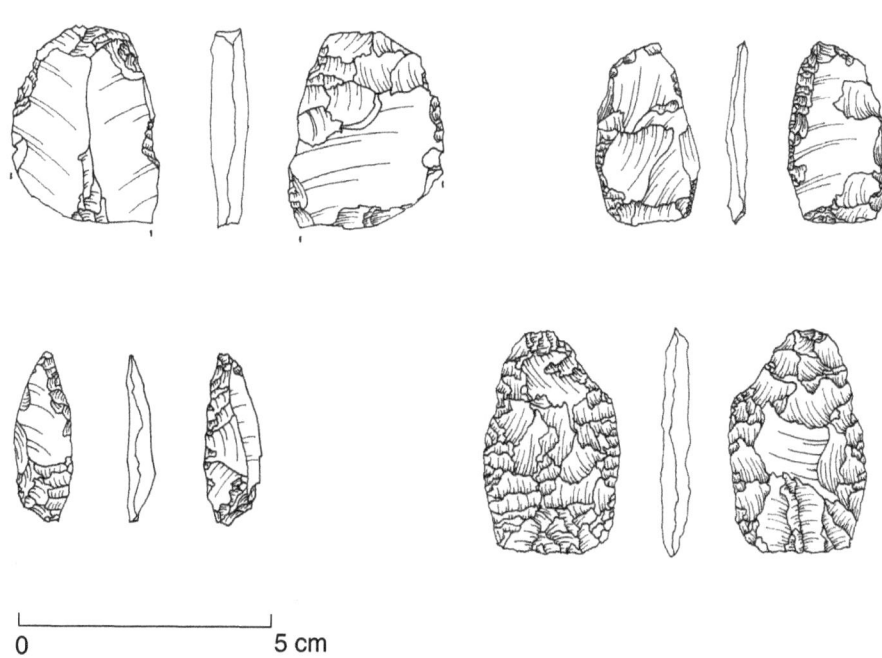

Figure 7.8: Bifaces that fit the provisional type J, which are probable preforms. Reproduced at 75 %.

artifact classes, our provisional biface typology suggests that economic differentiation was a much more salient factor in organizing material cultural at Cerro Baúl and, ostensibly, social dynamics as well. Diverse, bifacial forms are not distributed across the domestic contexts according to cultural affiliation, but rather are heavily loaded in Unit 9 (the context that has consistently shown the most elaborate material culture), as well as Units 24 and 25.

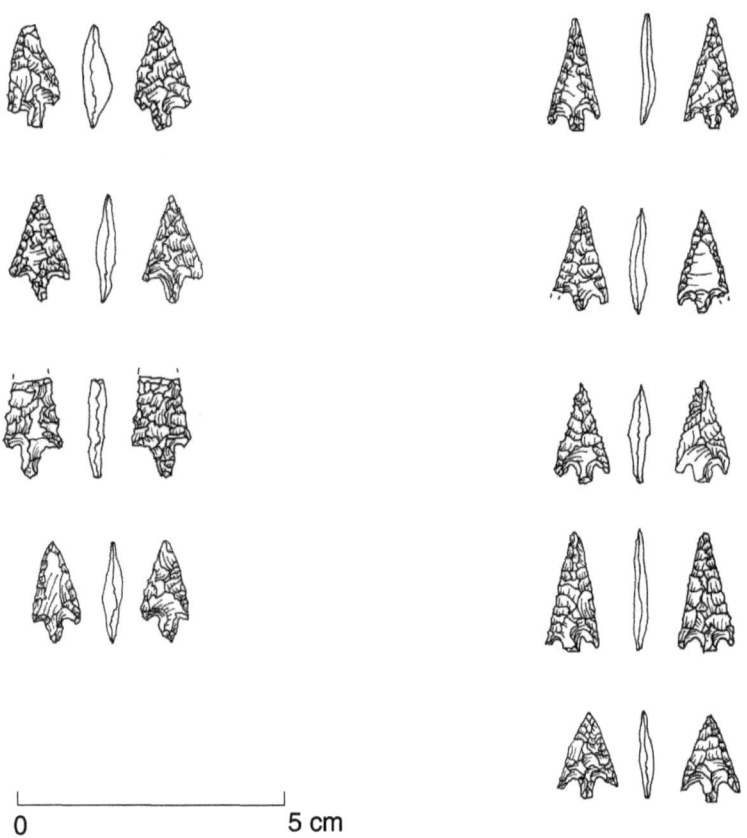

Figure 7.9: Bifaces from Unit 21, artifacts in left column fit provisional type G, and those in the right column fit type I with basal notching. These are likely a variation on the treatment given to stemmed points. Reproduced at 75 %.

Despite the large size of Unit 9, it has one of the highest densities of points per cubic meter and, by far, the greatest variety of biface types (Tables 7.7, 7.8). In keeping with the economic privilege of Unit 9, it also has the greatest abundance of obsidian points of Types A and B, which were likely linked to indirect procurement and elite networks, as suggested in the previous chapter.

Particularly striking is Unit 21, which consistently has been atypical in comparisons with other units for the high quantity but necessarily high quality of material that was exploited. By far, this context has the highest density of bifacial artifacts of any of the units, with an average of 2.83 points per cubic meter excavated (Table 7.8), and is rivaled only by the deposits in Unit 24. Unit 21 was identified securely during excavation as having Wari material culture, primarily ceramics. Most of the bifacial points from this context, however, are Type G which has elsewhere been linked to Tiwanaku sites, and Unit 21 is the only context from which basal-notched points were found (Table 7.7, Figure 7.9). These points likely are a variant of the stemmed points more commonly found at Cerro Baúl and other Middle Horizon sites, since they are characterized by two parallel and deep notches that form an incipient stem. The points in Unit 21, thus, represent a focus on a particular point type and most likely a particular economic activity in which they were employed. Given the high density of debitage in this context (see the densities of local material per unit, given in Table 5.8), Unit 21 was probably a locus of intensified production of these points. This does not accord with the interpretation that these points are explicitly Tiwanaku, but rather it suggests the economic singularity of this household and implies that the profusion of points in this household was a function of its occupants' activities.

Principal components analysis supports the divisions among residential units based on bifacial point morphology, and illustrates that the use of specific point types cannot be linked definitively to ethnic cultural criteria. Rather, households cluster together in a fashion that suggests neighborhoods or districts of shared economic activity. This analysis considered the criteria used above to describe provisional types, including morphological attributes, metric data, and material, to derive two components that would describe the majority of the variation seen in the bifaces from Cerro Baúl. Collectively these principal components account for

Table 7.3: Provisional biface typology based on frequent attribute combinations observed among the formal bifacial implements at Cerro Baúl.

Body shape	Basal shape concave	straight	convex	stemmed	bifurcate	basal notched	asymetrical
straight	A	C	E	G	H	I	J
excurvate	B	D	F	—	—	—	—

Table 7.4: Descriptive statistics for biface length and width (Types E, H, and J are not given as n≤2).

	Type A	B	C	D	F	G	I
N	32	27	7	10	3	18	5
Length							
μ (mm)	20.1	23.2	18.7	37.1	31.8	19.4	18.9
σ (mm)	5.0	10.3	4.3	15.0	7.8	3.7	1.7
Variance	25.0	106.2	18.4	225.6	60.2	13.3	2.8
95% confidence level (mm)							
upper	22.0	27.2	23.2	46.7	44.1	21.2	20.9
lower	18.3	19.2	14.2	27.6	19.4	17.6	16.8
Width							
μ (mm)	10.8	13.8	12.0	21.8	17.6	10.1	10.6
σ (mm)	1.7	4.9	2.6	5.6	5.7	1.0	0.4
Variance	2.8	23.9	6.8	31.6	31.9	1.1	0.16
95% confidence level (mm)							
upper	11.4	15.5	14.8	25.4	26.5	10.7	11.1
lower	10.1	11.9	9.3	18.3	8.6	9.6	10.1

Table 7.5: Observed frequencies of raw material types used for formal bifacial implements by morphological type.

Type	A	B	C	D	E	F	G	H	I	J
Obsidian	29	22	4	10		2	5	2		2
Dacite		1				1	1			
Rhyolite		2								
Chert	3	2	3		1		12		5	

Table 7.6: Summary descriptions of the 10 provisional biface types at Cerro Baúl that are outlined in Chapter 7.

Type	Description	
A	Small, straight-sided triangular points with concave base. Regularly sized μ of 20.1 x 10.8 mm. Most frequently of obsidian.	Figure 7.2
B	Diverse group of excurvate sided triangular and lanceolate points with concave base. Size ranges greatly, but μ of 23.2 x 13.8 mm. Most frequently of obsidian.	Figure 7.3
C	Small, straight-sided triangular points with straight base, related to Type A. Regularly sized μ of 18.7 x 12.0 mm. Sample from Cerro Baúl is entirely obsidian.	Figure 7.4
D	Diverse and irregular group of excurvate sided lanceolate points with straight bases, related to Type B. Wide range of sizes, but overall large w/ μ of 37.1 x 21.8. Entirely of obsidian, these are points typically referred to as "Wari" obsidian points.	Figure 7.5
E	Minor example of straight-sided triangular point with convex base. Only one case at Cerro Baúl, and so is questionable as a formal type. Moderately sized (27.2 x 16.8 mm) and made of chert.	
F	Diverse group of excurvate-sided, convex base points possibly related to Type B/D. Relatively large μ of 31.8 x 17.6 mm. Predominantly of obsidian, but also a case of local dacite.	Figure 7.6
G	Consistent group of small, straight-sided triangular points with stemmed bases. Regularly sized μ of 19.4 x 10.1 mm. Roughly two thirds of Cerro Baúl sample are chert, the remainder are obsidian. This type is typically referred to as "Tiwanaku," and chert is the most often cited material in the literature.	Figures 7.7, 7.9
H	Minor group (n=2) of straight-sided triangular points with a bifurcate base. Possibly related to Type I, except for material (both cases of H are obsidian).	
I	Consistent group of small, straight-sided triangular points with basal notches. Regularly sized μ of 18.9 x 10.6 mm. All examples are of chert, are found in Unit 21, and are likely an isolated variant of Type G.	Figure 7.9
J	Minor group (n=2) of relatively large, irregularly shaped obsidian bifaces. These may represent early stages of reduction.	Figure 7.8

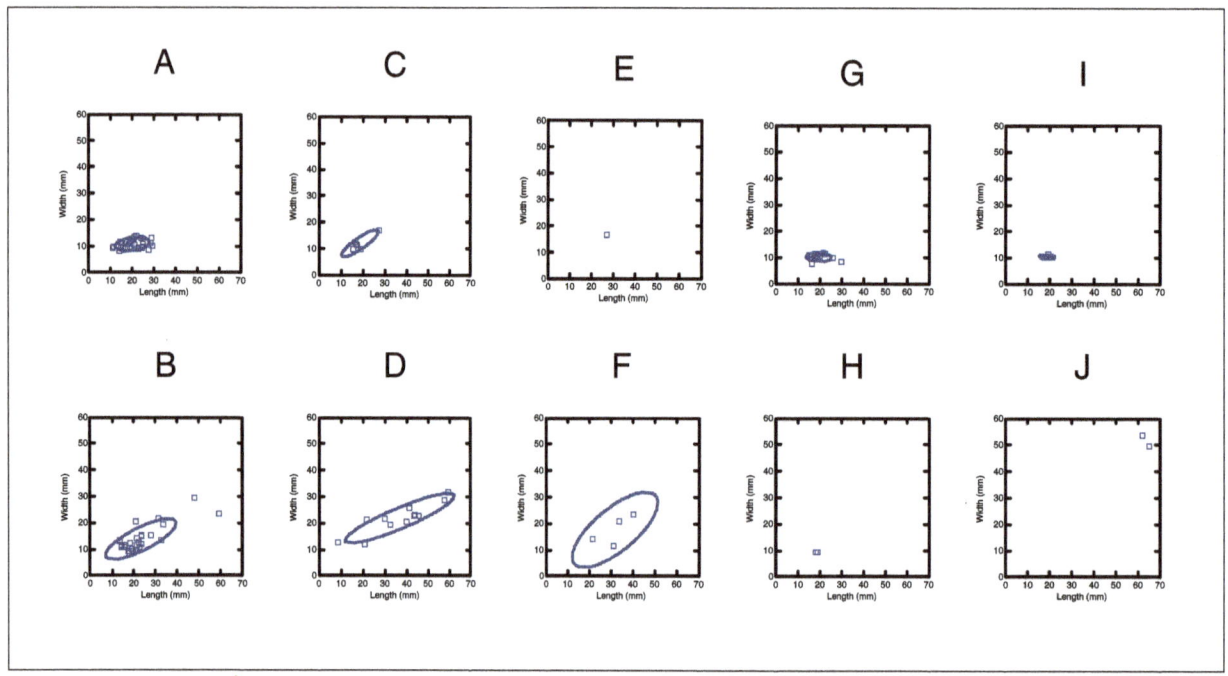

Figure 7.10: Scatterplots of biface length (mm) versus width (mm) for each morphological type as provisionally defined. Ellipses indicate 90 % confidence level.

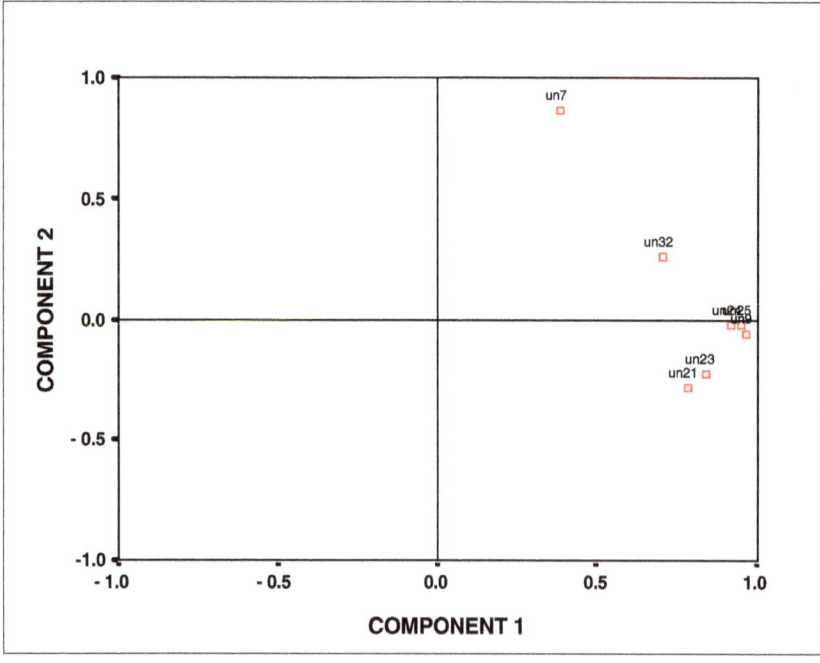

Figure 7.11: Principal components plot of bifacial types based on their technological and material attributes, per excavation unit. Groups of units have similar assemblages of bifaces, and therefore load similarly within the two components.

Table 7.7: The observed frequency of biface types per excavation unit.

	Un 7	Un 9	Un 21	Un 23	Un 24	Un 25	Un 32
A		24			4	3	
B		21		1	2	3	
C		6		1			
D		9			3		
E		1					
F		3				1	
G		4	11	1	1	1	
H		2					
I			5				
J		1			2	1	
NA*	1	30	1	1	7	8	1
Total	1	101	17	4	19	17	1

* NA represents non-diagnostic bifaces with missing portions not typed during the analysis.

Table 7.8: The average density of bifacial points per cubic meter.

Unidad	Un 7	Un 9	Un 21	Un 23	Un 24	Un 25	Un 32
m^3	22.5	190.4	6.0	6.0	12.6	67.5	17.5
Bifacial points/ m^3	0.04	0.53	2.83	0.17	1.51	0.25	0.06

80.1 % of the data variance (five components are necessary to describe over 94 % of the variance), and these components show the relationships between excavation units (Figure 7.11). The biface data can be reduced to cluster in two groups that include, 1) Units 9, 24, and 25 and 2) Units 21 and 23. Two additional units are isolated both from each other and from the principal clusters, Units 32 and 7. None of the other residential contexts appear, as they were without bifacial points.

The principal component plot points to two factors regarding the distribution of bifacial points at Cerro Baúl. First, those contexts which are most removed from the summit and center of archaeological occupation are not represented. Second, the summit and slope occupations are clearly separated in the components plot, with the exception of Unit 7 which was characterized during excavation as an auxiliary activity area and not principally a residence (Williams and Ruales 2002: 16). The three contexts on the summit have close associations, however, largely in the type and material of bifacial points that occur there. Units 21, 23, and 32 all load closely together on the axis of component one, suggesting strong similarities in the types of bifaces that were encountered, and Units 9, 24, and 25 fall closely together on both component axes, reflecting their similarity in culture vis-à-vis bifacial implements.

It is important to point out that all these units, with the exception of Unit 23, have been characterized as Wari, and so the division along ethnic lines may be stronger than is initially thought. As other, Tumilaca, residences are largely absent it is fair to say, however, that the use of point styles does not adhere to ethnic boundaries. Were this the case, Tumilaca residences should be represented by some, albeit distinct, form of artifact; moreover, the presence of points in Unit 23 (which has a moderate index of bifaces per cubic meter, see Table 7.8), precludes there having been draconian prohibitions against Tumilaca groups using or possessing any form of bifacial implement, for whatever purpose. Finally, an operative factor in how excavation units load within the components is, with the exception of Unit 7, distance from the summit of Cerro Baúl. As was seen with raw material diversity and the consumption of raw resources, wealth, status, and proximity to what appear to be economically privileged neighborhoods were elements which defined the distribution of bifacial tools. As has been suggested for Tiwanaku, point production and consumption may have constituted a form of taxation or elite-centered economy at strongly nucleated Middle Horizon sites (Giesso 2003: 383), although the evidence supporting this contention should be considered carefully. There is little lithic evidence in the households were points are absent to suggest that they were fabricating these artifacts but sending them off to be used elsewhere, and consequently the units where points are found appear to also have been the loci of production.

Unifacial Implements

Local and Exotic Materials

These implements constitute the smallest group of artifacts (n=22) that were distinguished during the lithic analysis, and this small overall sample size unfortunately precludes any rigorous statistical tests of these implements as a group. There is a strong likelihood that a large number of utilized flakes with more subtle expressions of use-wear and even edge modification passed through the analysis unnoticed or unacknowledged. I tended to be more conservative than generous when identifying possible unifacial implements, and particularly while assessing usewear and deliberate edge modification. A comprehensive evaluation of usewear is left for a specialist in order to ensure the integrity of the interpretation.

The difficulty of assessing utilized flakes was circumvented by using edge retouch as a defining criterion for unifacial implements. By definition, this class is composed of flaked lithics that were taken beyond their initial removal from a core and whose edges exhibit deliberate retouch only along one surface to modify the morphology or characteristics of the original flake. These implements subsequently were classified as either retouched flakes (where the original flake morphology was only marginally modified, Figures 7.12, 7.13) or as unifacially retouched implements (Figures 7.14, 7.15). Further, several of these implements have rather obvious use wear along their modified edges, which reinforces their classification as implements and—by suggesting specific activities—provides limited insight into aspects of economic behavior (Figures 7.12a, d, f; 7.13; 7.14d; 7.15). Beyond these defining criteria, unifacial implements comprise one of the more variable categories of lithic artifacts that can be found at Cerro Baúl. There is minimal consistency in their metric dimensions, morphological characteristics, and even mode of production. One aspect of their distribution is notable, however: unifacially retouched implements were prevalent across the different archaeological contexts, being represented by at least a single instance in most of the analyzed samples (Table 7.9).

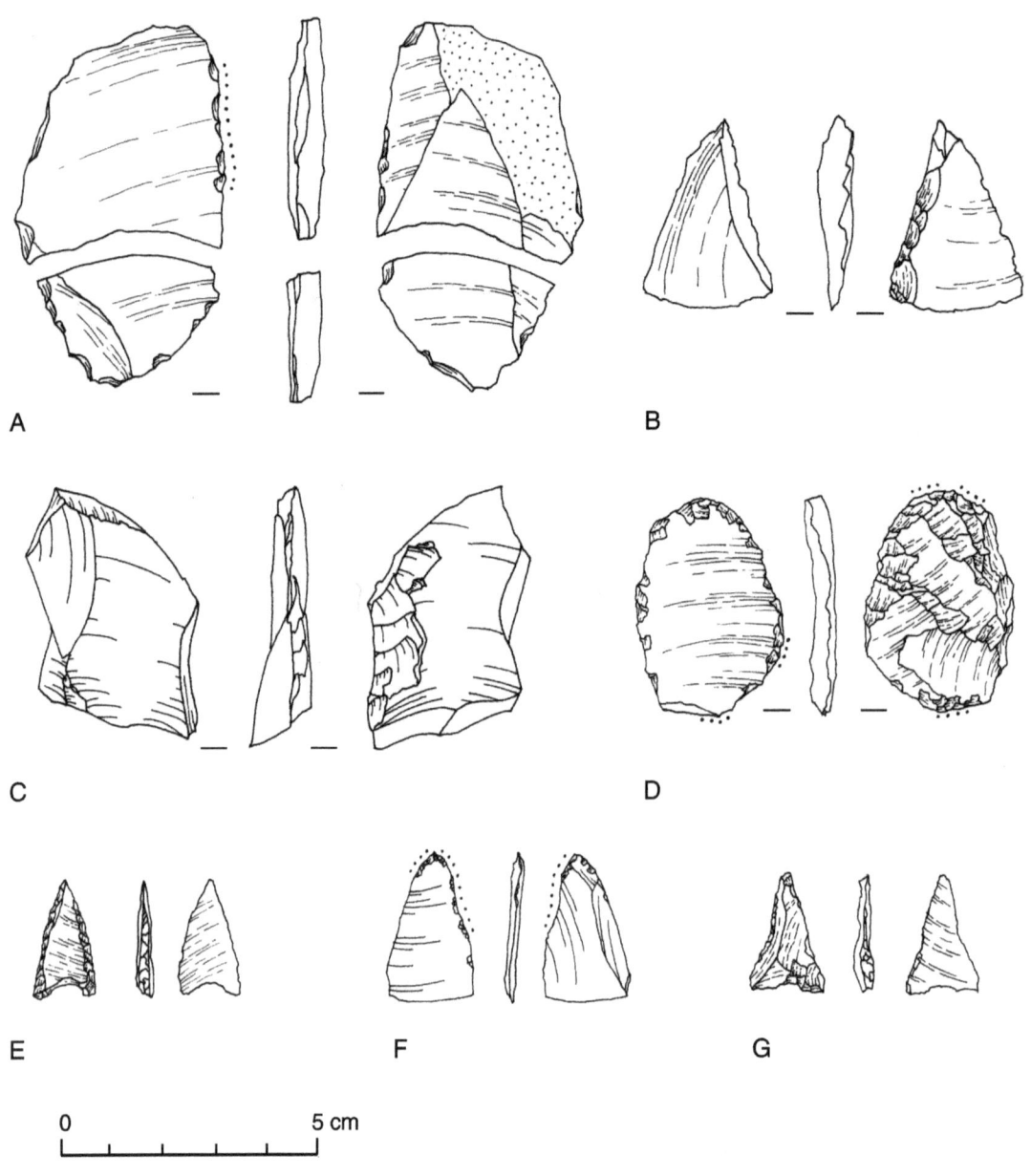

Figure 7.12: Unifacially-retouched flakes, all of local material. Use wear is indicated. The artifacts are reproduced at 75%.

A range of materials was used to fabricate unifacial implements, but a strong preference for fine-grained material is evident in those materials that were selected (Table 7.9). Some of the coarsest-grained volcanics that were locally and regionally available were not selected for uniface production. In contrast, cryptocrystalline cherts—a material that is regionally available and whose overall proportion is considerably smaller in the entire lithic assemblage—were frequently selected for the production of unifacial implements. By count, chert unifacial implements are the most common single class of material across the twelve units (n=9) and this compares favorably with the much more readily accessible group of volcanics, which collectively numbers 12 cases. When measured by weight (g), chert totals only 4.42

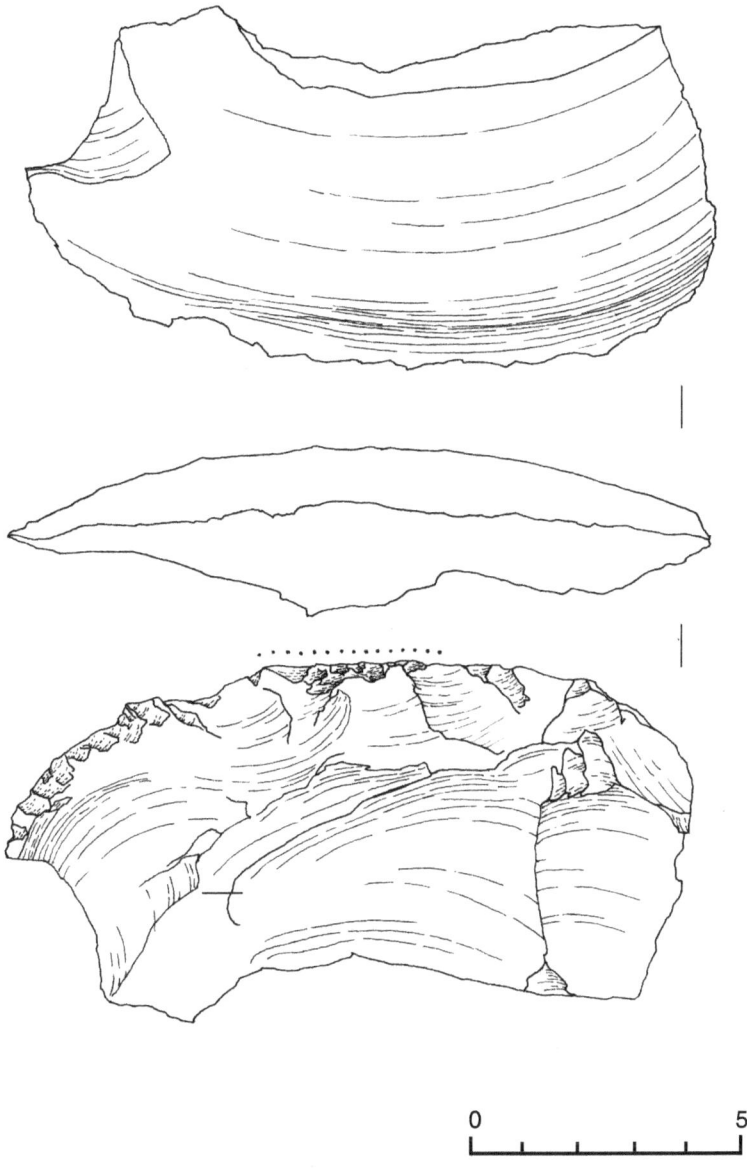

Figure 7.13: Unifacially-retouched flake of local rhyolite. Use wear is indicated on the distal edge. The artifact is reproduced at 75%.

percent of the total mass of raw material that was used to produce unifacial implements; local volcanics, in contrast, total over 95 percent, with fine-grained rhyolite making up the bulk of this at 63.7 percent. The discrepancy between chert's prevalence by count and the dominance of volcanic material by weight can be attributed to the very large size of a few rhyolite implements in excavation units 9, 27, and 32. Chert has a mean weight of 8.2 grams per implement while the implements made from local rhyolite have mean weights of 236, 95.4, and 45.3 grams for fine-grained, macrocrystalline, and microcrystalline varieties, respectively. Further, the mean length, width, and thickness for chert unifacial implements fall close to or within the lower end of the means for unifacial rhyolite tools, despite the great difference in mean weight (Table 7.10). Although they come close to overlapping, chert unifaces are overall more gracile than their rhyolite counterparts and were presumably made from smaller nodules of raw material.

Obsidian closes out the range of materials from which unifaces were made, but this material only makes minor contributions in terms of both numbers of artifacts and overall

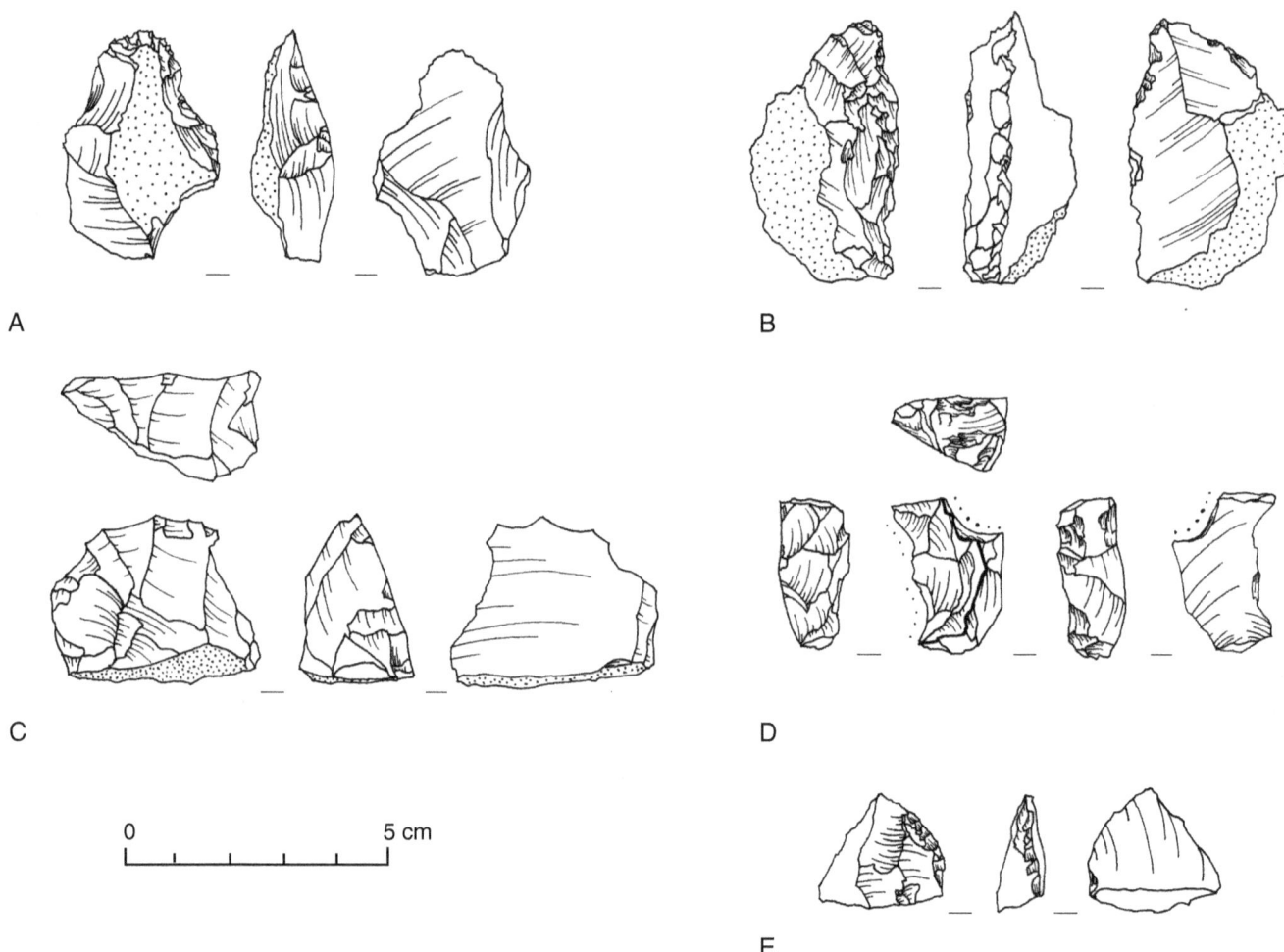

Figure 7.14: Unifacial implements, all of local material. Use wear and cortical surfaces are indicated. The artifacts are reproduced at 75%.

mass. Three unifacial implements were fabricated from exotic obsidian and together these implements total 4.1 grams, or only 0.27 percent of the total mass of raw material represented by unifacial implements. The mean length, width, and thickness for obsidian tools are considerably lower than those for other unifacial tools (Table 7.10). Moreover, unifacial obsidian implements are restricted exclusively to excavation units 9, 24, and 25—the dominance of these residential units in the disproportionate use of obsidian continues. Importantly, obsidian by weight represents only a minute proportion of the mass of unifacial implements. While obsidian was relatively more abundant in these residential contexts, it was apparently not preferred as a material for unifacial tools.

The best indication of this comes from Unit 9, which has the greatest number of unifacial implements (n=14) and which consistently has had the greatest number and variety of material and artifact types across all categories. This wealth of material is probably due to Unit 9's paramount position within the community at Cerro Baúl, and the residents of

this unit appear to have enjoyed privileged access to the widest range of local, regional, and exotic materials. Material selection in Unit 9, thus, was likely a matter of choice enabled by economic or social factors rather than a result of restraints imposed by these same factors. Despite this, only one unifacial implement from Unit 9 was made of obsidian. There was a stronger preference for local rhyolitic materials (n=7) or ones fabricated from chert (n=3). The disparities in material preference and the size of implements of different material may relate to functional differences between chert, volcanic, and the rare obsidian unifacial implements. This is suggested by statistical evidence, and awaits confirmation with use-wear analysis.

Obsidian's mechanical properties may have made it inappropriate for the activities that required unifacial implements, or else it may have been reserved for other uses due to cultural preferences. An additional limiting factor may have been that the bulk of exotic obsidian that was introduced to Cerro Baúl arrived in the form of bifacial preforms and/or finished artifacts, limiting the availability of preforms that

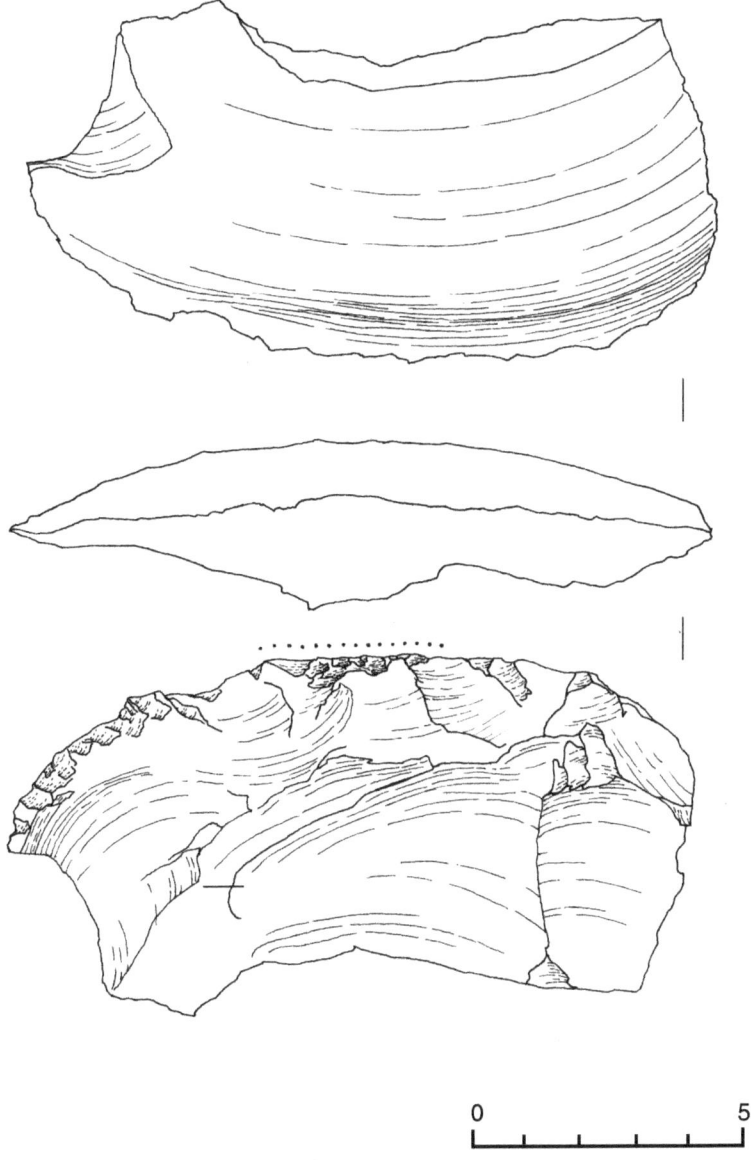

Figure 7.13: Unifacially-retouched flake of local rhyolite. Use wear is indicated on the distal edge. The artifact is reproduced at 75%.

percent of the total mass of raw material that was used to produce unifacial implements; local volcanics, in contrast, total over 95 percent, with fine-grained rhyolite making up the bulk of this at 63.7 percent. The discrepancy between chert's prevalence by count and the dominance of volcanic material by weight can be attributed to the very large size of a few rhyolite implements in excavation units 9, 27, and 32. Chert has a mean weight of 8.2 grams per implement while the implements made from local rhyolite have mean weights of 236, 95.4, and 45.3 grams for fine-grained, macrocrystalline, and microcrystalline varieties, respectively. Further,

the mean length, width, and thickness for chert unifacial implements fall close to or within the lower end of the means for unifacial rhyolite tools, despite the great difference in mean weight (Table 7.10). Although they come close to overlapping, chert unifaces are overall more gracile than their rhyolite counterparts and were presumably made from smaller nodules of raw material.

Obsidian closes out the range of materials from which unifaces were made, but this material only makes minor contributions in terms of both numbers of artifacts and overall

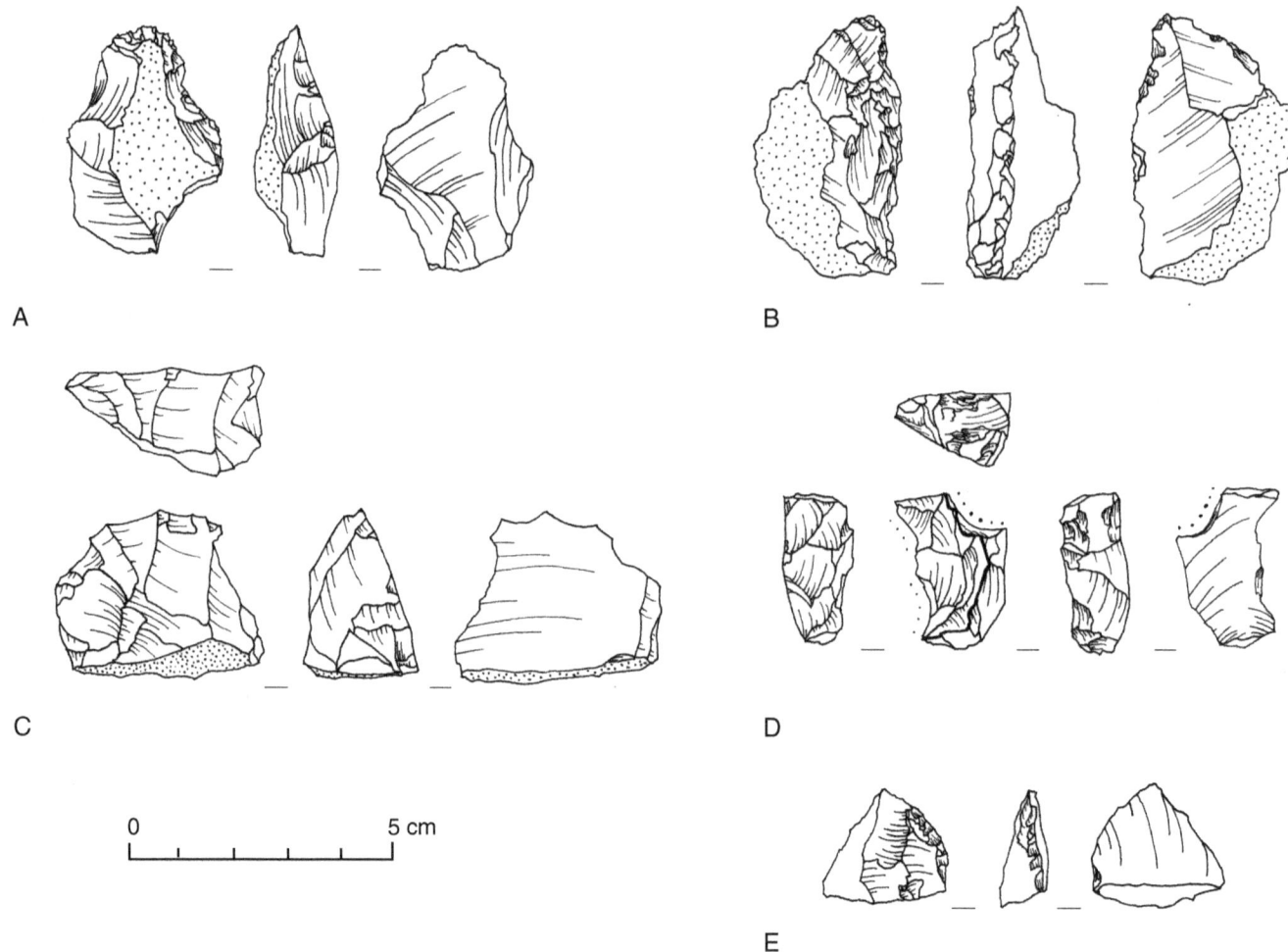

Figure 7.14: Unifacial implements, all of local material. Use wear and cortical surfaces are indicated. The artifacts are reproduced at 75%.

mass. Three unifacial implements were fabricated from exotic obsidian and together these implements total 4.1 grams, or only 0.27 percent of the total mass of raw material represented by unifacial implements. The mean length, width, and thickness for obsidian tools are considerably lower than those for other unifacial tools (Table 7.10). Moreover, unifacial obsidian implements are restricted exclusively to excavation units 9, 24, and 25—the dominance of these residential units in the disproportionate use of obsidian continues. Importantly, obsidian by weight represents only a minute proportion of the mass of unifacial implements. While obsidian was relatively more abundant in these residential contexts, it was apparently not preferred as a material for unifacial tools.

The best indication of this comes from Unit 9, which has the greatest number of unifacial implements (n=14) and which consistently has had the greatest number and variety of material and artifact types across all categories. This wealth of material is probably due to Unit 9's paramount position within the community at Cerro Baúl, and the residents of this unit appear to have enjoyed privileged access to the widest range of local, regional, and exotic materials. Material selection in Unit 9, thus, was likely a matter of choice enabled by economic or social factors rather than a result of restraints imposed by these same factors. Despite this, only one unifacial implement from Unit 9 was made of obsidian. There was a stronger preference for local rhyolitic materials (n=7) or ones fabricated from chert (n=3). The disparities in material preference and the size of implements of different material may relate to functional differences between chert, volcanic, and the rare obsidian unifacial implements. This is suggested by statistical evidence, and awaits confirmation with use-wear analysis.

Obsidian's mechanical properties may have made it inappropriate for the activities that required unifacial implements, or else it may have been reserved for other uses due to cultural preferences. An additional limiting factor may have been that the bulk of exotic obsidian that was introduced to Cerro Baúl arrived in the form of bifacial preforms and/or finished artifacts, limiting the availability of preforms that

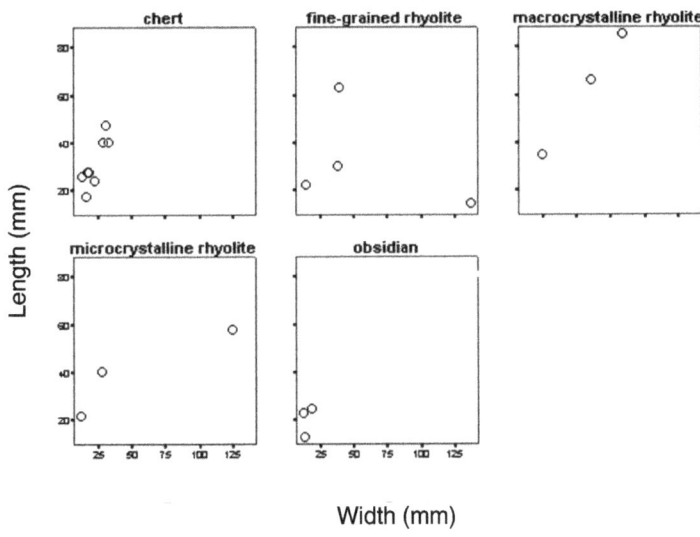

A

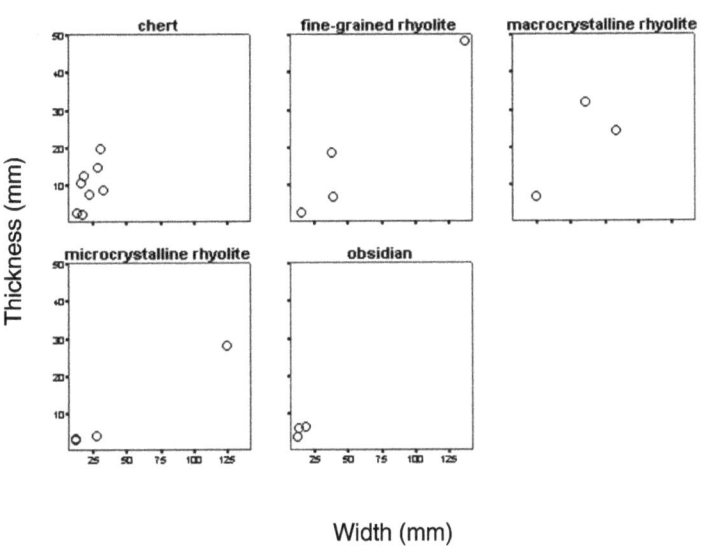

B

Figure 7.16: Bivariate correlations for the length, width and thickness (mm) of unifacial implements, organized by their material properties.

tion to other metric variables that describe unifacial tools, this was likely an operative factor in the design and use of unifacial implements at Cerro Baúl. One possible consideration in the selection of unifacial implements may have been the ability to withstand stress during their use, a property that would be enhanced with thicker implement profiles. This suggestion is reinforced by the relatively steep retouch seen on several of these implements. In addition, some are heavily carinated (e.g., Figures 7.14b, d). Further, 59 percent of the unifacial implements showed clear or probable evidence of use-wear—in the form of stepped micro-flaking, polish, or striations—compared to 9.9 percent of the bifacial artifacts. Unifacial implements, consequently, were subjected to a considerably larger amount of mechanical stress during their use life, resulting in differences in their design.

Morphological considerations other than thickness were less important, contributing to an under-emphasis on formal types. Unifacial artifacts thus take on a variety of irregular and inconstant morphologies. Some were based on the form of the original flake, while other preforms were consider-

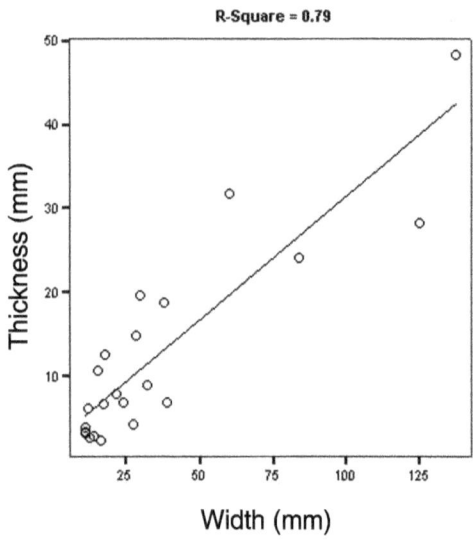
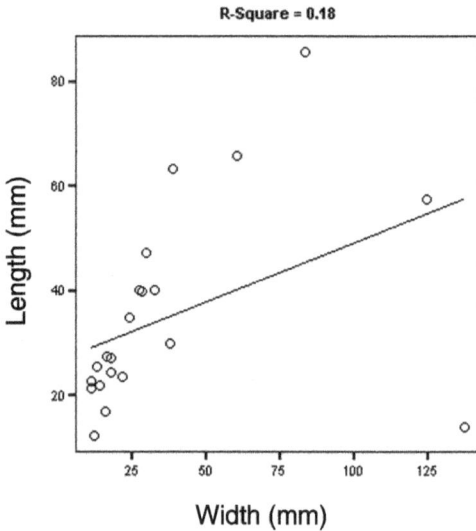

A   B

Figure 7.17: Scatterplots for the thickness and width, and length and width (mm) of all unifacial implements, with regression fit lines.

ably modified. Consequently, there are a number of denticulate and concave retouched margins found among the unifacial implements, a characteristic that is not seen so frequently in the bifacial artifacts. Use-wear is so visible on some implements that it can be readily identified macroscopically and this suggests heavy use. The analysis of these modified margins to determine the specific functions has not been undertaken.

Collectively, unifacial implements represent a small class of irregular artifacts that were used across the site of Cerro Baúl. The apparent lack of spatial concentrations and the small quantity suggest that these artifacts were common but not abundant objects in what were most likely quotidian activities. One of the more significant patterns can be seen in material selection where fine-grained material with a high mechanical tenacity was preferred and where the available material helped to determine the size of the implements. Despite the available material or the different uses for this class of artifact, the thickness of the implement was an important consideration in its final shape. In contrast to many Middle Horizon bifacial tools and even contrary to unifacial tool morphology in earlier periods (e.g., Aldenderfer 1998), the irregularity of artifact sizes and shapes implies that there was no formalized typology—either stylistic or functional—but that unifacial tools were fabricated on a particularistic and likely expedient basis to satisfy a wide range of industrial applications.

Table 7.9: Observed frequencies of raw material types that were used to fabricate unifacial implements. The petrographic variability in local materials is reduced to reflect general categories based on mechanical properties.

Material[1]	Un 7	Un 9	Un 19	Un 20	Un 21	Un 24	Un 25	Un 27	Un 28	Un 32	Total	Weight (g)	Percentage of weight
Obsidian (isotropic)		1			1	1					3	4.1	0.27
Rhyolite													
(crypto xstal)		3	1								4	944.3	63.74
(micro xstal)		2						1			3	180.5	12.18
(macro xstal)		2								1	3	286.3	19.32
Chert													
(crypto xstal)	1	3		1	1	1	1		1		9	65.5	4.42
Total	1	11	1	1	1	2	2	1	1	1	22	1480.7	100.00

[1]Material is organized an the basis of crystal development. "crypto xstal" is cryptocrystalline (e.g., fine dacites and rhyolites), "micro xstal" is microcrystalline (e.g., fine-grained rhyolites), and "macro xstal" is macrocrystalline (e.g., coarse rhyolites).

Table 7.10: Mean values for measurements on unifacial implements, organized by material properties (n=22).

Material	n	Length (mm)	Width (mm)	Thickness (mm)	Weight (g)
obsidian	3	19.67	13.93	5.57	1.37
rhyolite (crypto xstal)	4	32.1	57.18	19.23	236.08
rhyolite, (micro xstal)	3	35.00	43.95	9.80	45.30
rhyolite, (macro xstal)	3	62.07	56.20	20.93	95.43
chert, (crypto xstal)	9	30.9	22.14	9.9	8.19
Total	22	34.58	36.00	12.49	67.33

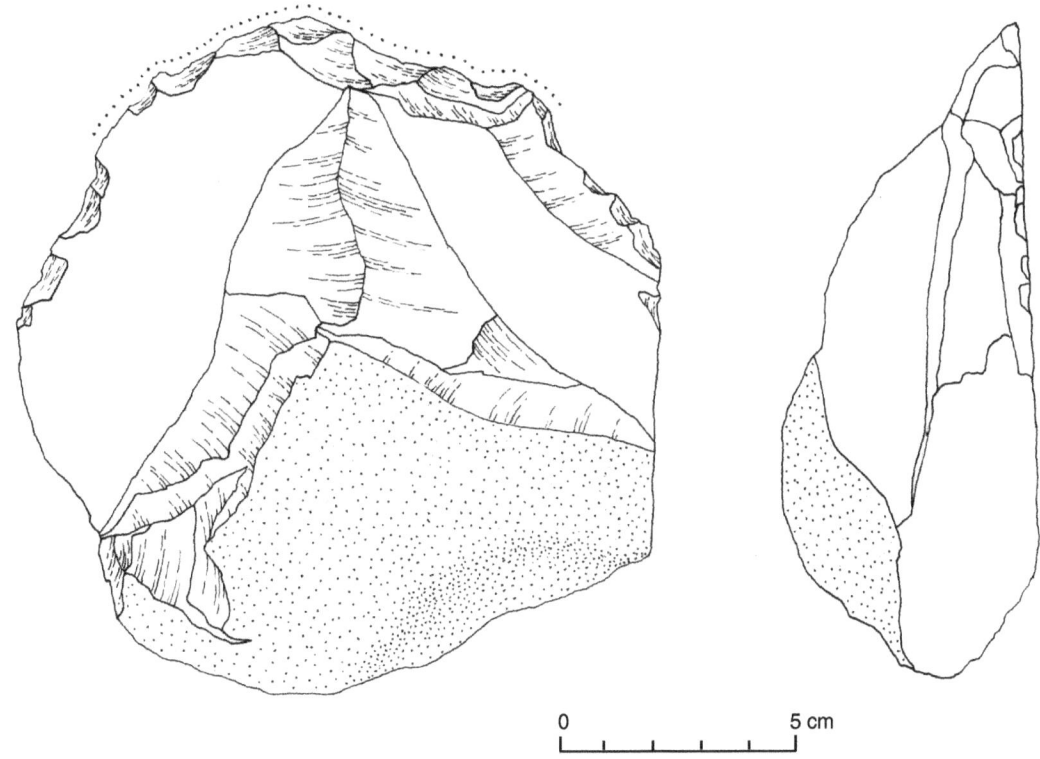

Figure 7.15: Unifacial implement flaked on a cobble of rhyolite. Use wear is indicated and cortex on the proximal end is indicated. The artifact is reproduced at 75%.

Table 7.11: Spearman's r_s correlation coefficients for measurements on unifacial implements. All correlations have a significance of .000, except that between length and thickness which has a significance of .024.

	Length (mm)	Width (mm)	Thickness (mm)	Weight (g)
Length (mm)	1.00	.696 *	.451	.653 *
Width (mm)	.696 *	1.00	.815 *	.956 *
Thickness (mm)	.451	.815 *	1.00	.907 *
Weight (g)	.653 *	.956 *	.907 *	1.00

*significant at a 0.01 level (2 tailed)

were themselves unifacial or large enough for unifacial implements (see Chapter 5). The small size (both weight and particularly the low mean thickness) and also morphological characteristics suggest that these artifacts were likely fashioned out of byproducts from the reduction of other obsidian artifacts and were not themselves primary products of the reduction of obsidian. Thus, the manufacture of unifacial obsidian tools was not an important economic niche at Cerro Baúl, but the occurrence of obsidian as a raw material does continue to suggest some important qualitative differences between the domestic sectors. Locally available materials were preferred more strongly.

Implement Morphology

The production of unifacial implements from readily available local material was an expedient and situational strategy where individual tools were modified for distinct and specialized purposes, but there was perhaps little curation between episodes of activity. This is suggested by the tools' morphological and technological characteristics. Significant cortical surfaces are preserved on almost a third (31.8 percent, n=7) of these implements. While retouched edges on these unifacial tools may show several generations of flake removals, the edges opposite retouched margins and the dorsal surfaces are frequently cortical (Figures 7.14a, b, c; 7.15). Worked edges are mostly marginally retouched, with short flake scars that do not measure longer than 10 percent of the implements' maximum dimension (Inizan et al. 1999: 141). Edges were not intensively refurbished, thus preserving cortical surfaces and limiting the extent to which flake scars modified the flaked surfaces of the implement.

The apparently ad hoc and situational approach to producing unifacial tools makes it difficult to describe any morphological typologies. Because of irregular sizes and shapes, length, width, and thickness measurements for these implements vary greatly and do not have normal distributions. Their metric dimensions do not correlate with the excavation unit from which the artifact was recovered. That is, there appears to be no relationship between the provenience of the artifact and its morphology, thus reflecting activities that were spatially separated. There is no obvious correlation between the artifact and its location, although the small sample size per excavation unit limits the utility of statistical tests.

There are stronger relationships, however, between the size of the implements and the material from which they are made, an association referred to above. Figure 7.16 shows bivariate relationships between the width and length and the width and thickness of unifacial implements based on five general material classes. The raw material has been divided into obsidian/isotropic, cryptocrystalline rhyolite, macrocrystalline rhyolite, microcrystalline rhyolite, and chert/cryptocrystalline. These categories primarily reflect the textural properties of the materials and consequently their amenability to conchoidal fracture. They also reflect, in a general way, categories of material that was immediately available or not. Obsidian and chert unifacial tools are some of the smallest that are found at Cerro Baúl. This may be due to their being fashioned from secondary reduction products.

There is a positive correlation between the length of the unifacial tools and their width (r=0.696), but this relationship is overshadowed by the much stronger positive correlation between thickness and width (r=0.815, Table 7.11). When unifacial tools are considered collectively, rather than dividing them on the basis of material properties, it is clear that width and length are poorly correlated. Collectively, however, the measurements for width and thickness are moderately to highly correlated. This is reflected in a Spearman's r value of 0.815 for the correlation between width and thickness for unifacial tools, compared to lower, less significant correlation coefficients when the length of tools is involved (Table 7.11). Width and thickness, in turn, are more important factors in determining implement weight and ultimately the size of the tools. The axes for determining length versus width were based on the orientation of the proximal end of the tool relative to its initial removal, rather than any position suggested by morphology. The bulbs of percussion, ripples, and/or radial fissures were important in orienting the artifact (Whittaker 1994: 17), and these are analytical criteria that likely had little cultural relevance in the use of the tool. The thickness and mass were likely more important factors during the tools' use.

This is reflected in a less constant relationship between length–width than between thickness–width. The relationship between thickness and width is especially constant in smaller unifacial implements. A linear regression describes the average thickness of unifacial implements as equal to 1.84 + 0.30 × width, with an R square value for all unifacial implements of 0.79 (Figure 7.17a). In contrast, best fit linear regression describes the length of unifacial implements as 26.46 + 0.23 × width, with an R square value of 0.18 (Figure 7.17b). The much lower R square statistic is likely due primarily to the considerable variability seen in the larger unifacial implements.

In this respect, unifacial tools contrast very strongly with bifacial tools, which have much more constant relationships between their length and width. In part, this lack of correlation is due to the considerable morphological variability seen in unifacial artifacts. As thickness has a strong correla-

Chapter 8: Conclusions

A Middle Horizon Context for Lithic Artifacts

To date there is an unfortunate shortage of literature that systematically addresses flaked lithic artifacts from the Andean Middle Horizon. There are sufficient data from Wari sites (Stone 1983; Bencic 2000; Nash 2002; Rivera Pineda 1978) as well as from Tiwanaku sites (Giesso 2000, 2003; Seddon 1994; Bencic 2000) to begin to compare and contextualize the lithic artifact assemblage at Cerro Baúl. Further, brief descriptions and illustrations of both Wari and Tiwanaku lithic artifacts are scattered in several other sources (e.g., Pozzi-Escot 1991: 87–89, figure 12; Klink and Aldenderfer 2005: 45–46; Burger, Chavéz and Chavéz 2000: 236–237, figures 12, 13; Goldstein 1993: 34, figure 3.7a; Owen and Goldstein 2001: figure 11; Seddon 1998: 187, figures 5.58, 5.60; Castillo 2000: 149, figure 8; see also Kolata 2003; Bermann 1994). Considered as a whole, the assemblage from Cerro Baúl shows several parallels with both Wari and Tiwanaku assemblages in terms of material selection and formal artifacts. This assemblage, however, demonstrates several strong departures from lithic assemblages described for other Middle Horizon sites. Cerro Baúl can thus be securely placed within the context of Middle Horizon culture, but these artifacts also point to significant differences in the economic organization of the community.

Throughout Middle Horizon sites, both Wari and Tiwanaku, a similar variety of tool types and raw material were exploited. The latter includes a suite of locally available material and a smaller group of exotic material that was transported over considerable distances. The local materials vary appreciably from site to site, due to the geological diversity of the Andean sierra and altiplano. Common types of raw material that were exploited include various volcanics (rhyolite and andesite), sedimentary rock (chert, quartz, and sandstone; Stone 1983 also lists "siliceous materials" but does not specify further), and metamorphic rocks (including quartzite, slate, and, at Tiwanaku, "fine metamorphic" rock, Giesso 2000: table 7.1). As these materials were transported over minimal distances, the diversity in each sample relates strongly to the heterogeneity of the proximate geological deposits. In many instances, this includes secondary colluvial and alluvial deposits.

Social dynamics also factor into the diversity of raw materials found in a given context. These dynamics are most significant for understanding the social milieu of Middle Horizon communities and also for distilling insights into the state mechanisms that impacted household production. Higher indices for material diversity are characteristic of Cerro Baúl elite residences. The material diversity in these residences is greater than would be anticipated on the basis of the geological environment alone, and it is clear from high resolution geological mapping that several of the elite houses were procuring and exploiting raw materials which are regionally available but not found in lower-status contexts. Those residences which are located more towards the periphery of the site have decreased diversity indices, and were exploiting local material that was directly available (i.e., in the immediate environment of the household) rather than transporting any significant amount of material. Transport distances for non-elite households are generally below several hundred meters, while elite households contain material that was transported distances up to several kilometers. As the different diversities of raw material in each context cannot be attributed wholly to localized geological deposits, differences in the scale and spatial dimension of each household's procurement network are implicated. By assuming that material diversity reflects the social mechanisms involved in procuring, transporting, and ultimately consuming material, greater diversity in the elite residences indicates extensive social networks which engaged more individuals. Material available at a regional scale was transported through multiple individuals and was used for specialized functions; the increase of such material in elite households speaks to their superior capacity to mobilize greater human resources relative to non-elite households. Raw material can be used as a coarse, relative measure of the capacity of individual households to direct and benefit from social capital.

In the sense that more extensive networks still functioned at or within the level of their community, they were local and the procurement of raw material through these networks was "direct" (e.g., McAnany 1989). Those artifacts fabricated from locally and regionally available raw materials do not exhibit technological attributes, including late reduction stages and constant morphologies, which would be consistent with formalized modes of lithic material procurement and distribution, which may have been administered according to state and/or elite concerns.

This is the case, however, for exotic materials that were transported to Cerro Baúl from outside the Osmore Drainage area—namely, obsidian. Such material was indirectly procured and a complex and established network was required to transport the exotic material from a limited number of distant geological sources to the consumer locus.

Several attributes of the exotic obsidian suggests that these networks were formalized, used repeatedly, and perhaps served as a component of state finance. Key among these attributes are low raw-material variability, indicating that one source and likely one network was preferred during repeated episodes of procurement and distribution, and late-stage, complex technological attributes of the artifacts found in the consumer assemblage (McAnany 1989). Obsidian at Cerro Baúl fits these criteria. Geological sourcing using INAA indicates that obsidian from Wari sources in central and southern Peru were used almost exclusively at Cerro Baúl and are predominate in other Middle Horizon sites in Moquegua (Burger, Chavéz, and Chavéz 2000). A single source, at Alca, accounts for 79 % of the sourced obsidian at Cerro Baúl and Wari sources collectively represent 97% of the sample (Burger, Chavéz, and Chavéz 2000: table 6). This heavy reliance on one geologic source emphasizes an established and centralized distribution network for Wari obsidian. It also supports the contention that the distribution and consumption of economic resources like agricultural produce and mineral deposits was administered in other regions (e.g., Schreiber 1987, 1992, 2000: 442). This resonates with the increasing literature suggesting that the administration of economic resources was a major aspect of Wari expansion (Williams and Nash 2002; Schreiber 1987, 1992; Moseley et al. 1991; Topic 1991).

Obsidian flakes at Cerro Baúl are small and have technologically complex attributes that are indicative of late stages of biface reduction. Several of the reduction stages that are found in local flaked material are absent in the sample of obsidian flakes, and the opposite is also true. Cortical surfaces are noticeably absent among obsidian. The proportion of obsidian flakes produced from soft-hammer reduction, pressure flaking, and bifacial retouch is considerably greater than similar flake types of locally available material. Principal components analysis shows that local and exotic materials were involved in markedly different reduction strategies, and not all of this difference is due to their use to fabricate different classes of tools. Rather, the primary reduction stages are underemphasized in the obsidian sample, pointing to a fundamental spatial separation in the loci of initial reduction and ultimate consumption of obsidian. In concert with the geological data and the regular morphology of obsidian implements, indirect procurement is the most plausible mechanism to explain obsidian distribution and consumption at Cerro Baúl. These data suggest an institutionalized system of artifact production, transport, and redistribution through, if not centralized, at least established and repeated network connections. While obsidian is well distributed among the households found at Wari sites, it is most prevalent in elite contexts—in these same sites as well as in contemporaneous elite contexts at non-Wari sites—and it was likely a medium of inter-elite exchange in general use during the Middle Horizon.

Jennings and Glascock (2002) have recently published a description of the Alca obsidian source, the main geological source of obsidian found at Cerro Baúl (Burger, Chavéz, and Chavéz 2000: table 6). They identified sixteen geological exposures that produce nodules of high-quality Alca-type obsidian in the Cotahuasi Valley, five of which were clearly exploited prehistorically. These quarries were places where obsidian was obtained but not reduced; large quantities of initial reduction debris common at prehistoric quarries are not present at these loci. The deposits are substantial, geographically dispersed, and obsidian nodules can be easily extracted with minimal technology. These characteristics suggest to Jennings and Glascock that direct control over the exploitation of Alca obsidian would have been difficult or impossible to establish and enforce, and that centralized, state-administered procurement was not likely (2002: 115–116). Given that control over raw material sources was likely not an aspect of Middle Horizon economic networks, at least in the case of Alca, institutionalization certainly occurred as indirect procurement. That is, the processes of reducing raw material into pre-established forms, transporting, and then introducing finished or near-finished artifacts into consumer loci could have provided opportunities for administration and oversight. Whether or not they in fact were is an aspect of Wari state organization that remains to be tested carefully using evidence from multiple archaeological sites and models that consider both production and consumer loci.

Exotic lithic materials at Huari and Tiwanaku show that long-distance indirect procurement networks were a common economic strategy in general use during the Middle Horizon. Stone (9183) attributes formalized obsidian tool types at Huari to specialized production. She finds no evidence in three surface-collected areas for the initial stages of reduction that produced these implements, however, suggesting that their production occurred elsewhere, either at Huari or at another site. This pattern contrasts with the generalized reduction of local materials in all areas of the site (Stone 1983: 293–295). The exotic material likely followed the mode of production and indirect procurement seen at Cerro Baúl, although Huari is closer to the Quispisisa obsidian source in Ayacucho (Burger and Glascock 2000a) and may have been more intimately involved in the production and distribution of obsidian. At Conchopata, similarly, obsidian is prevalent and flakes largely are the result of advanced stages of biface reduction (Bencic 2000: 105). In contrast to Cerro Baúl, however, a wider variety of artifact forms at Conchapata (including burins, expedient scrapers, and core-tools) were manufactured on obsidian, perhaps indicating that obsidian was more readily available, expendable, and functionally utilitarian (Bencic 2000: 113).

Obsidian had a slightly different role at Tiwanaku. The niche that obsidian occupied at Wari sites was occupied at Tiwanaku by black basalt from the Querimita source, near Lake Poopo to the south (Giesso 2000: 337–338, 2003: 363, 366).

Obsidian is found in quantities at Tiwanaku, but a greater variety of geological sources and artifact types are represented. Obsidian from the Chivay/Cotallalli source in Arequipa is the predominant type of obsidian associated with Tiwanaku and Tiwanaku-affiliated sites (Burger, Chavéz, and Chavéz 2000; Brooks, Glascock, and Giesso 1997; Giesso 2000: 204) while it is rarely associated with Wari sites. Obsidian varieties from nine other geological sources have been documented at Tiwanaku (Giesso 2000: 204, 2003: 335; Brooks, Glascock, and Giesso 1997: 450), a diversity that is not seen at Cerro Baúl or probably at other Wari sites. Individual residential sectors at Tiwanaku apparently established and maintained relations with different procurement networks that preferentially exploited some sources over others (Giesso 2003: 367–368). Quispisisa is represented in this sample, and it may indicate limited economic interaction between Wari and Tiwanaku (Giesso 2000: 200, 336). This and the remaining sources are located at least 200 kilometers from the site of Tiwanaku. Despite this transport distance and in contrast to the strategy seen at Wari sites, obsidian was introduced to Tiwanaku in nodular form and was reduced entirely on-site. Cortical flakes, primary reduction products, and microartifacts are abundant (Giesso 2000: 205, 2003: 366–367).

Basalt, on the other hand, was reduced into thin flakes prior to being transported to Tiwanaku where the flakes were themselves utilized or reduced into small points; basalt cortical flakes and microartifacts are more rare (Giesso 2003: 366). Giesso suggests that this is due to the practical mechanics of extracting and processing basalt, which does not occur naturally as nodules but rather was quarried from cuts into flow-deposits. Basalt is not a material found at Cerro Baúl, although it has been noted at Conchopata and Huari (Bencic 2000: 108; Stone 1983).

The different treatment of indirectly procured exotics may reflect substantive differences in the organization of Wari and Tiwanaku economies, in addition to suggesting substantive differences in how the polities themselves were organized. The lithic data suggest that Tiwanaku economic networks were decentralized relative to the organization of Wari networks. Giesso's interpretation that basalt was reduced into preforms merely due to practical constraints (rather than state motivations), the transport of obsidian in nodular form from a multiplicity of geological sources, and the preferential exploitation of variable sources by residential groups show more selection and less entrenchment of resource use at Tiwanaku. The formalization of Wari obsidian artifacts and the predominance of a few sources, on the other hand, make the possibility of centralized economic administration more plausible. Considered as a whole, both Wari and Tumilaca houses at Cerro Baúl conform more closely to the Wari rather than the Tiwanaku economic mode.

Within the site, though, there are qualitative and quantitative differences in the economies of each residence. The presence of obsidian in many households at Cerro Baúl demonstrates that several social segments could participate in the same economic system but at varying scales of intensity, and it suggests that draconian prohibitions were not in effect. Not all households participated in obsidian distribution networks equitably; while it is ubiquitous near the center of the site, obsidian—while present—decreases dramatically in quantity with distance from the site core. The households sampled in this analysis can be clustered into four groups based on the intensity of obsidian use and, by extension, the frequency of their interaction with long distance procurement networks. The relative intensity of social and economic interaction among households can also be compared.

Coincidentally, Giesso also divides the Tiwanaku populace into four macro- social segments that are spatially segregated, with elites residing at the monumental core of the site surrounded by concentric rings of urban commoner, urban periphery, and rural populations (2000: 333–334). These groups are economically differentiated. Elites enjoyed access to the greatest quantity and diversity of lithic materials. Exotic materials are rarer towards the periphery while functional specialization becomes more common. These groups constitute the social "concentric cline" discussed by Kolata (1993).

The intra-site social groups at Cerro Baúl also can be described by a spatially-concentric social cline, a point that I will return to below. Importantly, these groups are not organized principally by ethnic differentiation between Wari and Tumilaca. Rather, social segmentation was manifested economically. Taken together, the data on material use and other archaeological data indicate that the community at Cerro Baúl was organized according to considerations of ethnicity and economic status. These criteria were not directly correlated, however, but were in play simultaneously and complementarily. They described several intra-community clusters of households that represent intensive social and economic interaction. Neighborhood groupings included households with similar economic bases despite other apparent cultural differences.

Formal lithic artifacts serve to blur some of the cultural distinctions and reinforce economic differentiation. Several projectile point or biface types are recognizable at Cerro Baúl. These types match the biface types noted at other Middle Horizon sites and which have been linked to either Wari or Tiwanaku cultural styles. Raw material, size, and form are all criteria that determine the point types utilized in each residential context. As with the use of lithic artifacts in general, however, these factors did not coalesce to define sets of point types according to the apparent ethnicity of the household. Rather, the economics of acquiring and using these artifacts were more significant. For example, small triangular, stemmed point styles that have traditionally been attributed to Tiwanaku material culture were abundant in Wari contexts at Cerro Baúl and there is compelling evidence that at least one residence, Unit 21, was directly involved in the intensive manufacture of this style of point. Similarly, lanceolate point types that are most commonly described at Wari sites were recovered from households whose material culture otherwise was predominantly Tumilaca. Consequently, it is necessary to reevaluate the cultural attribution that traditionally has been attached to these artifact types. Middle Horizon point types do not, in general, appear to conform strongly to cultural or ethnic stylistic templates; rather, biface types and materials appear to have been mobilized relative to economic criteria, functional activity, and even exchange relationships that redistributed socially valuable materials. The assumption that they can be uncritically linked to particular cultural groups needs to be reconsidered.

Rivera Pineda provides a descriptive typology based on a sample of 300 projectile points from the surface of the Yanapunta sector at Huari. These points are small (between 1–4 cm in length) and come in five morphological types, with flat, concave, and stemmed bases and triangular or "leaf-shaped" (lanceolate) bodies (1978: 590–591). Although Rivera Pineda provides neither drawings nor photographs of these points, his description of these Wari points is as applicable to points at Cerro Baúl as they are to examples from Tiwanaku sites (e.g., Bencic 2000: figures 4, 5; Goldstein 1993: figure 3.7a; Seddon 1994: figures 172–174, 1994: figure 5.60; Giesso 2003: 378, figures 15.12–15.14; Couture 2003: figure 8.31). Burger, Chavéz, and Chavéz, in their detailed diachronic synthesis of Andean obsidian use, note that small, triangular stemmed and un-stemmed points are plentiful in Bolivian late Formative contexts at and near Tiwanaku (Tiwanaku epoch III, ca. AD 300 – 500) but are absent in highland Peru until later with Wari expansion during the Middle Horizon 1B epoch (ca. AD 600). They attribute the proliferation of such point types to the increased use of bow and arrow during the Middle Horizon, though this interpretation is based largely on correlations with iconographic evidence (Burger, Chavéz, and Chavéz 2000: 327). By the Middle Horizon, small-stemmed, chert points can be found regularly in both Wari and Tiwanaku contexts. Consequently, it is perhaps more productive to think of Middle Horizon biface morphologies as representing functional rather than cultural types, which suggests economic behavior rather than enculturated preference. This accounts for the mixing of morphologies seen Wari and Tumilaca contexts at Cerro Baúl.

At both Tiwanaku and Cerro Baúl, the density and diversity of bifacial types was greatest in the elite areas at the sites' cores. There is no compelling evidence at Cerro Baúl that biface production constituted a form of state taxation imposed on the individual households, as Giesso (2000, 2003) has proposed for Tiwanaku. If biface types are functional, and lithic raw material use is a factor of political and social connections, then the distribution of biface types supports the contention that economic differentiation was a salient factor in organizing social interaction and intra-community diversity. The assemblage of bifacial artifacts at Cerro Baúl shows similarities to both Wari and Tiwanaku sites; the intra-assemblage differences, however, cannot be attributed to such cultural divisions. Since types and cultural contexts are mixed, the presumed correlation between form and cultural complexes may be inappropriate. Functional preferences, instead, may more accurately explain the distribution of Middle Horizon point types.

The Cerro Baúl assemblage shares Wari and Tiwanaku elements, but it also departs dramatically from the suite of lithic artifacts that are seen at Middle Horizon sites. Large bifacial implements are common components of Tiwanaku assemblages in the Bolivian altiplano. Similar large bifaces are found in Wari assemblages, though their morphology is different and they appear to represent a distinct class of artifact. These formalized types of bifacial tools have been interpreted as agricultural hoes or alternatively as potter's implements. Such artifacts are conspicuously missing at Cerro Baúl. Their absence has substantial implications for how economic production may have been organized at Cerro Baúl.

Seddon provides a detailed discussion of such artifacts from the site of Tumatumani on the shores of Lake Titicaca (1994: 66–67). These bifaces are rectangular with a beveled, distal bit which is polished from use and exhibits distal-proximal use-striations. On the basis of metric criteria he has divided them into two minor classes: hoes (which tend to be longer, thicker, and wider) and adzes (Seddon interprets these artifacts as *q'orana*, the blades of traditional Andean footplows (*chakitaqlla*), though he conservatively ascribes their function to a "generic digging aspect" (1994: 67).

The Tumatumani lithic assemblage is similar to other, contemporaneous assemblages in the Bolivian altiplano (Seddon 1994: 65, 71). "Adzes" and "hoes" are found at the Tiwanaku sites of Chucaripupata on the Island of the Sun in Lake Titicaca (Seddon 1998: 187, figure 5.58), at Iwawi on the shores of Lake Titicaca (Bencic 2000: 100–101), in late Formative and Tiwanaku contexts at Lukurmata (Bermann 1994, 2003: 154; Janusek and Kolata 2003: 145), and in urban contexts at the site of Tiwanaku itself (Giesso 2003: 374). In most of these instances, excavators agree with Seddon that these adzes and hoes represent agricultural implements, though the urban examples also may have been used in residential construction (Giesso 2003: 374). During late Formative and Tiwanaku periods in the circum-Titicaca region, hoes are more abundant at sites located in lowland, 'alluvial' zones amenable to cultivation than they are at sites in upland 'colluvial' zones (Janusek and Kolata 2003: 145). They also become more frequent in Late Horizon assemblages in the Mantaro Valley of Peru (Giesso 2000: 66), where agricultural intensification under Inca influence has been documented archaeologically (e.g., D'Altroy and Hastorf 2001). Finally, the profusion of "crudely chipped stone hoe blades" at Chen Chen in Moquegua has likewise been attributed to agricultural intensification during the Tiwanaku V occupation (Goldstein 1990: 73, cited in Giesso 2000: 73).

Bifacial hoes at Wari sites are morphologically different than those found at Tiwanaku sites. The slate or andesite bifaces have a slender handle that runs perpendicular to a broad distal bit and are called "T"-shaped hoes, or *azadas* (Pozzi-Escot 1991: 88; Bencic 2000: 110). Their function also apparently differs from that of Tiwanaku hoes:

> Similar tools found by other archaeologists have been interpreted as agricultural tools. To test this, microscopic analysis of the use wear on five of the tools was conducted…The results suggest that more than farming tools, the mattocks and adzes were used to work clay, perhaps to excavate it and break clods before processing for ceramic manufacture (Pozzi-Escot 1991: 88)

These implements were found in association with quantities of ceramic wasters and burnishing tools, further cementing their relationship to ceramic production where they were used to process clay prior to levigation or for shaping vessels themselves (Pozzi-Escot 1991: 88; Cook and Benco 2000: 492, 498–500). T-shaped hoes are the most abundant artifact type at Conchopata, signifying their importance in Wari economic production; in one context, as many as 105 *azadas* were recovered (Cook and Benco 2000: 499).

Such large bifacial "hoes," whether related to agricultural or ceramic production, are absent from the entire sample of artifacts (N=1,972) analyzed in this study. It will be recalled that this sample represents all lithic material from twelve domestic contexts, yet no examples were recorded from either Wari or Tumilaca residences. On the other hand, hoes are reported from "a few domestic contexts" at Cerro Mejia, adjacent to Cerro Baúl (Nash 2002: 111). Nash cautions that these implements may have been discarded or further reduced as cores once broken, or stored or used in non-residential contexts (such as in fields). The complete lack of these implements in a sample of nearly two-thousand lithic artifacts, however, is problematic for understanding agrarian and craft production at Cerro Baúl. Extensive irrigation systems in the vicinity of Cerro Baúl and Cerro Mejia show that agricultural production was a significant concern at the Wari site and craft production was likely localized (Williams 2003; Williams and Nash 2002). As none of the artifact types typically associated with these activities at Wari and Tiwanaku sites appear in these residences at Cerro Baúl, different modes of production may have been in effect, particularly ones that occurred with lower intensity or which focused on other areas of the community, though all sectors of site have been sampled. Because these types are missing from this sample, however, it is difficult to make inferences about the social organization of agrarian and certain types of craft production, while the consumption of material does allow clear statements about socio-economic difference.

Social Order at Cerro Baúl

When lithic data are analyzed according to the social context of their particular archaeological provenience rather than as a homogenous class of material, they can provide key insights not only into the economic structure of a community but also the social structure of that economy. As an additional avenue of inquiry into social composition, lithic data complement other archaeological data and reveal additional aspects of the criteria that helped determine social communities. In this respect, lithic artifacts have a potential that is comparable to other lines of archaeological data conventionally relied on to reconstruct the socio-economic profile of a community. The social content is embedded in preferences expressed as differential modes of manufacture and use, and at Middle Horizon sites the inconstant distribution of materials reveals dissimilarities between societal segments vis-à-vis their economic stature and intensity of interaction.

The pattern of lithic artifact use at Cerro Baúl is continuous but not even, and this pattern suggests substantive differences in intra-site social structure. Individual households participated in the community's economy at different levels, likely with social and economic status as key criteria that governed the ability of each household to engage one another. Individual households can thus be grouped according to their lithic assemblages. As the membership of these groups includes households with different apparent ethnic affiliation, economic criteria which were mobilized to define group membership are suggested. The intensity of lithic material use indicates a concentric cline from complex economic behavior in the site core to more basic economies towards the edge of the site. Social status at Cerro Baúl probably followed a similar concentric cline, where the elite residences on the summit and the rustic households on the site periphery represent opposed ends of a status-differentiated spectrum. The elite residences in the core of the site enjoyed an advantaged and elaborate use of material, while non-elite residences towards the periphery are dominated by increasing quotidian and expedient assemblages. These multiethnic social groupings indicate that economy was an important aspect of the social life at Cerro Baúl and suggests that interaction may have been characterized more by social status rather than cultural background.

The evidence for a concentric, gradual social order at Cerro Baúl invites comparison with "a concentric cline" and the "concentric gradation of social status" that Kolata (1993: 93, 2003: 179) and Janusek (2003: 280) respectively have noted at the urban site of Tiwanaku. The two sites represent strikingly different magnitudes of population density and the urban organization that is noted for Tiwanaku likely did not characterize Cerro Baúl. Both share, however, a similar community structure. In both populaces, elite residence and ritual architecture constituted the community nucleus and the social status of residential groups appears to have decreased with distance away from this urban core (Janusek 2003: 280–281). The "concentric cline" of Tiwanaku was an amalgamation of the spatial and temporal priority of the residents; those on the edges of the city may have been among the latest to settle during the development of the center and these areas demonstrate some of the strongest ties to foreign, non-Tiwanaku communities (Janusek 2003: 294). With distance from the center of the site, there was greater latitude for strong assertions of disparate ethnic identities, perhaps because more recent arrivals at Tiwanaku were less assimilated and adsorbed into state culture (Janusek 2001: 284). This social gradient had strong political implications. It is also apparent economically in the consumption of material culture, with differences in ceramic wares, sanitation infrastructure, and archaeobotanical and archaeofuanal assemblages between the site's core and margins (Janusek 2003, Couture and Sampeck 2003, Webster and Janusek 2003).

The model of a concentric social cline to my knowledge has not been explicitly tested at Wari sites, with the exception of this current discussion of Cerro Baúl, although there are many discussions of intra-site status differentiation (e.g., Isbell 2004, 2000; Williams and Nash 2002) as well as regional ranked-site hierarchies (Isbell and Schreiber 1978; Schreiber 1987; Glowacki and McEwan 2001; McEwan 1991) which indicate for Wari sites a slightly different phenomenon of spatial social ordering. There is limited discussion of interethnic populations. Most attention is given to the possibility of direct contact between Wari and Tiwanaku, possibly with some exchange of ritual knowledge and technological expertise (e.g., Isbell 2000; Isbell et al. 1991: 50). Zapata notes ceramic forms, manufacture techniques, and decorative elements in the mortuary contexts at Batan Urqo that are related to both cultural traditions, and he suggests that the site, while primarily occupied by Wari, served as a contact point between diverse cultural groups (1997: 204). A few studies emphasize the role of local ethnic elites that were integrated into Wari expansionistic policies, or who actively manipulated theses policies to accomplish their own ends (Anders 1989; Jennings and Yepez 2001). Consequently, ethnic difference likely was accommodated but it is not clear how difference was managed at Wari sites. Cerro Baúl is an exception. These data suggest that ethnic and cultural difference was mitigated by scalar differences in the economic status of households within the community, such that intra-community social groups differentiated themselves and reproduced social ties through shared economic behaviors and a similar utilization of resources.

A similar mechanism for social integration via economy has been proposed for Tiwanaku, and this may provide a heuristic model by which to understand the mechanisms for social integration in play at Cerro Baúl, albeit on a smaller and more intimate scale. Tiwanaku increasingly has been shown to be a diverse and pluralistic society, where multiethnic populations were incorporated into the urban society through defined economic roles. The highland state was segmentary and integrated multiple *altiplano* traditions and residential groups with discrete stylistic preferences. Individual residential compounds with varied backgrounds continued to interact with each other under the auspices of an established state culture, largely through stylistic elements, behaviors, and modes of production associated with state economy (Janusek 2004, 1999; Janusek and Kolata 2003). Economic networks provided a mechanism for social interaction while simultaneously maintaining discrete and continuous cultural and ethnic affiliations (Haaland 1994). Ritual systems that focused on similar ideological elements may have also provided another shared facet of Middle Horizon life that could accommodate distinct cultural and ethnic identities (Cook 1994; Isbell and Cook 2002). The role that economy served at both sites as a mechanism for integrating their segmentary and pluralistic societies suggests that the two cultures may have shared additional organizational aspects, attesting to their participation in comparable cultural traditions.

Janusek (2001) notes a correlation between ethnic membership and economic specialization at Tiwanaku, where distinctive production modes were the domain of discrete, ethnically differentiated residential compounds. The lack of evidence for specialization in the lithic data at Cerro Baúl means that the Tiwanaku model cannot be translated directly as a model for Wari social order. None of the residential units at Cerro Baúl analyzed in this study, whether Wari or Tumilaca, appeared to have specialized in agrarian, craft, or other production. Rather, the lithic data suggest that production at the sub-urban site largely was generalized but differed in scale and intensity. In contrast to Tiwanaku, then, specialized modes of production were not a way of organizing and reinforcing ethnic difference at Cerro Baúl, but economic mechanisms were used to establishing inter-ethnic social networks that mitigated difference within the two communities.

What both sites (and ostensibly cultures) shared was an added layer of instrumental criteria which overlay ethnocultural difference and could be used to establish membership in sub-communal groups that shared similar socio-economic status if not cultural background. This enabled lateral social mobility across groups bounded by ethnic criteria to facilitate interactions defined by economic criteria. The range of individuals and households that potentially interacted expanded due to this additional layer of multifarious social criteria (e.g., Haaland 1998), resulting in a more complex and situational environment which may have characterized the Middle Horizon. Economic social criteria would have facilitated interaction at an elite level across cultural boundaries, such as would have existed between Wari, Tiwanaku, and other ethnic groups during expansive periods. Further, such criteria would have cemented relationships within pluralistic communities such as existed at Cerro Baúl, Tiwanaku, and likely many other Middle Horizon sites in later occupational phases.

At Cerro Baúl, ceramic and other archaeological data document the occupation and interaction of two cultural complexes, Wari and Tumilaca, in the latter half of the Middle Horizon. This study has shown that economy was an additional element that helped to characterize community structure and which determined membership in intra-community social groups that overlaid ethnic divisions. On a regional scale, there is considerable evidence to suggest that economic interaction was a primary concern during the spread of Wari influence and that exchange relationships were established and common place between Wari and non-Wari elites. On a community scale, the evidence from Cerro Baúl shows that similar economic relationships served to consolidate ties between residences and neighborhoods, and to minimize cultural differences between Wari and Tumilaca residents. On both scales, subsequently, multiple criteria—ethnic, economic, ideological, etc.—to establish and maintain social ties. In Andean South America, far-extending social and economic networks frequently mean that material culture was used in complex social settings. An understanding of these multifaceted criteria could likely be a powerful analytical tool for understanding the negotiation and mitigation of cultural difference during the development and maturation of Middle Horizon states.

Acknowledgements

Financial support for this research was provided principally by the Field Museum of Natural History, Chicago, through a CCC Research Internship Grant. The Department of Archaeology and the Center for Remote Sensing, Boston University also helped support this research.

As with any project, a number of people have contributed substantially towards the information and interpretation presented here, both with formal assistance and also while exchanging ideas more casually. I am indebted to Ryan Williams and Michael Moseley for the initial offer to be part of the Cerro Baúl Archaeological Project. Tricia McAnany, Norman Hammond, and Donna Nash read early drafts of this manuscript and it has benefited from their helpful and insightful comments. Tricia was also a great source of help during the statistical analyses that are presented here. Al Wesolowsky provided valuable advice during the production of this monograph. I am greatly indebted to Mutlu Ozdögan for his unparalleled patience for teaching and his expertise in processing remotely-sensed data. Finally, Evelyn Lopéz was an invaluable help in analyzing this sample of lithic artifacts and the scope of the discussion would not have been possible without her help. I am grateful to all of you for your contributions that have improved this research.

Bibliography

Addington, Lucile R.
1986 *Lithic Illustration: Drawing Flaked Stone Artifacts for Publication.* University of Chicago Press, Chicago.

Aldenderfer, Mark S.
1998 *Montane Foragers: Asana and the South-central Andean Archaic.* University of Iowa Press, Iowa City.

Aldenderfer, Mark S. and Charles Stanish
1993 Domestic Architecture, Household Archaeology, and the Past in the South-Central Andes. In *Domestic Architecture, Ethnicity, and Complementarity in the South-Central Andes,* edited by Mark Aldenderfer, pp. 1–12. University of Iowa Press, Iowa City.

Anders, Martha B.
1989 Evidence for the Dual Socio-Political Organisation and Administrative Structure of the Wari State. In *The Nature of Wari: A Reappraisal of the Middle Horizon Period in Peru,* edited by R. M. Czwarno, F. M. Meddens, and A. Morgan, pp. 35–52. BAR International Series 525, Oxford.

Ashmore, Wendy and A. Bernard Knapp (editors)
1999 *Archaeologies of Landscape.* Blackwell Publishers, Oxford.

Barth, Fredrik
1998 Introduction. In *Social Groups and Boundaries: The Social Organization of Cultural Difference,* edited by Fredrik Barth, pp. 9–38. Waveland Press, Prospect Heights, IL.

Bawden, Garth
1993 An Archaeological Study of Social Structure and Ethnic Replacement in Residential Architecture of the Tumilaca Valley. In *Domestic Architecture, Ethnicity, and Complementarity in the South-Central Andes,* edited by Mark Aldenderfer, pp. 42–54. University of Iowa Press, Iowa City.

Bencic, Catherine M.
2000 Industrias Líticas de Hauri y Tiwanaku. In *Boletín de Arqueología PUCP 4, Huari y Tiwanaku: Modelos vs. Evidencias,* edited by Peter Kaulicke and William H. Isbell, pp. 89–118. Pontifica Universidad Católica del Perú, Lima.

Bermann, Marc
1994 *Household Archaeology in Prehispanic Bolivia.* Princeton University Press, Princeton, NJ.

Berry, Kenneth J., Kenneth L. Kvamme, and Paul W. Mielke. Jr.
1983 Improvements in the Permutation Test for the Spatial Analysis of the Distribution of Artifacts into Classes. *American Antiquity* 48: 547–553.

Blanton, Richard E.
1994 *Houses and Households: A Comparative Study.* Plenum Publishers, New York.

Brooks, Sarah Osgood, Michael D, Glascock, and Martín Giesso
1997 Source of volcanic glass for ancient Andean tools. *Nature* 386: 449–450.

Burger, Richard L. and Michael Glascock
2000a Locating the Quispisisa Obsidian Source in the Department of Ayacucho, Peru. *Latin American Antiquity* 11: 258–268.

2000b The Puzolana Obsidian Source: Locating the Geological Source of Ayacucho Type Obsidian. *Andean Past* 6: 289–308.

Burger, Richard L., Karen L. Mohr Chávez, and Sergio J. Chávez
2000 Through the Glass Darkly: Prehispanic Obsidian Procurement and Exchange in Southern Peru and Northern Bolivia. *Journal of World Prehistory* 14: 267–362.

Castillo, Luis Jaime
2000 La Presencia de Huari en San José de Moro. In *Boletín de Arqueología PUCP 4, Huari y Tiwanaku: Modelos vs. Evidencias Primera Parte* edited by Peter Kaulicke and William H. Isbell, pp. 143–180. Pontifica Universidad Católica del Perú, Lima.

Clay, R.
1976 Typological Classification, Attribute Analysis, and Lithic Variability. *Journal of Field Archaeology* 3: 303–311.

Cook, Anita G.
1994 *Wari y Tiwanaku: Entre el Estilo y la Imagen.* Fondo Editorial, Pontifica Universidad Católica del Perú, Lima.

Cook, Anita G. and Nancy L. Benco
2000 Vasijas para la Fiesta y la Fama: Producción Artesanal en un Centro Urbano Huari. In *Boletín de Arqueología PUCP 4, Huari y Tiwanaku: Modelos vs. Evidencias,* edited by Peter Kaulicke and William H. Isbell, pp. 489–505. Pontifica Universidad Católica del Perú, Lima.

Coppus, R., A. C. Imeson, and J. Sevink
2003 Identification, distribution, and characteristics of erosion sensitive areas in three different Central Andean ecosystems. *Catena* 51: 315–328.

Couture, Nicole C.
2003 Ritual, monumentalism, and residence at Mollo Kontu, Tiwanaku. In *Tiwanaku and its Hinterland: Archaeology and Paleoecology of an Andean Ccivilization Volume 2, Urban and Rural Archaeology,* edited by Alan L. Kolata, pp. 202–225. Smithsonian Institution Press, Washington, D.C.

Couture, Nicole C. and Kathryn Sampeck
2003 Putuni: History of palace architecture at Tiwanaku. In *Tiwanaku and its Hinterland: Archaeology and Paleoecology of an Andean Civilization, Volume 2, Urban and Rural Archaeology,* edited by Alan L. Kolata, pp. 226–263. Smithsonian Institution Press, Washington, D.C.

Cowgill, George
1982 Clusters of Objects and Associations Between Variables: Two Approaches to Archaeological Classification. In *Essays on Archaeological Typology,* edited by Robert Whallon and James A. Brown, pp. 30–55. Center for American Archeology Press, Evanston, Il.

Czwarno, R. Michael
1989 Social Patterning and the Investigation of Political Control: the case for the Moche/Chimu area. In *The Nature of Wari: A Reappraisal of the Middle Horizon Period in Peru,* edited by R. M. Czwarno, F. M. Meddens, and A. Morgan, pp. 115–145. BAR International Series 525, Oxford.

Dacey, Michael F.
1973 Statistical Tests of Spatial Association in the Locations of Tool Types. *American Antiquity* 38: 320–328.

D'Altroy, Terence N. and Christine Hastorf
2001 *Empire and Domestic Economy.* Kluwer Academic Press, New York.

David, Nicholas and Carol Kramer
2001 *Ethnoarchaeology in Action.* Cambridge University Press, Cambridge.

DeBoer, Warren R.
1990 Interaction, Imitation, and Communication as Expressed in Style: the Ucayali Experience. In *The Uses of Style in Archaeology,* edited by M.W. Conkey and Christine A. Hastorf, pp. 82–104. Cambridge University Press, Cambridge.

Dobres, Marcia-Anne
   1995   Gender and Prehistoric Technology: On the Social Agency of Technical Strategies. *World Archaeology* 27: 25–49.

Drennan, Robert D.
   1996   *Statistics for Archaeologists: A Commonsense Approach.* Plenum Publishers, New York.

Eidheim, Harald
   1998   When Ethnic Identity is a Social Stigma. In *Social Groups and Boundaries: The Social Organization of Cultural Difference,* edited by Fredrik Barth, pp. 39–57. Waveland Press, Prospect Heights, IL.

Feldman, Robert A.
   1989   A speculative hypothesis of Wari southern expansion. In *The Nature of Wari: A Reappraisal of the Middle Horizon Period in Peru,* edited by R. M. Czwarno, F. M. Meddens, and A. Morgan, pp. 72–97. BAR International Series 525, Oxford.

Gamble, Clive and James Steele
   1999   Hominid Ranging Patterns and Dietary Strategies. In *Hominid Evolution: Lifestyles and Survival Strategies,* edited by Herbert Ulrich, pp. 396–409. Edition Archaea, Weimar, Germany.

Gero, Joan M.
   1989   Assessing the social information in material objects: how well do lithics measure up? In *Time, Energy, and Stone Tools,* edited by Robin Torrence, pp. 92–105. Cambridge University Press, Cambridge.

Giesso, Martin
   2000   Stone tool production in the Tiwanaku heartland: The impact of state emergence and expansion on local households. Unpublished PhD dissertation, Department of Anthropology, University of Chicago, Chicago. University Microfilms International, Ann Arbor, Michigan.

   2003   Stone Tool Production in the Tiwanaku Heartland. In *Tiwanaku and its Hinterland: Archaeology and Paleoecology of an Andean Civilization, Volume 2, Urban and Rural Archaeology,* edited by Alan L. Kolata, pp. 363–383. Smithsonian Institution Press, Washington, D.C.

Glowacki, Mary
   2002   The Huaro Archaeological Site Complex: Rethinking the Huari Occupation of Cuzco. In *Andean Archaeology I: Variations in Socio-political Organization,* edited by William H. Isbell and Helaine Silverman, pp. 267–285. Plenum Publishers, New York.

Glowacki, Mary and Michael Malpass
   2003   Water, Huacas, and Ancestor Worship: Traces of a Sacred Wari Landscape. *American Antiquity* 14: 431–448.

Glowacki, Mary, and Gordon F. McEwan
   2001   Pikillacta, Huaro, and the Greater Cuzco Region: New Interpretations of Wari Occupation in the Southern Highlands. In *Boletín de Arqueología PUCP 5, Huari y Tiwanaku: Modelos vs. Evidencias Segunda Parte,* edited by Peter Kaulicke and William H. Isbell, pp. 31–50. Pontifica Universidad Católica del Perú, Lima.

Goldstein, David J.
   2004   Putting Food on the Mesa. Paper presented at the 69th Annual Meeting of the Society for American Archaeology, Montreal, Canada.

Goldstein, Paul
   1989   The Tiwanaku occupation of Moquegua. In *Ecology, Settlement, and History in the Osmore Drainage,* edited by Don S. Rice, Charles Stanish, and Phillip Scarr, pp. 219–256. BAR International Series 545, Oxford.

   1993   House, Community, and State in the Earliest Tiwanaku Colony: Domestic Patterns and State Integration at Omo M12, Moquegua. In *Domestic Architecture, Ethnicity, and Complementarity in the South-Central Andes,* edited by Mark S. Aldenderfer, pp. 25–41. University of Iowa Press, Iowa City.

Goldstein, Paul S. and Bruce Owen
   2001   Tiwanaku en Moquegua: Las Colonias Altiplánicas. In *Boletín de Arqueología PUCP 5, Huari y Tiwanaku: Modelos vs. Evidencias Segunda Parte* edited by Peter Kaulicke and William H. Isbell, pp. 139–168. Pontifica Universidad Católica del Perú, Lima.

Goodchild, Michael F.
   1996   Geographic Information Systems and Spatial Analysis in the Social Sciences. In *Anthropology, Space, and Geographic Information Systems,* edited by Mark Aldenderfer and Herbert D.G. Maschner, pp. 241–257. Oxford University Press, New York.

Haaland, Gunnar
   1998   Economic Determinants in Ethnic Processes. In *Social Groups and Boundaries: The Social Organization of Cultural Difference,* edited by Fredrik Barth, pp. 59–73. Waveland Press, Prospect Heights, IL.

Hurst Thomas, David
   1986   Points on Points: A Reply to Flenniken and Raymond. *American Antiquity* 51: 619–627.

Inizan, M. L., M. Reduron-Ballinger, H. Roche, J. Tixier
   1999   *Technology and Terminology of Flaked Stone Tools.* Cerlce de Recherches et d'Etudes Préhitoriques, Naterre, France.

INGEMMET (Instituto Geológico Minero y Metalúrgico)
   2003   *501 Cuadrángulos Geológicos Digitales de la Carta Nacional 1960 – 1999.* Instituto Geológico Minero y Metalúrgico, Sector de Energía y Minas. República del Perú.

Isbell, William
   2000   Repensando el Horizonte Medio: el caso de Conchapata, Ayacucho, Peru. In *Boletín de Arqueología PUCP 4, Huari y Tiwanaku: Modelos vs. Evidencias Primera Parte* edited by Peter Kaulicke and William H. Isbell, pp. 9–68. Pontifica Universidad Católica del Perú, Lima.

   2004   Mortuary Preferences: A Wari Culture Case Study from Middle Horizon Peru. *Latin American Antiquity* 15: 3–32.

Isbell, William H., and Katherine Schreiber
   1978   Was Huari a State? *American Anthropologist* 43: 372–389.

Isbell, William H. and Anita G. Cook
   2002   A New Perspective on Conchapata and the Andean Middle Horizon. In *Andean Archaeology II: Art, Landscape, and Society,* edited by Helaine Silverman and William H. Isbell, pp. 249–305. Kluwer Academic Press, New York.

Isbell, William H., Christine Brewster-Wray, and Lynda E. Spickard
   1991   Architecture and Spatial Organization at Huari. In *Huari Administrative Structure: Prehistoric Monumental Architecture and State Government,* edited by William H. Isbell and Gordon F. McEwan, pp. 19–53. Dumbarton Oaks Research Library and Collection, Washington, D.C.

Janusek, John Wayne
   1999   Craft and Local Power: Embedded Specialization in Tiwanaku Cities. *Latin American Antiquity* 10: 107–131.

   2001   Diversidad Residencial y el Surgimiento de la Complejidad en Tiwanaku. In *Boletín de Arqueología PUCP 5, Huari y Tiwanaku: Modelos vs. Evidencias Segunda Parte* edited by Peter Kaulicke and William H. Isbell, pp. 251–294. Pontifica Universidad Católica del Perú, Lima.

2003 The Changing Face of Tiwanaku Residential Life: State and Local Identity in an Andean City. In *Tiwanaku and its Hinterland: Archaeology and Paleoecology of an Andean Civilization, Volume 2, Urban and Rural Archaeology*, edited by Alan L. Kolata, pp. 264–295. Smithsonian Institution Press, Washington, D.C.

2004 Tiwanaku and its Precursors: Recent Research and Emerging Perspectives. *Journal of Archaeological Research* 12: 121–183.

Janusek, John Wayne, and Alan L. Kolata
2003 Prehispanic Rural History in the Katari Valley. In *Tiwanaku and its Hinterland: Archaeology and Paleoecology of an Andean Civilization, Volume 2, Urban and Rural Archaeology*, edited by Alan L. Kolata, pp. 264–295. Smithsonian Institution Press, Washington, D.C.

Jennings, Justin and Michael D. Glascock
2002 Description and Method of Exploitation of the Alca Obsidian Source, Peru. *Latin American Antiquity* 13: 107–118.

Jennings, Justin and Willey Yépez
2001 Collata, Netahaha, y el Desarrollo del Poder Wari en el Valle de Cotahuasi, Arequipa, Peru. In *Boletín de Arqueología PUCP 5, Huari y Tiwanaku: Modelos vs. Evidencias Primera Parte* edited by Peter Kaulicke and William H. Isbell, pp. 13–29. Pontifica Universidad Católica del Perú, Lima.

Jones, George T. and Robert D. Leonard
1989 The Concept of Diversity: an Introduction. In *Quantifying Diversity in Archaeology*, edited by Robert D. Leonard and George T. Jones, pp. 1–3. Cambridge University Press, Cambridge.

Julien, Catherine J.
1993 Finding a Fit: Archaeology and Ethnohistory of the Incas. In *Provincial Inca: Archaeological and Ethnohistorical Assessment of the Impact of the Inca State*, edited by Michael A. Malpass, pp. 177–233. University of Iowa Press, Iowa City.

Keefer, D. K., S. D. deFrance, M. E. Moseley, J. B. Richardson, D. R. Satterlee, and A. Day-Lewis
1998 Early maritime economy and El Niño events at Quebrada Tacahuay, Peru. *Science* 281: 1833–1835.

Kintigh, Keith W.
1989 Sample Size, Significance, and Measures of Diversity. In *Quantifying Diversity in Archaeology*, edited by Robert D. Leonard and George T. Jones, pp. 25–36. Cambridge University Press, Cambridge.

1990 Intrasite Spatial Analysis: A Commentary on Major Methods. In *Mathmatics and Information Science in Archaeology: A Flexible Framework, Studies in Modern Archaeology 3*, edited by Albertus Voorrips, pp. 165–200. HOLOS-Verlag, Bonn.

Klink, Cynthia and Mark Aldenderfer
2005 A Projectile Point Chronology for the South-Central Andean Highlands. In *Advances in Lake Titicaca Basin Archaeology 1*, edited by Charles Stanish, Amanda B. Cohen, and Mark S. Aldenderfer, pp. 25–54. Cotsen Institute of Archaeology at UCLA, Los Angeles.

Kolata, Alan
1993 *The Tiwanaku: Portrait of an Andean Civilization*. Blackwell Publishers, Cambridge, Massachusetts.

2003 Tiwanaku Ceremonial Architecture and Urban Organization. In *Tiwanaku and its Hinterland: Archaeology and Paleoecology of an Andean Civilization, Volume 2, Urban and Rural Archaeology*, edited by Alan L. Kolata, pp. 175–201. Smithsonian Institution Press, Washington D. C.

Kooistra, L., J. Wanders, G.F. Epema, R.S.E.W. Leuven, R. Wehrens, L.M.C. Buydens
2003 The potential of field spectroscopy for the assessment of sediment properties in river floodplains. *Analytica Chimica Acta* 484: 189–200.

Kvamme, Kenneth L.
1990 One-sample tests in Regional Archaeological Analysis: New Possibilities through Computer Technology. *American Antiquity* 55: 367–381.

Lillesand, Thomas W. and Ralph W. Kiefer
2000 *Remote Sensing and Image Interpretation, Fourth Edition*. John Wiley and Sons, Inc., New York.

McAnany, Patricia A
1989 Stone-tool production and exchange in the eastern Maya Lowlands: the consumer perspective from Pulltrouser Swamp, Belize. *American Antiquity* 54: 332–346.

McEwan, Gordon F.
1989 The Wari Empire in the Southern Peruvian highlands: a view from the provinces. In *The Nature of Wari: A Reappraisal of the Middle Horizon Period in Peru*, edited by R. M. Czwarno, F. M. Meddens, and A. Morgan, pp. 53–71. BAR International Series 525, Oxford.

1991 Investigations at the Pikillacta Site: A Provincial Huari Center in the Valley of Cuzco. In *Huari Administrative Structure: Prehistoric Monumental Architecture and State Government*, edited by William H. Isbell and Gordon F. McEwan, pp. 93–120. Dumbarton Oaks Research Library and Collection, Washington, D.C.

1996 Archaeological Investigations at Pikillacta, a Wari Site in Peru. *Journal of Field Archaeology* 23: 169–186.

Meltzer, David
1981 A Study of Style and Function in a Class of Tools. *Journal of Field Archaeology* 8: 313–326.

Moholy-Nagy, Hattula
1997 Middens, Construction Fill, and Offerings: Evidence for the Organization of Classic Period Craft Production at Tikal, Guatemala. *Journal of Field Archaeology* 24: 293–313.

Moseley, Michael E., Robert A. Feldman, Paul S. Goldstein, and Luis Watanabe
1991 Colonies and Conquest: Tihuanaco and Huari in Moquegua. In *Huari Administrative Structure: Prehistoric Monumental Architecture and State Government*, edited by William H. Isbell and Gordon F. McEwan, pp. 121–140. Dumbarton Oaks Research Library and Collection, Washington, D.C.

Nash, Donna J.
2002 The Archaeology of Space: Places of Power in the Wari Empire. Unpublished PhD dissertation. Gainesville, Florida: University of Florida.

Ochatoma Paravicino, José and Martha Cabrera Romero
2002 Religious Ideology and Military Organization in the Iconography of a D-Shaped Ceremonial Precint at Conchopata. In *Andean Archaeology II: Art, Landscape, and Society*, edited by Helaine Silverman and William H. Isbell, pp. 225–247. Kluwer Academic Press, New York.

ONERN (Oficina Nacional de Evaluación de Recursos Naturales)
1976 *Inventario, Evaluacion, y Uso Racional de los Recursos Nat-*

urales de la Costa. Oficina Nacional de Evaluacion de Recursos Naturales. Republica del Perú, Lima, Perú.

Owen, Bruce
1994 Were Wari and Tiwanaku in Conflict, Competition, or Complementary Coexistence? Survey Evidence from the Upper Osmore Drainage, Peru. Paper presented at the 59th annual meeting of the Society for American Archaeology, Anaheim.

Owen, Bruce and Paul S. Goldstein
2001 Tiwanaku en Moquegua: interacciones regionales y colapso. In *Boletín de Arqueología PUCP 5, Huari y Tiwanaku: Modelos vs. Evidencias Segunda Parte* edited by Peter Kaulicke and William H. Isbell, pp. 169–188. Pontifica Universidad Católica del Perú, Lima.

Pinder, David, Izumi Shimada, and David Gregory
1979 The Nearest-Neighbor Statistic: Archaeological Application and New Developments. *American Antiquity* 44: 430–445.

Peterson, Christian E. and Robert D. Drennen
2005 Communities, Settlements, Sites, and Surveys: Regional Scale Analysis of Prehistoric Human Interaction. *American Antiquity* 70: 5–30.

Popper, Virginia S.
1988 Selecting Quantitative Measures in Paleoethnobotany. In *Current Paleoethnobotany: Analytical Methods and Cultural Interpretations of Archaeological Plant Remains,* edited by Christine A Hastorf and Virginia S. Popper, pp. 53–71. University of Chicago Press, Chicago.

Pozzi-Escot, Denise
1991 Conchapata: A Community of Potters. In *Huari Administrative Structure: Prehistoric Monumental Architecture and State Government,* edited by William H. Isbell and Gordon F. McEwan, pp. 81–92. Dumbarton Oaks Research Library and Collection, Washington, D.C.

Prentiss, William C.
1998 The Reliability and Validity of a Lithic Debitage Typology: Implications for Archaeological Interpretation. *American Antiquity* 63: 635–650.

Read, Dwight W.
1974 Some Comments on Typologies in Archaeology and an Outline of a Methodology. *American Antiquity* 39: 216–242.

Rivera Pineda, Fermín
1978 Análisi tipológico de las puntas de proyectil Wari. *Hombre y la Cultura Andina, Congreso Peruano del hombre y la cultural Andina, volumen 3.* pp. 584–593. Secretaria General del III Congreso Peruano: Lima.

Rouse, Irving
1960 The Classification of Artifacts in Archaeology. *American Antiquity* 25: 313–323.

Rowan, Lawrence C. and John C. Mars
2003 Lithological Mapping in the Mountain Pass, California area using Advanced Spaceborne Thermal Emission and Reflection Radiometer (ASTER) data. *Remote Sensing of Environment* 84: 350–366.

Rozen, Kenneth C. and Alan P. Sullivan
1989 The Nature of Lithic Reduction and Lithic Analysis: Stage Typologies Revisited. *American Antiquity* 54: 179–184.

Sahlins, Marshall
1976 *Culture and Practical Reason.* University of Chicago Press, Chicago.

Sackett, J.R.
1986 Isochrestism and Style: A Clarification. *Journal of Anthropological Archaeology* 5: 266–277.

Samuel, M. D., and R. E. Green
1988 A Revised Test Procedure for Identifying Core Areas within the Home Range. *Journal of Animal Ecology* 57: 1067–1068.

Schreiber, Katherine J.
1987 Conquest and Consolidation: A Comparison of the Wari and Inka Occupations of A Highland Peruvian Valley. *American Antiquity* 52: 266–284.

1991 Jincamocco: A Huari Administrative Center in the South Central Highlands of Peru. In *Huari Administrative Structure: Prehistoric Monumental Architecture and State Government,* edited by William H. Isbell and Gordon F. McEwan, pp. 199–214. Dumbarton Oaks Research Library and Collection, Washington, D.C.

1992 *Wari Imperialism in Middle Horizon Peru.* Anthropological Papers of the Museum of Anthropology, University of Michigan, Ann Arbor, Michigan.

2000 Los Wari en su Contexto Local: Nasca y Sondondo. In *Boletín de Arqueología PUCP 4, Huari y Tiwanaku: Modelos vs. Evidencias Primera Parte* edited by Peter Kaulicke and William H. Isbell, pp. 425–447. Pontificia Universidad Católica del Perú, Lima.

Schuster, Robert L., Alberto S. Nieto, Thomas D. O'Rouke, Esteban Crespo, and Galo Plaza-Nieto
1996 Mass wasting triggered by the 5 March 1987 Ecuador earthquakes. *Engineering Geology* 42: 1–23.

Seddon, Matthew
1994 Lithic Artifacts. In *Archaeological Research at Tumatumani, Juli, Peru* by Charles Stanish and Lee Steadman. Fieldiana: Anthropology no. 23. Field Museum of Natural History, Chicago.

Shady Solís, Ruth
1988 La época Huari como interacción de las sociedades regionales. *Revista Andina* 6: 67–99.

Shelley, Phillip H.
1993 A Geoarchaeological Approach to the Analysis of Secondary Lithic Deposits. *Geoarchaeology* 8: 59–72.

Shennan, Stephen J.
1989 Introduction. In *Archaeological Approaches to Cultural Identity,* edited by Stephen J. Shennan, pp. 1–32. Unwin Hyman, London.

Sheets, Payson
1975 Behavioral Analysis and the Structure of a Prehistoric Industry. *Current Anthropology* 16: 369–391.

Sliva, R. Jane
1997 *Introduction to the Study and Analysis of Flaked Stone Artifacts and Lithic Technology.* Center for Desert Archaeology, Tucson, Arizona.

Stanish, Charles
2002 Tiwanaku Political Economy. In *Andean Archaeology I: Variations in Socio-political Organization,* edited by William H. Isbell and Helaine Silverman, pp. 169–198. Plenum Publishers, New York.

Stone, Barbara Jane
1983 The Socio-Economic Implications of Lithic Evidence from Huari, Peru. Unpublished PhD dissertation. State University of New York at Binghamton, Binghamton, New York. University Microfilms International, Ann Arbor, Michigan.

Thouret, J. C., E. Juvigné, A Gourgaud, P. Boivin, and J. Dávila
2002 Reconstruction of the AD 1600 Huaynaputina eruption based on the correlation of geologic evidence with early Spanish

chronicles. *Journal of Volcanology and Geothermal Research* 115: 529–570.

Thouret, Jean-Claude, Jasmine Dávila, Marco Rivera, Alain Gourgaud, Jean-Philippe Eissen, Jean-Luc Le Pennec, and Etienne Juvigné
1997 L'éruption explosive de 1600 au Huaynaputina (Pérou), la plus volumineuse de l'histoire dans les Andes centrals. *Géomatériaux* 325: 931–938.

Tosdal, R. M., Clark, A. H., Farrah, E.
1985 Cenozoic polyphase landscape and tectonic evolution of the Cordillera Occidental, southernmost Peru. *Geological Society of America Bulletin* 95: 1318–1332.

Topic, John R.
1991 Huari and Huamachuco. In *Huari Administrative Structure: Prehistoric Monumental Architecture and State Government*, edited by William H. Isbell and Gordon F. McEwan, pp. 141–164. Dumbarton Oaks Research Library and Collection, Washington, D.C.

Toth, Nicholas
1985 The Oldowan Reassessed: A Close Look at Early Stone Artifacts. *Journal of Archaeological Science* 12: 101–120.

1987 Behavioral Inferences from Early Stone artifact assemblages: an experimental model. *Journal of Human Evolution* 16: 763–787.

Trauth, Martin H., Bodo Bookhagen, Norbert Marwan, and Manfred R. Strecker
2003 Multiple landslide clusters record Quaternary climate in the Northwestern Argentine Andes. *Palaeogeography, Palaeoclimatology, Palaeoecology* 194: 109–121.

Webster, Ann Demuth and John Wayne Janusek
2003 Tiwanaku Camelids: Subsistence, Sacrifice, and Social Reproduction. In *Tiwanaku and its Hinterland: Archaeology and Paleoecology of an Andean Civilization, Volume 2, Urban and Rural Archaeology*, edited by Alan L. Kolata, pp. 343–362. Smithsonian Institution Press, Washington, D.C.

Whallon, Robert
1974 Spatial Analysis of Occupation Floors II: The Application of Nearest Neighbor Analysis. *American Antiquity* 39: 15–34.

1984 Unconstrained Clustering for the Analysis of Spatial Distributions in Archaeology. In *Intrasite Spatial Analysis in Archaeology*, edited by H. Hietala, pp. 242–277. Cambridge University Press, Cambridge.

Whittaker, John C.
1987 Individual Variation as an Approach to Economic Organization: Projectile Point Production at Grasshopper Pueblo, Arizona. *Journal of Field Archaeology* 14: 465–479.

1994 *Flintknapping: Making and Understanding Stone Tools.* University of Texas Press, Austin.

Wiessner, Poly
1983 Style and Social Information in Kalahari San Projectile Points. *American Antiquity* 48: 253–276.

1990 Is There Unity in Style? In *The Uses of Style in Archaeology*, edited by M.W. Conkey and Christine A. Hastorf, pp. 105–112. Cambridge University Press, Cambridge.

Williams, Patrick Ryan
1997 The Role of Disaster in the Development of Agriculture and the Evolution of Social Complexity in the South-central Andes. Unpublished PhD dissertation, University of Florida, Gainsville, Florida.

1999 *Informe de Campo e Informe Final: Proyecto Cerro Baúl 1998.* Museo Contisuyu and University of Florida, Moquegua, Peru and Gainsville, Florida.

2001 Cerro Baúl: A Wari Center on the Tiwanaku Frontier. *Latin American Antiquity* 12: 67–83.

2002 Rethinking disaster-induced collapse in the demise of the Andean highland states: Wari and Tiwanaku. *World Archaeology* 33: 361–374.

2003 Hydraulic Landscapes and Social Relations in the Middle Horizon Andes. In *The reconstruction of archaeological landscapes through digital technologies: proceedings of the 1st Italy-United States workshop, Boston, Massachusetts, USA, November 1-3, 2001*, edited by Maurizio Forte and P. Ryan Williams, pp. 163–172. BAR Publishing, Oxford.

Williams, P. Ryan and Johny Isla
1998 *Proyecto Arqueológico Cerro Baúl: Informe Final Temporada 1997.* Museo Contisuyu and University of Florida, Moquegua, Peru and Gainsville, Florida.

Williams, Patrick Ryan and Donna J. Nash
2002 Imperial Interaction in the Andes: Huari and Tiwanaku at Cerro Baúl. In *Andean Archaeology I: Variations in Socio-political Organization*, edited by William H. Isbell and Helaine Silverman, pp. 243–265. Plenum Publishers, New York.

Williams, Patrick R., Johny A. Isla, and Donna J. Nash
2001 Cerro Baúl: Un Enclave Wari en Interacción con Tiwanaku. In *Boletín de Arqueología PUCP 5, Huari y Tiwanaku: Modelos vs. Evidencias Segunda Parte* edited by Peter Kaulicke and William H. Isbell, pp. 69–87. Pontifica Universidad Católica del Perú, Lima.

Williams, Patrick Ryan and Mario Ruales M.
2002 *Informe de Campo e Informe Final: Proyecto Cerro Baúl 2001.* Museo Contisuyu and The Field Museum of Natural History, Moquegua, Peru and Chicago, Illinois.

2004 *Informe de Campo e Informe Final: Proyecto Cerro Baúl 2002.* Museo Contisuyu and The Field Museum of Natural History, Moquegua, Peru and Chicago, Illinois.

Wobst, Martin
1977 Stylistic Behavior and Information Exchange. In *Papers for the Director: Research Essays in Honor of James B. Griffin, Museum of Anthropology Papers 61*, edited by Charles E. Clelend, pp. 317–342. Anthropology Museum, University of Michigan, Ann Arbor.

Wörner, Gerhard, Dieter Uhlig, Ingrid Kohler, and Hartmut Seyfried
2002 Evolution of the Western Andean Escarpment at 18ºS (N. Chile) during the last 25 Ma: uplift, erosion, and collapse through time. *Technophysics* 345: 183–198.

Yamaguchi, Yasushi, Anne B. Kahle, Hiroji Tsu, Toru Kawakami, and Moshe Pniel
1998 Overview of Advanced Spaceborne Thermal Emission and Reflection Radiometer (ASTER). *IEEE Transactions on Geoscience and Remote Sensing* 36: 1062–1071.

Yamaguchi, Y., H. Fujisada, M. Kudoh, T. Kawakami, H. Tsu, A.B. Kahle, and M. Pniel
1999 ASTER Instrument Characterization and Operation Scenario. *Advanced Space Research* 23: 1415–1424.

Yamaguchi, Y. H. Fujisada, H. Tsu, I. Sate, H. Watanabe, M. Kate, M. Kudoh, A.B. Kahlc, and M. Pniel
2001 ASTER early image evaluation. *Advanced Space Research* 28: 69–76.

Zapata Rodriguez, Julinho
1997 Arquitectura y Contextos Funerarios Wari en Batan Urqo,

Cusco. In *Boletin de Arqueología PUCP 1, La Muerte en el Antiguo Perú: Contextos y Conceptos Funerarios,* edited by Peter Kaulicke, pp. 165–206. Pontifica Universidad Católica del Perú, Lima.

Appendix A: Coded Lithic Debitage

no_especimen	sector	unidad	recinto	cuadro	corteza	huellas de uso	tipo plataforma	bordes	tipo techno	tamano	peso
CB02-25-0971	A	25	A	52	0	0	0	0	0	0.0	0.0
CB01-2346	A	7	G	42	0	0	0	0	0	0.0	
CB01-3578	A	9	B	104	0	0	0	0	0	0.0	5.0
CB01-3585	A	9	B	119	0	0	0	0	0	0.0	13.8
CB01-3642	A	9	B	137	0	0	0	0	0	0.0	0.0
CB01-3536	A	9	B	134	0	0	0	0	0	12.0	9.9
CB02-09-0930	A	9	D	142	0	0	0	0	0	0.0	
CB01-2355	A	7	H	63	0	0	0	0	0	10.0	0.2
CB02-25-1033	A	25	A	65	0	1	0	540	110	10.0	2.6
CB02-25-1045	A	25	A	90	0	0	1	0	540	10.0	1.5
CB01-2351	A	7	H	63	0	0	0	1	110	12.0	33.0
CB01-3606	A	9	B	166	0	0	0	1	110	10.0	0.1
CB02-25-0978	A	25	A	70	0	0	1	6	111	11.0	27.5
CB01-6156	L	20	A	36	0	0	0	6	111	11.0	7.8
CB01-2316	A	7	F	61	0	0	0	6	111	10.0	2.5
CB02-25-0957	A	25	A	24	0	0	0	6	111	13.0	57.1
CB02-24-1832	A	24	A	8	0	30	0	6	111	12.0	25.2
CB02-27-0185	N	27	B	32	0	0	0	1	111	11.0	7.4
CB01-6150	L	20	A	23	0	0	0	6	111	12.0	17.2
CB01-3591	A	9	B	132	0	0	0	6	111	10.0	1.2
CB01-6415	H	21	A	7	0	0	1	6	111	11.0	10.5
CB01-6415	H	21	A	7	0	0	1	6	111	11.0	3.0
CB01-6419	H	21	A	15	0	0	0	1	111	10.0	1.0
CB02-25-1105	A	25	A	52	0	0	0	1	111	10.0	0.2
CB02-25-1127	A	25	A	98	0	0	0	1	111	10.0	0.6
CB02-32-0201	F	32	A	23	0	0	0	6	111	11.0	6.5
CB01-6159	L	20	A	28	0	0	0	6	111	11.0	13.5
CB01-3647	A	9	B	153	0	0	0	6	111	10.0	0.4
CB01-6411	H	21	A	14	0	0	0	6	111	11.0	3.9
CB01-6419	H	21	A	15	0	0	1	6	111	10.0	1.7
CB01-2319	A	7	F	71	0	0	0	6	111	10.0	0.4
CB01-2327	A	7	F	71	0	0	0	6	111	10.0	0.8
CB02-25-1038	A	25	A	79	0	0	0	0	111	10.0	8.6
CB02-32-0214	F	32	A	17	0	0	1	6	111	12.0	17.9
CB02-32-0214	F	32	A	17	0	0	1	6	111	11.0	5.8
CB02-32-0219	F	32	A	27	0	0	1	6	111	11.0	4.3
CB01-6165	L	20	A	33	0	0	0	6	111	12.0	17.8
CB02-25-0974	A	25	A	64	0	0	1	1	112	13.0	51.5
CB01-6419	H	21	A	15	0	0	1	1	112	10.0	1.2
CB01-2762	A	9	A	18	0	0	1	6	121	12.0	18.2
CB01-6411	H	21	A	14	0	0	1	6	121	11.0	2.5
CB01-6588	H	22	B	14	0	0	0	0	520	12.0	19.7
CB01-6589	H	22	B	16	0	0	0	0	520	11.0	7.6
CB02-25-1071	A	25	A	16	0	0	0	0	540	10.0	0.2
CB02-25-1048	A	25	A	94	0	0	0	0	540	11.0	2.0
CB02-09-1041	A	9	F	250	0	0	0	0	540	10.0	
CB02-24-1888	A	24	A	6	0	0	0	6	540	10.0	0.4
CB01-2356	A	7	I	24	0	0	0	0	540	11.0	4.7
CB01-4075	A	9	C	36	0	0	0	6	540	11.0	18.1
CB01-4486	A	9	E	12	0	0	0	6	540	10.0	1.4

Appendix A: Coded Lithic Debitage

no_especimen	sector	unidad	recinto	cuadro	corteza	huellas de uso	tipo plataforma	bordes	tipo techno	tamano	peso
CB02-25-1148	A	25	A	91	0	0	0	6	540	10.0	0.2
CB01-4474	A	9	E	12	0	0	0	6	540	10.0	3.2
CB01-4486	A	9	E	12	0	0	0	6	540	10.0	3.5
CB01-6419	H	21	A	15	0	0	1	6	540	10.0	1.7
CB01-2339	A	7	G	41	0	0	0	0	540	10.0	0.4
CB01-2352	A	7	H	43	0	0	0	0	540	10.0	
CB01-2725	A	9	A	1	0	0	0	6	540	10.0	0.7
CB01-2735	A	9	A	18	0	0	0	6	540	10.0	0.2
CB01-2736	A	9	A	33	0	0	0	6	540	10.0	0.1
CB01-2739	A	9	A	33	0	0	0	6	540	10.0	0.1
CB01-2741	A	9	A	49	0	0	0	6	540	10.0	1.0
CB01-2756	A	9	A	129	0	0	0	6	540	10.0	0.4
CB01-2757	A	9	A	131	0	0	0	6	540	12.0	15.6
CB01-2758	A	9	A	145	0	0	0	6	540	10.0	1.8
CB01-2759	A	9	A	146	0	0	0	6	540	10.0	1.6
CB01-3566	A	9	B	68	0	0	0	6	540	10.0	0.1
CB01-3543	A	9	B	69	0	0	0	6	540	10.0	0.3
CB01-3638	A	9	B	75	0	0	0	6	540	10.0	0.6
CB01-3547	A	9	B	76	0	0	0	6	540	10.0	0.6
CB01-3568	A	9	B	76	0	0	0	6	540	10.0	0.3
CB01-3532	A	9	B	108	0	0	0	6	540	10.0	0.1
CB01-3532	A	9	B	108	0	0	0	6	540	10.0	0.2
CB01-3585	A	9	B	119	0	0	0	6	540	10.0	0.4
CB01-3556	A	9	B	124	0	0	0	6	540	10.0	0.7
CB01-3534	A	9	B	132	0	0	0	6	540	10.0	0.5
CB01-3598	A	9	B	149	0	0	0	6	540	10.0	0.1
CB01-3604	A	9	B	164	0	0	0	6	540	10.0	0.1
CB01-3636	A	9	B	185	0	0	0	6	540	10.0	0.1
CB01-3617	A	9	B	188	0	0	0	6	540	11.0	3.7
CB01-3618	A	9	B	196	0	0	0	6	540	10.0	3.2
CB01-3565	A	9	B	204	0	0	0	6	540	10.0	1.0
CB01-4241	A	9	C	21	0	0	0	6	540	10.0	2.4
CB01-4214	A	9	C	22	0	0	0	6	540	10.0	2.8
CB01-4234	A	9	C	24	0	0	0	6	540	10.0	3.5
CB01-4217	A	9	C	25	0	0	0	6	540	37905.0	21.7
CB01-4218	A	9	C	26	0	0	0	6	540	10.0	0.1
CB01-4219	A	9	C	27	0	0	0	6	540	10.0	0.9
CB01-4208	A	9	C	36	0	0	0	6	540	10.0	0.1
CB01-4235	A	9	C	36	0	0	0	6	540	10.0	1.6
CB01-4221	A	9	C	37	0	0	0	6	540	10.0	1.0
CB01-4224	A	9	C	40	0	0	0	6	540	10.0	0.2
CB01-4210	A	9	C	43	0	0	0	6	540	10.0	2.1
CB01-4237	A	9	C	54	0	0	0	6	540	10.0	2.6
CB01-4244	A	9	C	55	0	0	0	6	540	10.0	1.5
CB01-4229	A	9	C	57	0	0	0	6	540	10.0	0.1
CB01-4243	A	9	C	40/41	0	0	0	6	540	10.0	0.1
CB02-09-0920	A	9	D	62	0	0	0	0	540	10.0	0.1
CB02-09-1020	A	9	D	95	0	0	0	6	540	10.0	0.2
CB02-09-1026	A	9	D	95	0	0	0	6	540	10.0	0.8
CB02-09-0950	A	9	D	125	0	0	0	6	540	10.0	0.2

Appendix A: Coded Lithic Debitage

no_especimen	sector	unidad	recinto	cuadro	corteza	huellas de uso	tipo plataforma	bordes	tipo techno	tamano	peso
CB02-09-0990	A	9	D	125	0	0	0	6	540	10.0	0.5
CB02-09-0954	A	9	D	127	0	0	0	6	540	10.0	0.1
CB02-09-0955	A	9	D	141	0	0	0	6	540	10.0	0.8
CB02-09-0956	A	9	D	141	0	0	0	6	540	10.0	1.1
CB02-09-0993	A	9	D	141	0	0	0	6	540	10.0	0.2
CB02-09-1006	A	9	D	173	0	0	0	6	540	11.0	5.8
CB02-09-1008	A	9	D	174	0	0	0	6	540	10.0	0.3
CB02-09-0935	A	9	D	191	0	0	0	6	540	10.0	0.4
CB02-09-0980	A	9	D	222	0	0	0	0	540	10.0	0.3
CB01-4470	A	9	E	12	0	0	0	6	540	10.0	6.2
CB01-4473	A	9	E	12	0	0	0	6	540	10.0	1.6
CB01-4486	A	9	E	12	0	0	0	6	540	10.0	7.7
CB01-4476	A	9	E	15	0	0	0	6	540	10.0	2.6
CB01-4481	A	9	E	31	0	0	0	6	540	10.0	1.5
CB01-4482	A	9	E	44	0	0	0	6	540	10.0	1.7
CB02-09-1091	A	9	F	147	0	0	0	6	540	10.0	0.4
CB02-09-1042	A	9	F	196	0	0	0	6	540	10.0	0.7
CB02-09-1051	A	9	F	212	0	0	0	6	540	10.0	0.2
CB02-09-1052	A	9	F	213	0	0	0	6	540	10.0	0.6
CB02-09-1054	A	9	F	214	0	0	0	6	540	11.0	8.0
CB02-09-1103	A	9	F	232	0	0	0	6	540	10.0	0.8
CB02-09-1077	A	9	F	233	0	0	0	6	540	11.0	2.9
CB02-09-1110	A	9	F1	233	0	0	0	6	540	10.0	0.1
CB02-09-1137	A	9	F2	253	0	0	0	6	540	10.0	0.1
CB02-09-1143	A	9	G	146	0	0	0	6	540	10.0	0.3
CB02-09-1152	A	9	G	163	0	0	0	6	540	10.0	0.6
CB02-09-1160	A	9	G	210	0	0	0	6	540	10.0	0.2
CB01-6383	H	21	A	6	0	0	0	6	540	10.0	0.1
CB01-6417	H	21	A	11	0	0	0	6	540	11.0	4.4
CB01-6404	H	21	A	15	0	0	0	6	540	10.0	0.1
CB01-6743	F	23	A	12	0	0	0	6	540	11.0	2.5
CB01-6743	F	23	A	12	0	0	0	6	540	11.0	0.2
CB02-24-1864	A	24	A	1	0	0	0	6	540	10.0	0.2
CB02-24-1871	A	24	A	1	0	0	0	6	540	10.0	0.7
CB02-24-1861	A	24	A	1	0	0	0	6	540	10.0	0.1
CB02-24-1879	A	24	A	2	0	0	0	6	540	10.0	0.1
CB02-24-1805	A	24	A	8	0	0	0	6	540	10.0	0.2
CB02-24-1832	A	24	A	10	0	0	0	6	540	10.0	0.2
CB02-24-1916	A	24	A	10	0	0	0	6	540	10.0	0.7
CB02-24-1839	A	24	A	11	0	0	0	6	540	10.0	0.1
CB02-24-1941	A	24	A	12	0	0	0	6	540	10.0	0.3
CB02-24-1945	A	24	A	16	0	0	0	6	540	10.0	2.2
CB02-24-1850	A	24	A	18	0	0	0	6	540	10.0	0.2
CB02-25-1099	A	25	A	42	0	0	0	6	540	11.0	2.6
CB02-25-1101	A	25	A	46	0	0	0	6	540	10.0	0.1
CB02-25-0973	A	25	A	55	0	0	0	6	540	10.0	0.2
CB02-25-1109	A	25	A	56	0	0	0	6	540	10.0	0.3
CB02-25-1133	A	25	A	107	0	0	0	6	540	10.0	0.4
CB02-25-1141	A	25	A	120	0	0	0	6	540	10.0	0.5
CB02-25-1164	A	25	A2	115	0	0	0	6	540	10.0	2.5

Appendix A: Coded Lithic Debitage

no_especimen	sector	unidad	recinto	cuadro	corteza	huellas de uso	tipo plataforma bordes	tipo techno	tamano	peso
CB02-27-0217	N	27	C	54	0	0	0	6	540	10.0	0.2
CB02-32-0234	F	32	A	13	0	0	0	6	540	10.0	0.2
CB02-32-0207	F	32	A	48	0	0	0	6	540	12.0	32.1
CB01-2354	A	7	H	53	0	0	0	0	540	12.0	22.6
CB01-3546	A	9	B	75	0	0	0	6	540	10.0	0.4
CB01-3530	A	9	B	92	0	0	0	6	540	10.0	2.5
CB01-3653	A	9	B	172	0	0	0	6	540	10.0	2.7
CB01-4243	A	9	C	40/41	0	0	0	6	540	10.0	0.1
CB02-09-0925	A	9	D	80	0	0	0	6	540	10.0	1.3
CB02-25-1007	A	25	A	28	0	0	1	0	540	11.0	11.3
CB02-25-1087	A	25	A	32	0	0	0	6	540	10.0	0.5
CB01-2740	A	9	A	35	0	0	0	6	540	10.0	0.1
CB01-3592-WB	A	9	B	133	0	0	0	6	540	10.0	0.4
CB01-4216	A	9	C	24	0	0	0	6	540	10.0	0.4
CB02-09-0958	A	9	D	142	0	0	0	6	540	10.0	0.4
CB02-24-1898	A	24	A	8	0	0	1	6	540	10.0	0.4
CB02-09-0976	A	9	D	205	0	0	0	0	540	10.0	0.5
CB02-09-0988	A	9	D	253	0	0	0	1	540	10.0	0.1
CB02-09-1130	A	9	F2	204	0	0	0	6	540	10.0	0.5
CB02-25-1113	A	25	A	70	0	0	0	6	540	10.0	0.4
CB02-25-1039	A	25	A	80	0	0	1	0	540	10.0	38.0
CB02-32-0199	F	32	A	12	0	0	0	6	540	10.0	0.2
CB02-32-0205	F	32	A	33	0	0	0	6	540	10.0	3.7
CB02-32-0206	F	32	A	36	0	0	0	6	540	10.0	1.1
CB02-02-0225	F	32	A	49	0	0	0	6	540	10.0	0.1
CB02-24-1854	A	24	A	1	0	0	0	1	540	10.0	0.1
CB02-24-1860	A	24	A	1	0	0	0	6	540	10.0	0.1
CB02-24-1863	A	24	A	1	0	0	0	6	540	10.0	0.1
CB02-24-1869	A	24	A	1	0	0	0	6	540	10.0	0.1
CB02-24-1873	A	24	A	2	0	0	0	6	540	10.0	0.2
CB02-24-1881	A	24	A	3	0	0	0	6	540	10.0	0.1
CB02-24-1885	A	24	A	5	0	0	0	6	540	10.0	0.1
CB02-24-1891	A	24	A	6	0	0	0	6	540	10.0	0.1
CB02-24-1893	A	24	A	8	0	0	0	6	540	10.0	0.3
CB02-24-1895	A	24	A	8	0	0	0	6	540	10.0	0.1
CB02-24-1896	A	24	A	8	0	0	0	6	540	10.0	0.1
CB02-24-1835	A	24	A	9	0	0	0	1	540	10.0	0.1
CB02-24-1901	A	24	A	9	0	0	0	6	540	10.0	0.1
CB02-24-1907	A	24	A	9	0	0	0	6	540	10.0	0.1
CB02-24-1909	A	24	A	10	0	0	0	6	540	10.0	0.1
CB02-24-1911	A	24	A	10	0	0	0	6	540	10.0	0.1
CB02-24-1938	A	24	A	11	0	0	0	6	540	10.0	0.1
CB02-24-1845	A	24	A	13	0	0	0	6	540	10.0	0.1
CB02-25-1077	A	25	A	21	0	0	0	1	540	11.0	0.1
CB02-25-1096	A	25	A	41	0	0	0	1	540	10.0	0.1
CB02-25-1146	A	25	A	62	0	0	0	1	540	10.0	0.1
CB02-25-1128	A	25	A	98	0	0	0	1	540	10.0	<0.1
CB02-25-1124	A	25	A	102	0	0	0	1	540	11.0	<0.1
CB02-25-1134	A	25	A	107	0	0	0	6	540	10.0	0.1
CB02-25-1138	A	25	A	114	0	0	0	6	540	10.0	0.1

Appendix A: Coded Lithic Debitage

no_especimen	sector	unidad	recinto	cuadro	corteza	huellas de uso	tipo plataforma	bordes	tipo techno	tamano	peso
CB02-25-1142	A	25	A	130	0	0	0	1	540	11.0	0.1
CB02-25-1165	A	25	A2	120	0	0	0	6	540	10.0	0.1
CB02-25-1167	A	25	A2	121	0	0	0	6	540	10.0	0.1
CB02-25-1178	A	25	A3	124	0	0	0	1	540	10.0	0.1
CB02-09-1009	A	9	D	174	0	0	0	1	540	10.0	0.1
CB02-09-1107	A	9	F1	217	0	0	0	1	540	10.0	<0.1
CB01-2350	A	7	H	43	0	0	0	0	540	10.0	0.1
CB02-09-1061	A	9	F	216	0	0	0	6	540	10.0	3.0
CB01-2759	A	9	A	146	0	0	0	6	540	10.0	0.2
CB01-3569	A	9	B	85	0	0	0	1	540	10.0	0.1
CB01-3611	A	9	B	180	0	0	0	6	540	10.0	0.2
CB01-3657	A	9	B	188	0	0	0	6	540	11.0	6.8
CB01-3618	A	9	B	196	0	0	0	6	540	10.0	0.2
CB02-09-0994	A	9	D	141	0	0	0	6	540	11.0	23.9
CB02-09-0994	A	9	D	141	0	0	0	6	540	10.0	0.6
CB02-09-1005	A	9	D	173	0	0	0	0	540	11.0	21.4
CB02-09-1042	A	9	F	196	0	0	0	6	540	10.0	1.4
CB02-09-1150	A	9	G	163	0	0	0	6	540	10.0	0.8
CB02-09-1163	A	9	G	227	0	0	0	6	540	10.0	0.6
CB02-25-1087	A	25	A	32	0	0	0	6	540	10.0	0.1
CB02-25-1153	A	25	A2	1	0	0	0	6	540	11.0	14.8
CB01-3573	A	9	B	89	0	0	0	6	540	10.0	2.4
CB01-4219	A	9	C	27	0	0	0	6	540	10.0	0.1
CB01-2744	A	9	A	65	0	0	0	0	600	10.0	0.7
CB01-2313	A	7	F	73	1	0	1	1	110	12.0	30.7
CB01-2355	A	7	H	63	1	0	1	0	110	10.0	1.0
CB02-09-1150	A	9	G	163	1	0	1	6	111	12.0	15.6
CB01-2131	A	7	F	73	1	0	0	6	111	11.0	1.1
CB02-24-1790	A	24	A	4	1	0	1	6	111	11.0	25.8
CB02-24-1832	A	24	A	8	1	0	1	6	111	11.0	
CB02-25-1131	A	25	A	104	1	0	1	6	111	12.0	23.5
CB01-2312	A	7	F	53	1	0	1	1	111	11.0	11.4
CB01-2335	A	7	G	42	1	0	1	6	111	12.0	23.8
CB02-24-1857	A	24	A	1	1	0	1	6	111	12.0	37.1
CB02-24-1857	A	24	A	1	1	0	1	6	111	11.0	6.0
CB02-09-0978	A	9	D	206	1	0	1	1	112	12.0	11.5
CB02-25-1004	A	25	A	18	1	0	1	1	112	13.0	30.9
CB01-2747	A	9	A	89	1	0	1	1	112	10.0	0.3
CB01-6397	H	21	A	7	1	0	1	1	112	12.0	38.7
CB02-25-1012	A	25	A	33	1	0	1	0	112	11.0	5.7
CB02-25-1149	A	25	A	91	1	0	1	1	112	15.0	84.2
CB01-2313	A	7	F	73	1	0	1	1	112	13.0	66.7
CB01-2313	A	7	F	73	1	0	1	1	112	12.0	8.4
CB01-2731	A	9	A	17	1	0	1	1	112	13.0	115.5
CB02-09-0976	A	9	D	205	1	0	1	1	112	11.0	4.5
CB02-09-1015	A	9	D	205	1	0	1	1	112	12.0	14.4
CB02-09-1052	A	9	F	213	1	0	1	1	112	10.0	0.8
CB02-09-1073	A	9	F	231	1	0	1	1	112	13.0	36.4
CB02-09-1075	A	9	F	232	1	0	1	1	112	11.0	5.5
CB02-09-1113	A	9	F1	218	1	0	1	1	112	10.0	0.9

Appendix A: Coded Lithic Debitage

no_especimen	sector	unidad	recinto	cuadro	corteza	huellas de uso	tipo plataforma bordes	tipo techno	tamano	peso
CB01-6371	H	21	A	14	1	0	1	1	112	14.0	127.4
CB01-6749	F	23	A	10	1	0	1	1	112	11.0	5.0
CB01-6761	F	23	A	13	1	0	1	1	112	11.0	6.3
CB02-24-1806	A	24	A	2	1	0	1	1	112	11.0	2.6
CB02-25-1144	A	25	A	51	1	0	1	2	112	12.0	28.5
CB02-25-1025	A	25	A	55	1	0	1	1	112	11.0	9.3
CB02-25-1131	A	25	A	104	1	0	1	1	112	11.0	1.8
CB01-2741	A	9	A	49	1	0	1	1	112	10.0	0.7
CB02-09-1097	A	9	F	217	1	0	1	1	112	12.0	11.2
CB02-24-1806	A	24	A	2	1	0	1	1	112	10.0	1.2
CB02-09-1035	A	9	F	212	1	0	1	1	112	12.0	16.3
CB02-25-1084	A	25	A	30	1	0	1	1	112	12.0	31.5
CB01-6391	H	21	A	17	1	0	1	1	112	10.0	0.2
CB02-27-0217	N	27	C	54N	1	0	1	1	112	10.0	0.5
CB02-25-1210	A	25	A	43	1	0	1	1	112	10.0	0.9
CB02-09-1082	A	9	F	247	1	0	1	1	112	11.0	1.8
CB02-09-1073	A	9	F	231	1	0	1	1	112	11.0	4.2
CB01-3550	A	9	B	92	1	0	1	6	121		
CB02-25-0996	A	25	A	123	2	0	0	1	110	10.0	0.4
CB02-25-1151	A	25	A	108	2	0	1	6	110	15.0	252.6
CB02-27-0159	N	27	A	15	2	0	1	6	111	12.0	47.8
CB01-2308	A	7	F	74	2	0	0	0	111	11.0	0.0
CB02-27-0212	N	27	B	47	2	0	0	1	111	10.0	0.3
CB01-6401	H	21	A	11	2	0	1	6	111	11.0	2.8
CB02-25-1047	A	25	A	93	2	0	0	1	111	11.0	6.6
CB02-09-1141	A	9	G	146	2	0	1	1	112	12.0	32.4
CB02-09-1166	A	9	G	243	2	0	1	1	112	11.0	2.5
CB02-25-0955	A	25	A	1	2	0	1	1	112	11.0	0.9
CB01-6158	L	20	A	26	2	0	1	1	112	13.0	61.7
CB01-3594	A	9	B	137	2	0	1	1	112	10.0	0.5
CB01-4213	A	9	C	21	2	0	1	1	112	11.0	1.2
CB02-09-0956	A	9	D	141	2	0	1	1	112	12.0	20.4
CB02-09-1049	A	9	F	204	2	0	1	1	112	10.0	0.4
CB02-09-1031	A	9	F	231	2	0	1	1	112	12.0	9.0
CB02-09-1161	A	9	G	211	2	0	1	1	112	12.0	13.7
CB02-09-1166	A	9	G	243	2	0	1	1	112	11.0	1.9
CB01-6380	H	21	A	2	2	0	1	1	112	12.0	45.9
CB01-6752	F	23	A	1	2	0	1	1	112	11.0	6.0
CB02-24-1905	A	24	A	9	2	0	1	1	112	11.0	1.2
CB02-25-1009	A	25	A	29	2	0	1	1	112	15.0	126.6
CB02-25-1010	A	25	A	30	2	0	1	1	112	12.0	12.0
CB02-25-1010	A	25	A	30	2	0	1	2	112	13.0	70.4
CB02-25-1025	A	25	A	31	2	0	1	2	112	13.0	46.0
CB02-25-1104	A	25	A	51	2	0	1	1	112	13.0	37.9
CB02-25-1042	A	25	A	83	2	0	0	1	112	11.0	5.2
CB02-24-1799	A	24	A	10	2	0	1	1	112	13.0	30.3
CB01-3595-7	A	9	B	138	2	0	1	1	112	15.0	204.1
CB02-24-1912	A	24	A	10	2	0	1	1	112	11.0	1.3
CB02-25-1057	A	25	A	97	2	0	1	1	112	13.0	47.8
CB01-2317	A	7	F	62	2	0	1	0	112	10.0	1.1

Appendix A: Coded Lithic Debitage

no_especimen	sector	unidad	recinto	cuadro	corteza	huellas de uso	tipo plataforma bordes	tipo techno	tamano	peso
CB02-25-1125	A	25	A	97	2	0	1	1	112	11.0	2.5
CB02-09-0961	A	9	D	157	2	0	1	1	112	13.0	8.6
CB01-6401	H	21	A	11	2	0	1	1	112	10.0	0.9
CB02-24-1797	A	24	A	9	2	0	1	1	112	11.0	2.2
CB02-27-0195	N	27	B	41	2	0	1	1	112	12.0	12.2
CB01-3608	A	9	B	169	2	0	1	1	112	12.0	15.2
CB02-09-1046	A	9	F	199	2	0	2	1	113	10.0	1.2
CB02-32-0200	F	32	A	13	2	0	1	1	121	13.0	41.2
CB01-2327	A	7	F	71	3	0	1	1	110	10.0	0.6
CB01-2313	A	7	F	73	3	0	0	1	110	11.0	1.2
CB02-25-1014	A	25	A	38	3	0	1	0	110	14.0	76.0
CB01-2318	A	7	F	71	3	0	0	6	111	10.0	0.9
CB02-25-1119	A	25	A	84	3	0	0	2	111	11.0	3.1
CB02-09-1124	A	9	F2	235	3	0	1	1	112	10.0	0.8
CB02-09-1128	A	9	F2	252	3	0	1	1	112	10.0	1.2
CB02-24-1806	A	24	A	2	3	0	1	1	112	11.0	5.8
CB02-09-1124	A	9	F2	235	3	0	1	1	112	12.0	16.7
CB01-6400	H	21	A	11	3	0	1	1	112	10.0	1.6
CB02-24-1875	A	24	A	2	3	0	1	1	112	10.0	0.9
CB01-6158	L	20	A	26	3	0	1	1	112	13.0	66.7
CB01-6158	L	20	A	26	3	0	1	1	112	12.0	33.0
CB01-2762	A	9	A	18	3	0	1	1	112	12.0	18.4
CB02-09-0924	A	9	D	79	3	0	1	1	112	12.0	7.5
CB02-09-1097	A	9	F	217	3	0	1	1	112	12.0	1.1
CB01-6380-1	H	21	A	2	3	0	1	1	112	12.0	19.6
CB01-6396-10	H	21	A	6	3	0	1	1	112	12.0	17.9
CB01-6417	H	21	A	11	3	0	1	1	112	11.0	1.0
CB01-6403	H	21	A	15	3	0	1	1	112	11.0	2.4
CB01-6392	H	21	A	18	3	0	1	1	112	12.0	13.7
CB01-6739	F	23	A	1	3	0	1	1	112	12.0	31.9
CB01-6740	F	23	A	4	3	0	1	1	112	11.0	4.0
CB01-6742	F	23	A	10	3	0	1	1	112	11.0	4.2
CB02-24-1921	A	24	A	10	3	0	1	6	112	10.0	0.2
CB02-25-1154	A	25	A	4	3	0	1	1	112	11.0	
CB02-27-0157	N	27	A	3	3	0	1	1	112	12.0	15.4
CB01-6157	L	20	A	19	3	0	1	1	112	11.0	4.4
CB01-6157	L	20	A	19	3	0	1	1	112	11.0	5.2
CB02-09-1145	A	9	G	147	3	0	1	1	112	14.0	53.0
CB02-25-0957	A	25	A	24	3	0	1	1	112	10.0	0.8
CB02-25-1084	A	25	A	30	3	0	1	1	112	11.0	3.7
CB02-25-1097	A	25	A	42	3	0	1	1	112	10.0	0.6
CB01-2728	A	9	A	17	3	0	1	1	112	10.0	0.1
CB01-3603	A	9	B	154	3	0	1	1	112	11.0	6.8
CB02-09-1123	A	9	F2	220	3	0	1	1	112	12.0	17.6
CB02-09-1123	A	9	F2	220	3	0	1	1	112	10.0	0.6
CB01-6382	H	21	A	5	3	0	1	1	112	12.0	19.8
CB01-6396-9	H	21	A	6	3	0	1	1	112	11.0	7.4
CB02-24-1790	A	24	A	4	3	0	1	1	112	11.0	2.4
CB02-24-1912	A	24	A	10	3	0	1	1	112	10.0	0.4
CB02-25-1159	A	25	A2	78	3	0	1	1	112	12.0	4.4

Appendix A: Coded Lithic Debitage

no_especimen	sector	unidad	recinto	cuadro	corteza	huellas de uso	tipo plataforma bordes	tipo techno	tamano	peso
CB02-27-0175	N	27	B	21	3	0	1	1	112	15.0	148.4
CB02-27-0175	N	27	B	21	3	0	1	1	112	11.0	1.9
CB02-28-0013	N	28	A	3	3	0	1	1	112	11.0	1.9
CB01-6002	L	19	A	12	3	0	1	1	112	13.0	56.5
CB01-3662	A	9	B	204	3	0	1	1	112	10.0	0.2
CB01-6414	H	21	A	6	3	0	1	1	112	10.0	0.2
CB01-6419	H	21	A	15	3	0	1	1	112	10.0	0.6
CB02-241886	A	24	A	5	3	0	1	1	112	11.0	3.1
CB02-24-1841	A	24	A	11	3	0	1	1	112	10.0	0.1
CB02-32-0226	F	32	A	3	3	0	1	1	112	10.0	0.1
CB02-09-1025	A	9	D	95	3	0	1	2	112	12.0	9.9
CB01-2752	A	9	A	99	3	0	1	1	112	10.0	0.9
CB02-09-0950	A	9	D	125	3	0	1	2	112	10.0	0.5
CB01-6399	H	21	A	10	3	0	1	1	112	10.0	0.2
CB02-09-0926	A	9	D	109	3	0	1	1	112	10.0	0.6
CB02-09-0952	A	9	D	126	3	0	1	1	112	10.0	0.3
CB02-09-1162	A	9	G	226	3	0	1	1	112	10.0	0.3
CB01-2753	A	9	A	113	3	0	1	1	112	10.0	0.2
CB02-09-1058	A	9	F	215	3	0	1	1	112	11.0	2.2
CB01-2730	A	9	A	2	3	0	1	1	112	11.0	8.6
CB01-2313	A	7	F	73	3	0	1	1	112	11.0	5.7
CB01-3562	A	9	B	172	3	0	1	1	112	10.0	0.5
CB01-6758	F	23	A	10	3	0	1	1	112	13.0	49.5
CB01-2313	A	7	F	73	3	0	1	1	112	12.0	7.6
CB02-09-1062	A	9	F	217	3	0	1	1	112	10.0	0.4
CB02-09-1031	A	9	F	231	3	0	1	1	112	13.0	21.9
CB02-09-1131	A	9	F2	204	3	0	1	1	112	12.0	8.1
CB01-2734	A	9	A	18	3	0	1	1	112	12.0	9.3
CB01-2757	A	9	A	99	3	0	1	1	112	11.0	0.7
CB01-6742	F	23	A	2	3	0	1	1	112	12.0	4.3
CB01-6767	F	23	A	8	3	0	1	1	112	12.0	8.0
CB01-6758	F	23	A	10	3	0	1	1	112	11.0	6.8
CB02-24-1915	A	24	A	10	3	0	1	1	112	12.0	17.4
CB02-25-1097	A	25	A	42	3	0	1	1	112	13.0	37.0
CB02-25-1020	A	25	A	48	3	0	1	1	112	10.0	0.1
CB02-25-1021	A	25	A	51	3	0	1	1	112	12.0	7.6
CB02-25-1147	A	25	A	85	3	0	1	1	112	15.0	160.4
CB02-25-1050	A	25	A	96	3	0	1	1	112	10.0	1.0
CB02-25-1127	A	25	A	98	3	0	1	1	112	11.0	3.4
CB02-25-1175	A	25	A2	78A	3	0	1	1	112	12.0	15.8
CB02-27-0194	N	27	B	40	3	0	1	1	112	14.0	159.5
CB02-32-0217	F	32	A	23	3	0	1	6	112	10.0	1.3
CB01-3605-W	A	9	B	165	3	0	1	1	110-1	10.0	0.1
CB01-6404	H	21	A	15	4	0	0	1	110	11.0	14.3
CB02-09-0963	A	9	D	158	4	0	1	1	110	18.0	1291.7
CB01-2327	A	7	F	71	4	0	1	1	110	10.0	0.3
CB02-25-0972	A	25	A	53	4	0	1	6	111	11.0	3.5
CB02-25-0972	A	25	A	53	4	0	1	6	111	11.0	2.5
CB02-25-1057	A	25	A	105	4	0	1	6	111	13.0	43.1
CB02-25-1047	A	25	A	93	4	0	0	0	111	11.0	6.3

Appendix A: Coded Lithic Debitage

no_especimen	sector	unidad	recinto	cuadro	corteza	huellas de uso	tipo plataforma	bordes	tipo techno	tamano	peso
CB02-09-0984	A	9	D	237	4	0	1	1	111	10.0	0.3
CB02-09-1141	A	9	G	146	4	0	1	6	111	11.0	19.4
CB02-09-1025	A	9	D	95	4	0	1	1	112	11.0	2.6
CB02-09-0981	A	9	D	222	4	0	1	1	112	13.0	45.7
CB02-25-1077	A	25	A	25	4	0	1	1	112	11.0	0.4
CB02-25-0994	A	25	A	115	4	0	1	1	112	11.0	0.9
CB01-2728	A	9	A	2	4	0	1	1	112	13.0	25.3
CB01-6154	L	20	A	9	4	0	1	1	112	13.0	41.3
CB02-09-1150	A	9	G	163	4	0	1	1	112	12.0	16.6
CB02-25-1056	A	25	A	104	4	0	1	1	112	11.0	11.5
CB02-25-1131	A	25	A	104	4	0	1	2	112	10.0	7.3
CB01-2739	A	9	A	33	4	0	1	1	112	11.0	2.3
CB01-2750	A	9	A	97	4	0	1	1	112	15.0	337.5
CB02-09-0944	A	9	D	77	4	0	1	1	112	11.0	2.2
CB02-09-0928	A	9	D	127	4	0	1	1	112	13.0	34.6
CB02-09-1032	A	9	F	232	4	0	1	1	112	12.0	15.2
CB02-09-1156	A	9	G	179	4	0	1	1	112	10.0	0.9
CB01-6753	F	23	A	2	4	0	1	1	112	11.0	2.4
CB02-27-0158	N	27	A	8	4	0	1	1	112	13.0	18.7
CB01-3539	A	9	B	148	4	0	1	1	112	11.0	1.3
CB02-24-1832	A	24	A	8	4	0	1	1	112	11.0	1.7
CB02-27-0166	N	27	A	14	4	1	1	1	112	11.0	3.8
CB02-27-0202	N	27	B	48	4	0	1	1	112	12.0	20.9
CB01-6419	H	21	A	15	4	0	1	1	112	11.0	2.2
CB02-09-0941	A	9	D	61	4	0	1	1	112	10.0	0.3
CB02-24-1779	A	24	A	18	4	0	1	3	112	13.0	95.5
CB02-27-0217	N	27	C	54N	4	0	1	1	112	10.0	0.5
CB01-2322	A	7	F	82	4	0	1	0	112	10.0	0.6
CB01-2314	A	7	F	74	4	0	1	1	112	11.0	1.5
CB02-09-1163	A	9	G	227	4	0	1	1	112	11.0	1.0
CB01-2318	A	7	F	71	4	0	1	1	112	12.0	6.8
CB01-2744	A	9	A	65	4	0	1	1	112	10.0	1.0
CB01-6373	H	21	A	18	4	0	1	1	112	13.0	27.2
CB01-3610	A	9	B	171	4	0	1	1	112	11.0	3.0
CB01-3615	A	9	B	185	4	0	1	1	112	10.0	0.4
CB02-09-1128	A	9	F2	252	5	0	0	1	110	13.0	56.9
CB01-6371	H	21	A	14	5	0	1	6	110	14.0	161.0
CB01-6371	H	21	A	14	5	0	1	1	110	13.0	55.3
CB01-6399	H	21	A	10	5	0	0	1	110	11.0	1.8
CB02-27-0199	N	27	B	44	5	0	0	1	110	10.0	1.6
CB02-24-1853	A	24	A	1	5	0	0	6	111	10.0	0.7
CB02-09-1097	A	9	F	217	5	0	0	6	111	11.0	10.5
CB02-25-1150	A	25	A	106	5	0	1	6	111	12.0	30.6
CB02-25-1066	A	25	A	120	5	0	0	1	111	11.0	3.3
CB01-2131	A	7	F	73	5	0	0	1	111	11.0	2.6
CB01-2325	A	7	F	61	5	0	1	6	111	10.0	0.9
CB02-09-1000	A	9	D	157	5	0	1	1	112	11.0	
CB02-24-1825	A	24	A	2	5	0	1	1	112	11.0	1.1
CB01-6416-2	H	21	A	10	5	0	1	1	112	12.0	25.5
CB02-25-1132	A	25	A	105	5	0	1	1	112	14.0	45.8

Appendix A: Coded Lithic Debitage

no_especimen	sector	unidad	recinto	cuadro	corteza	huellas de uso	tipo plataforma bordes	tipo techno	tamano	peso
CB01-2751	A	9	A	98	5	0	1	1	112	12.0	11.6
CB01-3634	A	9	B	156	5	0	1	1	112	13.0	39.8
CB01-6383	H	21	A	6	5	0	1	1	112	11.0	5.0
CB02-24-1806	A	24	A	2	5	0	1	1	112	11.0	6.6
CB02-25-1073	A	25	A	18	5	0	1	1	112	11.0	2.0
CB02-25-1019	A	25	A	44	5	0	1	1	112	11.0	1.8
CB02-32-0212	F	32	A	13	5	0	1	1	112	12.0	12.3
CB01-2728	A	9	A	2	5	0	1	1	112	11.0	4.1
CB01-2758	A	9	A	145	5	0	1	1	112	14.0	135.7
CB01-3545	A	9	B	72	5	0	1	1	112	13.0	57.7
CB01-3578	A	9	B	104	5	0	1	1	112	11.0	2.0
CB01-3554	A	9	B	120	5	0	1	1	112	11.0	4.5
CB01-3588-10	A	9	B	121	5	0	1	1	112	13.0	60.0
CB01-3602	A	9	B	153	5	0	1	1	112	11.0	4.9
CB01-3626	A	9	B	203	5	0	1	1	112	13.0	29.5
CB02-09-0946	A	9	D	110	5	0	1	1	112	10.0	0.4
CB02-09-0966	A	9	D	173	5	0	1	1	112	12.0	10.7
CB02-09-1022	A	9	D	175	5	0	1	1	112	13.0	43.3
CB02-09-1069	A	9	F	229	5	0	1	1	112	11.0	3.0
CB02-09-1099	A	9	F	229	5	0	1	1	112	12.0	18.1
CB02-09-1141	A	9	G	146	5	0	1	1	112	13.0	79.1
CB01-6362	H	21	A	1	5	0	1	1	112	11.0	2.7
CB01-6401	H	21	A	11	5	0	1	1	112	12.0	8.6
CB01-6417	H	21	A	11	5	0	1	1	112	11.0	1.0
CB01-6411	H	21	A	14	5	0	1	1	112	12.0	11.0
CB01-6403	H	21	A	15	5	0	1	1	112	11.0	4.8
CB01-6392	H	21	A	18	5	0	1	1	112	11.0	3.8
CB01-6769	F	23	A	10	5	0	1	1	112	11.0	4.7
CB01-6744	F	23	A	13	5	0	1	1	112	12.0	18.4
CB01-6761	F	23	A	13	5	0	1	1	112	11.0	4.1
CB02-24-1792	A	24	A	5	5	0	1	1	112	10.0	2.7
CB02-25-1005	A	25	A	20	5	0	1	1	112	12.0	10.0
CB02-25-1024	A	25	A	54	5	0	0	1	112	11.0	6.3
CB02-25-0984	A	25	A	94	5	0	1	1	112	14.0	123.7
CB02-25-1050	A	25	A	96	5	0	0	1	112	12.0	9.9
CB02-25-1177	A	25	A3	121	5	0	1	1	112	12.0	27.7
CB01-6000	L	19	A	5	5	0	1	1	112	12.0	19.5
CB01-6001	L	19	A	8	5	0	1	1	112	12.0	17.2
CB01-6148	L	20	A	9	5	0	1	1	112	13.0	45.5
CB01-6150	L	20	A	23	5	0	1	1	112	11.0	6.6
CB01-3603	A	9	B	154	5	0	1	1	112	13.0	81.2
CB02-25-1057	A	25	A	97	5	0	1	1	112	12.0	20.1
CB01-3602	A	9	B	153	5	0	1	1	112	14.0	145.1
CB01-6413	H	21	A	3	5	0	1	1	112	13.0	54.6
CB01-6414	H	21	A	6	5	0	1	1	112	11.0	1.8
CB01-6416	H	21	A	10	5	0	1	1	112	13.0	39.4
CB01-6416-1	H	21	A	10	5	0	1	1	112	12.0	25.6
CB01-6403	H	21	A	15	5	0	1	1	112	11.0	1.8
CB01-6761	F	23	A	13	5	0	1	1	112	11.0	4.2
CB02-25-1115	A	25	A	75	5	0	1	1	112	11.0	5.8

Appendix A: Coded Lithic Debitage

no_especimen	sector	unidad	recinto	cuadro	corteza	huellas de uso	tipo plataforma bordes	tipo techno	tamano	peso
CB02-25-1046	A	25	A	92	5	0	0	1	112	12.0	24.7
CB02-27-0176	N	27	B	23	5	0	1	1	112	13.0	54.1
CB02-27-0176	N	27	B	23	5	0	1	1	112	11.0	1.0
CB02-27-0182	N	27	B	29	5	0	1	1	112	12.0	15.3
CB02-27-0200	N	27	B	46	5	0	1	1	112	10.0	0.5
CB02-27-0216	N	27	C	54N	5	0	1	1	112	11.0	2.9
CB02-27-0216	N	27	C	54N	5	0	1	1	112	12.0	21.4
CB02-28-0016	N	28	A	10	5	0	1	1	112	12.0	14.8
CB01-2322	A	7	F	82	5	0	1	0	112	12.0	16.3
CB01-3659	A	9	B	203	5	0	0	1	112	11.0	3.8
CB02-09-1163	A	9	G	227	5	0	1	1	112	10.0	0.7
CB01-6399	H	21	A	10	5	0	1	1	112	10.0	0.5
CB02-25-0991	A	25	A	107	5	0	1	1	112	10.0	0.3
CB02-24-1883	A	24	A	5	5	0	1	1	112	11.0	8.7
CB02-25-1168	A	25	A2	121	5	0	1	1	112	10.0	1.7
CB02-09-1097	A	9	F	217	5	0	1	1	112	10.0	0.3
CB01-6770	F	23	A	11	5	0	1	1	112	10.0	
CB02-09-1066	A	9	F	228	5	0	1	1	112	10.0	0.6
CB02-09-0970	A	9	D	174	5	0	1	1	112	11.0	4.0
CB01-3540	A	9	B	155	5	0	1	1	112	10.0	0.7
CB01-3635	A	9	B	183	5	0	1	1	112	11.0	1.6
CB02-24-1903	A	24	A	9	5	0	1	6	112	10.0	0.1
CB02-09-1062	A	9	F	217	5	0	1	1	112	10.0	0.5
CB01-6396	H	21	A	6	5	0	1	1	112	12.0	16.2
CB02-32-0215	F	32	A	18	5	0	1	1	112	12.0	19.3
CB02-25-0987	A	25	A	101	5	0	1	1	112	10.0	0.9
CB01-2740	A	9	A	35	5	0	1	1	112	11.0	1.8
CB01-2760	A	9	A	147	5	0	1	1	112	11.0	0.7
CB01-3550	A	9	B	92	5	0	1	1	112	13.0	23.1
CB01-3641	A	9	B	122	5	0	1	1	112	12.0	6.7
CB01-3604	A	9	B	164	5	0	1	1	112	10.0	0.4
CB01-3608	A	9	B	169	5	0	1	1	112	11.0	1.5
CB01-4229	A	9	C	57	5	0	1	1	112	14.0	69.6
CB01-6380	H	21	A	2	5	0	1	1	112	12.0	30.9
CB01-6390	H	21	A	15	5	0	1	1	112	13.0	82.1
CB01-6769	F	23	A	10	5	0	1	1	112	12.0	5.7
CB01-6769	F	23	A	10	5	0	1	1	112	12.0	18.9
CB02-24-1875	A	24	A	2	5	0	1	1	112	10.0	0.9
CB02-24-1797	A	24	A	9	5	0	1	1	112	11.0	1.8
CB02-25-1168	A	25	A2	121	5	0	1	1	112	11.0	1.9
CB01-2751	A	9	A	98	5	0	1	1	112	12.0	6.8
CB01-2751	A	9	A	98	5	0	1	1	112	13.0	52.8
CB01-6413	H	21	A	3	5	0	1	1	112	13.0	32.1
CB01-6415	H	21	A	7	5	0	1	1	112	12.0	13.8
CB02-27-0162	N	27	A	9	5	0	1	1	112	13.0	78.9
CB02-27-0168	N	27	A	15	5	0	1	1	112	14.0	93.6
CB02-27-0178	N	27	B	25	5	0	1	1	112	12.0	16.1
CB02-27-0179	N	27	B	27	5	0	1	1	112	12.0	17.1
CB02-27-0201	N	27	B	47	5	0	1	1	112	13.0	47.9
CB02-32-0229	F	32	A	18	5	0	1	1	112	10.0	0.4

Appendix A: Coded Lithic Debitage

no_especimen	sector	unidad	recinto	cuadro	corteza	huellas de uso	tipo plataforma	bordes	tipo techno	tamano	peso
CB02-09-1162	A	9	G	152	5	0	1	1	115	12.0	23.0
CB02-09-1109	A	9	F1	232	5	0	1	6	400	12.0	19.3
CB02-25-1088	A	25	A	32	6	0	3	1	100	10.0	<0.1
CB02-09-0965	A	9	D	159	6	0	1	1	100	10.0	0.1
CB01-4483	A	9	E	45	6	0	1	1	110	10.0	0.1
CB02-24-1937	A	24	A	11	6	0	1	1	110	10.0	0.1
CB02-09-1073	A	9	F	231	6	0	1	1	110	11.0	0.8
CB02-09-1150	A	9	G	163	6	0	0	1	110	10.0	0.3
CB02-25-1172	A	25	A2	132	6	0	0	6	110	12.0	25.8
CB01-2319	A	7	F	71	6	0	1	1	110	11.0	3.2
CB01-2314	A	7	F	74	6	0	1	1	110	12.0	9.7
CB02-09-1045	A	9	F	198	6	0	1	1	110	10.0	0.6
CB02-09-0950	A	9	D	125	6	0	1	1	110	10.0	0.7
CB02-25-1169	A	25	A2	123	6	0	1	1	110	10.0	1.1
CB02-24-1843	A	24	A	12	6	0	0	6	111	11.0	5.0
CB01-3571	A	9	B	88	6	0	1	1	111	10.0	0.1
CB02-09-0995	A	9	D	141	6	0	1	6	111	10.0	0.1
CB02-09-1010	A	9	D	174	6	0	1	6	111	10.0	1.0
CB02-09-1066	A	9	F	229	6	0	0	6	111	10.0	0.1
CB02-24-1836	A	24	A	9	6	0	0	6	111	10.0	0.3
CB02-25-1001	A	25	A	8	6	0	0	6	111	10.0	1.1
CB02-25-1003	A	25	A	18	6	0	0	6	111	10.0	0.5
CB02-25-1088	A	25	A	32	6	0	1	6	111	10.0	0.1
CB02-25-1090	A	25	A	35	6	0	0	6	111	10.0	0.3
CB02-25-0993	A	25	A	110	6	0	0	6	111	11.0	3.3
CB02-09-1???	A	9	F	214	6	0	0	6	111	10.0	0.2
CB02-09-1048	A	9	F	203	6	0	0	6	111	11.0	4.6
CB02-09-0945	A	9	D	78	6	0	1	6	111	10.0	0.7
CB02-09-0950	A	9	D	125	6	0	1	6	111	10.0	0.6
CB02-09-0994	A	9	D	141	6	0	1	6	111	11.0	6.5
CB02-24-1857	A	24	A	1	6	0	1	6	111	11.0	4.1
CB02-25-1057	A	25	A	105	6	0	0	6	111	11.0	9.6
CB02-09-0965	A	9	D	159	6	0	0	6	111	10.0	1.8
CB02-09-1052	A	9	F	213	6	0	0	6	111	10.0	1.5
CB02-09-1058	A	9	F	215	6	0	0	6	111	10.0	2.7
CB02-09-1132	A	9	F2	235	6	0	0	6	111	10.0	0.7
CB02-09-1133	A	9	F2	236	6	0	1	6	111	10.0	0.3
CB01-2314	A	7	F	74	6	0	1	3	111	11.0	2.4
CB02-09-1131	A	9	F2	204	6	0	0	6	111	11.0	3.6
CB02-27-0216	N	27	C	54N	6	0	0	6	111	10.0	0.1
CB02-09-0950	A	9	D	125	6	0	1	6	111	10.0	3.4
CB02-09-0994	A	9	D	141	6	0	1	6	111	10.0	0.3
CB02-09-0966	A	9	D	173	6	0	0	6	111	10.0	0.7
CB01-6419	H	21	A	15	6	0	1	6	111	11.0	7.1
CB01-6406	H	21	A	18	6	0	1	1	111	10.0	0.5
CB02-09-0994	A	9	D	141	6	0	1	0	111	10.0	0.7
CB02-09-0975	A	9	D	191	6	0	1	6	111	10.0	3.2
CB02-09-1145	A	9	G	147	6	0	0	6	111	10.0	1.9
CB01-6404	H	21	A	15	6	0	1	1	111	10.0	0.4
CB-2-09-1044	A	9	F	197	6	0	0	6	111	10.0	0.2

Appendix A: Coded Lithic Debitage

no_especimen	sector	unidad	recinto	cuadro	corteza	huellas de uso	tipo plataforma bordes	tipo techno	tamano	peso
CB02-09-1098	A	9	F	228	6	0	0	6	111	10.0	0.1
CB02-25-1002	A	25	A	17	6	0	1	6	111	10.0	0.7
CB02-09-0950	A	9	D	125	6	0	1	6	111	10.0	0.8
CB02-24-1857	A	24	A	1	6	0	0	6	111	12.0	56.6
CB01-6405	H	21	A	18	6	0	1	1	111	10.0	2.0
CB02-09-0941	A	9	D	61	6	0	1	6	111	11.0	4.7
CB01-6770	F	23	A	11	6	0	1	1	111	10.0	1.5
CB01-3636	A	9	B	185	6	0	1	1	111	10.0	0.4
CB02-25-1043	A	25	A	84	6	0	1	1	111	13.0	25.8
CB01-6400	H	21	A	11	6	0	1	2	112	10.0	0.6
CB01-6773	F	23	A	14	6	0	1	1	112	10.0	0.3
CB01-2747	A	9	A	89	6	0	1	1	112	10.0	0.1
CB01-2723	A	9	A	130	6	0	1	1	112	11.0	0.5
CB01-3546	A	9	B	75	6	0	1	1	112	10.0	0.1
CB01-3549	A	9	B	92	6	0	1	1	112	10.0	0.1
CB01-3679	A	9	B	105	6	0	1	1	112	10.0	0.7
CB01-3622	A	9	B	200	6	0	1	1	112	10.0	0.1
CB01-3662	A	9	B	204	6	0	1	1	112	11.0	1.0
CB01-4216	A	9	C	24	6	0	1	1	112	10.0	0.1
CB01-4216	A	9	C	24	6	0	1	1	112	10.0	0.1
CB02-09-0995	A	9	D	141	6	0	1	1	112	10.0	0.1
CB02-09-0997	A	9	D	142	6	0	1	1	112	10.0	0.1
CB02-09-1000	A	9	D	157	6	0	1	1	112	10.0	
CB02-09-1028	A	9	D	175	6	0	1	1	112	10.0	1.1
CB02-09-0987	A	9	D	238	6	0	1	1	112	10.0	0.2
CB01-4480	A	9	E	30	6	0	1	1	112	10.0	0.7
CB02-09-1060	A	9	F	216	6	0	1	2	112	10.0	0.1
CB02-09-1038	A	9	F	228	6	0	1	1	112	10.0	0.1
CB02-09-1074	A	9	F	232	6	0	1	1	112	10.0	0.1
CB01-6768	F	23	A	10	6	0	1	1	112	10.0	0.4
CB02-24-1808	A	24	A	2	6	0	1	1	112	10.0	0.1
CB02-24-1874	A	24	A	2	6	0	1	2	112	10.0	0.1
CB02-24-1810	A	24	A	5	6	0	1	1	112	10.0	0.1
CB02-24-1821	A	24	A	16	6	0	1	1	112	10.0	0.1
CB02-25-1072	A	25	A	17	6	0	1	1	112	10.0	0.6
CB02-25-1088	A	25	A	32	6	0	1	1	112	10.0	0.9
CB02-25-1017	A	25	A	64	6	0	1	1	112	10.0	0.4
CB02-25-1034	A	25	A	73	6	0	1	1	112	11.0	0.9
CB02-25-0995	A	25	A	120	6	0	1	2	112	10.0	0.4
CB02-32-0211	F	32	A	12	6	0	1	1	112	10.0	0.3
CB01-2733	A	9	A	17	6	0	1	1	112	10.0	0.2
CB01-3626	A	9	B	204	6	0	1	1	112	10.0	0.3
CB01-4230	A	9	C	5	6	0	1	1	112	10.0	0.4
CB02-09-1021	A	9	D	175	6	0	1	1	112	10.0	0.2
CB02-09-1135	A	9	F2	252	6	0	1	1	112	10.0	0.1
CB02-09-1163	A	9	G	227	6	0	1	1	112	10.0	0.1
CB01-6748	F	23	A	1	6	0	1	1	112	10.0	1.3
CB01-6770	F	23	A	11	6	0	1	1	112	10.0	0.4
CB02-24-1855	A	24	A	1	6	0	1	1	112	10.0	0.1
CB02-24-1874	A	24	A	2	6	0	1	1	112	10.0	0.1

Appendix A: Coded Lithic Debitage

no_especimen	sector	unidad	recinto	cuadro	corteza	huellas de uso	tipo plataforma bordes	tipo techno	tamano	peso
CB02-24-1874	A	24	A	2	6	0	1	1	112	10.0	0.5
CB02-24-1825	A	24	A	2	6	0	1	1	112	10.0	0.1
CB02-24-1899	A	24	A	8	6	0	1	1	112	11.0	0.5
CB02-24-1847	A	24	A	17	6	0	1	1	112	12.0	5.2
CB02-25-1090	A	25	A	35	6	0	1	1	112	11.0	1.4
CB02-25-0964	A	25	A	39	6	0	1	1	112	10.0	0.1
CB02-32-0213	F	32	A	15	6	0	1	1	112	10.0	0.3
CB02-32-0228	F	32	A	17	6	0	1	1	112	10.0	0.2
CB01-2751	A	9	A	48	6	0	1	1	112	12.0	6.8
CB01-2747	A	9	A	89	6	0	1	1	112	10.0	0.7
CB02-09-1025	A	9	D	95	6	0	1	1	112	13.0	35.9
CB02-09-0986	A	9	D	238	6	0	1	6	112	11.0	3.4
CB01-4481	A	9	E	31	6	0	1	1	112	11.0	1.5
CB01-4481	A	9	E	31	6	0	1	1	112	11.0	2.2
CB01-4485	A	9	E	47	6	0	1	1	112	10.0	0.6
CB02-09-1044	A	9	F	197	6	0	1	1	112	11.0	0.8
CB02-09-1052	A	9	F	213	6	0	1	1	112	10.0	0.3
CB02-09-1069	A	9	F	229	6	0	1	1	112	10.0	0.6
CB02-09-1082	A	9	F	247	6	0	1	1	112	11.0	2.2
CB02-09-1134	A	9	F2	252	6	0	1	1	112	10.0	3.0
CB02-24-1790	A	24	A	4	6	0	1	1	112	11.0	5.1
CB02-25-1059	A	25	A	107	6	0	1	1	112	10.0	0.5
CB02-25-1171	A	25	A2	128	6	0	1	1	112	11.0	1.8
CB02-27-0160	N	27	A	8	6	0	1	1	112	13.0	49.1
CB02-27-0185	N	27	B	32	6	0	1	1	112	12.0	7.8
CB02-27-0207	N	27	B	42	6	0	1	1	112	10.0	0.7
CB02-27-0216	N	27	C	54N	6	0	1	1	112	12.0	17.3
CB02-09-1088	A	9	F	246	6	0	1	1	112	11.0	3.1
CB01-5996	L	19	A	14	6	0	1	1	112	11.0	4.3
CB01-6157	L	20	A	19	6	0	1	1	112	11.0	4.9
CB01-3577	A	9	B	103	6	0	1	1	112	11.0	6.1
CB01-3601	A	9	B	152	6	0	1	1	112	11.0	3.9
CB01-4216	A	9	C	24	6	0	1	1	112	12.0	5.6
CB01-4224	A	9	C	40	6	0	1	1	112	12.0	14.2
CB02-09-0923	A	9	D	77	6	0	1	1	112	10.0	0.6
CB02-09-0928	A	9	D	127	6	0	1	2	112	11.0	4.7
CB02-09-0996	A	9	D	142	6	0	1	1	112	11.0	1.5
CB02-09-0975	A	9	D	191	6	0	1	1	112	11.0	0.8
CB02-09-1104	A	9	F	233	6	0	1	1	112	13.0	47.4
CB02-09-1155	A	9	G	178	6	0	1	1	112	11.0	2.0
CB02-09-1161	A	9	G	211	6	0	1	1	112	10.0	0.6
CB02-09-1163	A	9	G	227	6	0	1	2	112	10.0	1.8
CB01-6380	H	21	A	2	6	0	1	1	112	11.0	1.2
CB01-6394-4	H	21	A	2	6	0	1	1	112	11.0	4.9
CB01-6383	H	21	A	6	6	0	1	1	112	11.0	12.7
CB01-6366	H	21	A	7	6	0	1	1	112	11.0	3.3
CB01-6397	H	21	A	7	6	0	1	1	112	10.0	1.0
CB01-6399	H	21	A	10	6	0	1	2	112	11.0	4.1
CB01-6405	H	21	A	18	6	0	1	1	112	11.0	7.6
CB01-6757	F	23	A	8	6	0	1	1	112	10.0	0.5

Appendix A: Coded Lithic Debitage

no_especimen	sector	unidad	recinto	cuadro	corteza	huellas de uso	tipo plataforma bordes	tipo techno	tamano	peso
CB01-6736	F	23	A	11	6	0	1	1	112	13.0	55.1
CB02-24-1853	A	24	A	1	6	0	1	1	112	10.0	0.3
CB02-24-1790	A	24	A	4	6	0	1	1	112	10.0	1.3
CB02-24-1797	A	24	A	9	6	0	1	1	112	11.0	8.6
CB02-24-1799	A	24	A	10	6	0	1	1	112	10.0	1.0
CB02-24-1784	A	24	A	15	6	0	1	1	112	11.0	4.8
CB02-25-1002	A	25	A	17	6	0	1	1	112	11.0	5.6
CB02-25-1076	A	25	A	20	6	0	1	1	112	11.0	1.7
CB02-25-1006	A	25	A	24	6	0	1	1	112	13.0	8.9
CB02-25-1097	A	25	A	42	6	0	1	1	112	11.0	1.4
CB02-25-1144	A	25	A	51	6	0	1	2	112	11.0	8.7
CB0'2-25-1124	A	25	A	96	6	0	1	1	112	10.0	2.0
CB02-25-1130	A	25	A	103	6	0	1	1	112	11.0	2.4
CB02-25-1131	A	25	A	104	6	0	1	1	112	10.0	0.7
CB02-27-0159	N	27	A	15	6	0	1	1	112	12.0	12.4
CB02-32-0208	F	32	A	49	6	0	1	1	112	11.0	3.3
CB01-2316	A	7	F	61	6	0	1	1	112	11.0	2.0
CB01-2328	A	7	F	71	6	0	1	1	112	11.0	1.3
CB01-2313	A	7	F	73	6	0	1	1	112	12.0	6.1
CB01-2313	A	7	F	73	6	0	1	1	112	10.0	0.4
CB01-2314	A	7	F	74	6	0	1	1	112	10.0	1.4
CB01-2321	A	7	F	81	6	0	1	1	112	10.0	0.5
CB01-2725	A	9	A	1	6	0	1	1	112	11.0	9.1
CB01-2729	A	9	A	2	6	0	1	1	112	10.0	0.7
CB01-2740	A	9	A	35	6	0	1	1	112	12.0	5.3
CB01-3581	A	9	B	108	6	0	1	1	112	11.0	2.3
CB01-3581	A	9	B	108	6	0	1	1	112	11.0	3.9
CB01-3553	A	9	B	119	6	0	1	1	112	12.0	6.5
CB01-3592	A	9	B	133	6	0	1	1	112	11.0	1.8
CB01-3599	A	9	B	150	6	0	1	1	112	10.0	0.5
CB01-3599	A	9	B	150	6	0	1	1	112	11.0	1.2
CB01-3560	A	9	B	153	6	0	1	1	112	12.0	6.4
CB01-3540	A	9	B	155	6	0	1	1	112	11.0	2.9
CB01-3540	A	9	B	155	6	0	1	1	112	11.0	9.1
CB01-3652	A	9	B	170	6	0	1	1	112	11.0	1.4
CB01-4220	A	9	C	36	6	0	1	1	112	11.0	1.5
CB02-09-0946	A	9	D	110	6	0	1	1	112	10.0	0.2
CB02-09-0952	A	9	D	126	6	0	1	1	112	10.0	1.2
CB02-09-0954	A	9	D	127	6	0	1	1	112	10.0	0.2
CB02-09-0956	A	9	D	141	6	0	1	1	112	10.0	0.4
CB02-09-0956	A	9	D	141	6	0	1	1	112	11.0	2.9
CB02-09-0959	A	9	D	143	6	0	1	1	112	11.0	6.0
CB02-09-0959	A	9	D	143	6	0	1	1	112	10.0	0.2
CB02-09-0965	A	9	D	159	6	0	1	1	112	11.0	2.3
CB02-09-0966	A	9	D	173	6	0	1	1	112	11.0	2.1
CB02-09-0971	A	9	D	189	6	0	1	1	112	12.0	13.8
CB02-09-0971	A	9	D	189	6	0	1	1	112	10.0	0.6
CB02-09-1012	A	9	D	189	6	0	1	1	112	11.0	7.3
CB02-09-0972	A	9	D	190	6	0	1	1	112	13.0	11.6
CB02-09-1023	A	9	D	190	6	0	1	1	112	10.0	0.3

Appendix A: Coded Lithic Debitage

no_especimen	sector	unidad	recinto	cuadro	corteza	huellas de uso	tipo plataforma	bordes	tipo techno	tamano	peso
CB02-09-1029	A	9	D	190	6	0	1	1	112	10.0	2.6
CB02-09-0976	A	9	D	205	6	0	1	1	112	11.0	1.1
CB02-09-1018	A	9	D	222	6	0	1	1	112	10.0	1.3
CB02-09-0984	A	9	D	237	6	0	1	2	112	11.0	3.0
CB01-4481	A	9	E	31	6	0	1	1	112	11.0	0.7
CB01-4482	A	9	E	44	6	0	1	1	112	12.0	15.3
CB01-4482	A	9	E	44	6	0	1	1	112	13.0	18.7
CB01-4487	A	9	E	44	6	0	1	1	112	13.0	45.1
CB02-09-1034	A	9	F	203	6	0	1	1	112	10.0	1.0
CB02-09-1048	A	9	F	203	6	0	1	1	112	12.0	7.7
CB02-09-1048	A	9	F	203	6	0	1	1	112	10.0	0.2
CB02-09-1035	A	9	F	212	6	0	1	1	112	10.0	1.4
CB02-09-1052	A	9	F	213	6	0	0	1	112	11.0	4.7
CB02-09-1036	A	9	F	214	6	0	1	1	112	11.0	0.7
CB02-09-1058	A	9	F	215	6	0	1	1	112	10.0	2.3
CB02-09-1058	A	9	F	215	6	0	1	1	112	11.0	14.1
CB02-09-1094	A	9	F	215	6	0	1	1	112	12.0	11.9
CB02-09-1061	A	9	F	216	6	0	1	1	112	11.0	2.2
CB02-09-1097	A	9	F	217	6	0	1	1	112	11.0	11.0
CB02-09-1066	A	9	F	228	6	0	1	1	112	11.0	1.8
CB02-09-1070	A	9	F	230	6	0	1	6	112	12.0	71.6
CB02-09-1075	A	9	F	232	6	0	1	1	112	10.0	0.4
CB02-09-1076	A	9	F	233	6	0	1	1	112	10.0	0.5
CB02-09-1080	A	9	F	244	6	0	1	1	112	10.0	0.8
CB02-09-1126	A	9	F2	236	6	0	1	1	112	11.0	9.1
CB02-09-1162	A	9	G	226	6	0	1	1	112	10.0	0.3
CB02-09-1163	A	9	G	227	6	0	1	1	112	12.0	12.9
CB02-09-1163	A	9	G	227	6	0	1	1	112	11.0	0.5
CB01-6380	H	21	A	2	6	0	1	1	112	11.0	7.8
CB01-6394-7	H	21	A	2	6	0	1	1	112	13.0	28.8
CB01-6413	H	21	A	3	6	0	1	1	112	11.0	2.4
CB01-6414	H	21	A	6	6	0	1	1	112	11.0	2.0
CB01-6366	H	21	A	7	6	0	1	1	112	11.0	6.7
CB01-6416	H	21	A	10	6	0	1	1	112	10.0	0.5
CB01-6401	H	21	A	11	6	0	1	1	112	12.0	16.3
CB01-6417	H	21	A	11	6	0	1	1	112	11.0	6.4
CB01-6370	H	21	A	13	6	0	1	1	112	11.0	4.2
CB01-6402	H	21	A	13	6	0	1	1	112	11.0	0.8
CB01-6411	H	21	A	14	6	0	1	1	112	11.0	7.1
CB01-6411	H	21	A	14	6	0	1	1	112	11.0	2.7
CB01-6393	H	21	A	19	6	0	1	1	112	11.0	0.5
CB01-6766	F	23	A	7	6	0	1	1	112	12.0	26.3
CB01-6746	F	23	A	8	6	0	1	1	112	11.0	1.5
CB01-6746	F	23	A	8	6	0	1	1	112	12.0	6.4
CB01-6767	F	23	A	8	6	0	1	1	112	11.0	1.2
CB01-6742	F	23	A	10	6	0	1	1	112	12.0	27.6
CB01-6769	F	23	A	10	6	0	1	1	112	13.0	25.4
CB01-6769	F	23	A	10	6	0	1	1	112	13.0	21.8
CB01-6769	F	23	A	10	6	0	1	1	112	12.0	25.8
CB01-6769	F	23	A	10	6	0	1	1	112	12.0	17.2

Appendix A: Coded Lithic Debitage

no_especimen	sector	unidad	recinto	cuadro	corteza	huellas de uso	tipo plataforma bordes	tipo techno	tamano	peso
CB01-6744	F	23	A	13	6	0	1	1	112	13.0	48.3
CB01-6744	F	23	A	13	6	0	1	1	112	12.0	20.7
CB02-24-1868	A	24	A	1	6	0	1	1	112	10.0	0.5
CB02-24-1875	A	24	A	2	6	0	1	1	112	10.0	1.2
CB02-24-1790	A	24	A	4	6	0	1	1	112	11.0	2.6
CB02-24-1797	A	24	A	9	6	0	1	1	112	11.0	2.0
CB02-24-1849	A	24	A	17	6	0	1	1	112	12.0	9.3
CB02-25-1016	A	25	A	41	6	0	1	1	112	12.0	14.5
CB02-25-1111	A	25	A	64	6	0	1	1	112	11.0	6.1
CB02-25-0989	A	25	A	105	6	0	1	2	112	11.0	4.8
CB02-25-0994	A	25	A	115	6	0	1	1	112	10.0	0.9
CB02-27-0178	N	27	B	25	6	0	1	1	112	10.0	0.6
CB02-27-0179	N	27	B	27	6	0	1	1	112	11.0	3.6
CB02-27-0180	N	27	B	28	6	0	1	1	112	10.0	0.1
CB02-27-0185	N	27	B	32	6	0	1	1	112	10.0	0.6
CB02-27-0197	N	27	B	43	6	0	1	1	112	13.0	53.4
CB02-27-0202	N	27	B	48	6	0	1	1	112	11.0	3.5
CB02-32-0215	F	32	A	18	6	0	1	1	112	13.0	34.8
CB01-5998	L	19	A	15	6	0	1	1	112	11.0	1.5
CB01-6155	L	20	A	19	6	0	1	1	112	11.0	1.9
CB01-6149	L	20	A	25	6	0	1	1	112	12.0	30.2
CB01-6165	L	20	A	33	6	0	1	1	112	12.0	11.0
CB01-2313	A	7	F	73	6	0	1	1	112	10.0	0.5
CB01-2736	A	9	A	33	6	0	1	1	112	11.0	2.7
CB01-2744	A	9	A	65	6	0	1	1	112	11.0	7.6
CB01-2748	A	9	A	82	6	0	1	1	112	11.0	3.2
CB01-2748	A	9	A	82	6	0	1	1	112	11.0	6.4
CB01-3539	A	9	B	148	6	0	1	1	112	11.0	1.6
CB01-3652	A	9	B	170	6	0	1	1	112	10.0	0.2
CB01-4484	A	9	E	46	6	0	1	1	112	11.0	2.3
CB01-6412	H	21	A	2	6	0	1	1	112	11.0	1.6
CB01-6365	H	21	A	6	6	0	1	1	112	11.0	3.9
CB01-6414	H	21	A	6	6	0	1	1	112	11.0	5.0
CB01-6367	H	21	A	9	6	0	1	1	112	12.0	4.6
CB01-6385	H	21	A	9	6	0	0	1	112	13.0	35.0
CB01-6398	H	21	A	9	6	0	1	1	112	11.0	4.5
CB01-6401	H	21	A	11	6	0	1	1	112	11.0	3.8
CB01-6401	H	21	A	11	6	0	1	1	112	11.0	6.5
CB01-6411	H	21	A	14	6	0	1	1	112	12.0	17.6
CB01-6403	H	21	A	15	6	0	1	1	112	10.0	0.8
CB01-6407	H	21	A	18	6	0	1	1	112	10.0	0.5
CB01-6408	H	21	A	19	6	0	1	1	112	11.0	4.1
CB01-6748	F	23	A	1	6	0	1	1	112	11.0	1.2
CB01-6758	F	23	A	10	6	0	1	1	112	12.0	13.4
CB01-6770	F	23	A	11	6	0	1	1	112	12.0	6.7
CB02-25-0987	A	25	A	101	6	0	1	1	112	11.0	1.3
CB02-25-1160	A	25	A2	100	6	0	1	1	112	12.0	21.7
CB02-27-0175	N	27	B	21	6	0	1	1	112	11.0	5.6
CB02-27-0185	N	27	B	32	6	0	1	1	112	11.0	1.6
CB02-27-0185	N	27	B	32	6	0	1	1	112	10.0	1.1

Appendix A: Coded Lithic Debitage

no_especimen	sector	unidad	recinto	cuadro	corteza	huellas de uso	tipo plataforma bordes	tipo techno	tamano	peso
CB02-27-0185	N	27	B	32	6	0	1	1	112	11.0	1.4
CB02-27-0208	N	27	B	44	6	0	1	1	112	10.0	0.3
CB02-27-0202	N	27	B	48	6	0	1	1	112	10.0	0.9
CB02-27-0183	N	27	B	31E	6	0	1	1	112	11.0	2.7
CB02-27-0216	N	27	C	54N	6	0	1	1	112	11.0	8.1
CB01-3553	A	9	B	119	6	0	1	1	112	11.0	1.7
CB02-09-1045	A	9	F	198	6	0	1	2	112	11.0	3.1
CB01-2762	A	9	A	18	6	0	1	1	112	10.0	0.2
CB01-3597	A	9	B	140	6	0	1	1	112	10.0	0.3
CB01-3649	A	9	B	167	6	0	1	1	112	10.0	0.4
CB01-3654	A	9	B	172	6	0	1	1	112	11.0	3.7
CB01-3612	A	9	B	181	6	0	1	1	112	10.0	6.5
CB01-4219	A	9	C	27	6	0	1	1	112	11.0	1.4
CB02-09-0933	A	9	D	190	6	0	1	1	112	10.0	
CB02-09-0975	A	9	D	191	6	0	1	1	112	11.0	1.4
CB02-09-1122	A	9	F2	220	6	0	1	2	112	11.0	1.9
CB01-6413	H	21	A	3	6	0	1	1	112	11.0	0.9
CB01-6414	H	21	A	6	6	0	1	1	112	11.0	0.9
CB01-6415	H	21	A	7	6	0	1	1	112	10.0	0.5
CB01-6415	H	21	A	7	6	0	1	1	112	11.0	1.4
CB01-6416	H	21	A	10	6	0	1	2	112	10.0	0.6
CB01-6416	H	21	A	10	6	0	1	1	112	10.0	0.1
CB01-6416	H	21	A	10	6	0	1	1	112	10.0	0.3
CB01-6417	H	21	A	11	6	0	1	1	112	11.0	4.6
CB01-6417	H	21	A	11	6	0	1	1	112	11.0	1.8
CB01-6418	H	21	A	14	6	0	1	1	112	10.0	0.4
CB02-24-1875	A	24	A	2	6	0	1	1	112	10.0	0.1
CB02-25-1097	A	25	A	42	6	0	1	1	112	10.0	0.2
CB02-25-1116	A	25	A	79	6	0	1	1	112	11.0	1.4
CB02-25-0990	A	25	A	106	6	0	1	1	112	10.0	0.2
CB02-27-0172	N	27	A	22	6	0	1	1	112	10.0	0.2
CB02-32-0231	F	32	A	28	6	0	1	1	112	10.0	1.1
CB01-5994	L	19	A	12	6	0	1	1	112	11.0	3.8
CB01-3615	A	9	B	185	6	0	1	1	112	10.0	0.8
CB01-6772	F	23	A	13	6	0	1	1	112	10.0	0.1
CB01-2318	A	7	F	71	6	0	1	1	112	11.0	1.6
CB01-2318	A	7	F	71	6	0	1	2	112	10.0	0.7
CB01-2321	A	7	F	81	6	0	1	1	112	11.0	1.8
CB01-2743	A	9	A	51	6	0	1	1	112	10.0	0.2
CB02-09-0925	A	9	D	80	6	0	1	1	112	10.0	0.2
CB02-09-0928	A	9	D	127	6	0	1	1	112	10.0	0.1
CB02-09-0971	A	9	D	189	6	0	1	1	112	11.0	1.3
CB02-09-0986	A	9	D	238	6	0	1	1	112	10.0	0.1
CB02-09-1058	A	9	F	215	6	0	1	1	112	10.0	0.8
CB02-09-1063	A	9	F	218	6	0	1	1	112	11.0	3.4
CB02-09-1063	A	9	F	218	6	0	1	1	112	10.0	0.4
CB02-09-1071	A	9	F	230	6	0	1	1	112	10.0	0.3
CB02-09-1073	A	9	F	231	6	0	1	1	112	10.0	0.1
CB01-6380	H	21	A	2	6	0	1	1	112	10.0	0.1
CB02-27-0161	N	27	A	8	6	0	1	1	112	10.0	0.6

Appendix A: Coded Lithic Debitage

no_especimen	sector	unidad	recinto	cuadro	corteza	huellas de uso	tipo plataforma bordes	tipo techno	tamano	peso
CB02-32-0204	F	32	A	22	6	0	1	1	112	11.0	8.6
CB01-3563	A	9	B	180	6	0	1	1	112	11.0	2.7
CB02-09-0938	A	9	D	223	6	0	1	1	112	10.0	0.2
CB02-09-1052	A	9	F	213	6	0	1	2	112	10.0	1.2
CB01-2321	A	7	F	81	6	0	1	1	112	10.0	0.8
CB02-09-1093	A	9	F	213	6	0	1	1	112	10.0	0.1
CB02-09-1066	A	9	F	228	6	0	1	1	112	10.0	1.6
CB02-09-1098	A	9	F	228	6	0	1	1	112	10.0	0.2
CB02-09-1073	A	9	F	231	6	0	1	1	112	10.0	0.4
CB02-09-1087	A	9	F	245	6	0	1	1	112	10.0	0.5
CB02-09-1093	A	9	F	213	6	0	1	1	112	10.0	0.2
CB02-09-1111	A	9	F1	232	6	0	1	1	112	10.0	0.3
CB02-09-1110	A	9	F1	233	6	0	1	1	112	10.0	0.4
CB02-27-0204	N	27	B	28	6	0	1	1	112	10.0	0.1
CB02-27-0185	N	27	B	32	6	0	1	1	112	10.0	0.4
CB02-09-0999	A	9	D	157	6	0	1	2	112	10.0	0.3
CB02-09-1004	A	9	D	159	6	0	1	1	112	10.0	0.3
CB02-09-1069	A	9	F	229	6	0	1	1	112	10.0	7.0
CB02-09-1160	A	9	G	210	6	0	1	1	112	10.0	1.0
CB02-09-1160	A	9	G	210	6	0	1	1	112	11.0	8.9
CB02-09-0977	A	9	D	205	6	0	1	1	112	10.0	0.2
CB02-09-1061	A	9	F	216	6	0	1	1	112	10.0	0.1
CB01-4485	A	9	E	47	6	0	0	1	112	10.0	1.1
CB01-2312	A	7	F	53	6	0	1	1	112	11.0	3.1
CB02-09-0946	A	9	D	110	6	0	1	1	112	11.0	2.2
CB02-09-0938	A	9	D	223	6	0	1	1	112	11.0	1.1
CB02-09-1061	A	9	F	216	6	0	1	1	112	10.0	0.9
CB02-09-1083	A	9	F	248	6	0	1	1	112	10.0	0.7
CB02-09-1166	A	9	G	243	6	0	1	1	112	11.0	2.4
CB01-2725	A	9	A	1	6	0	1	1	112	11.0	4.7
CB01-3589	A	9	B	122	6	0	1	1	112	11.0	2.1
CB01-4238	A	9	C	55	6	0	1	1	112	11.0	2.9
CB02-09-1005	A	9	D	173	6	0	1	2	112	11.0	2.8
CB02-09-1015	A	9	D	205	6	0	1	1	112	10.0	0.5
CB01-6397	H	21	A	7	6	0	1	1	112	11.0	2.3
CB01-6411	H	21	A	14	6	0	1	1	112	11.0	1.7
CB01-6748	F	23	A	1	6	0	1	1	112	11.0	1.4
CB01-6764	F	23	A	5	6	0	1	1	112	11.0	7.4
CB01-6756	F	23	A	7	6	0	1	1	112	11.0	0.5
CB01-6757	F	23	A	8	6	0	1	1	112	10.0	0.3
CB01-6742	F	23	A	10	6	0	1	1	112	11.0	4.8
CB01-6742	F	23	A	10	6	0	1	1	112	11.0	4.5
CB01-6742	F	23	A	10	6	0	1	1	112	10.0	0.9
CB01-6742	F	23	A	10	6	0	1	1	112	12.0	25.2
CB01-6749	F	23	A	10	6	0	1	1	112	11.0	1.5
CB01-6758	F	23	A	10	6	0	1	1	112	11.0	2.6
CB01-6769	F	23	A	10	6	0	1	1	112	11.0	2.0
CB01-6769	F	23	A	10	6	0	1	1	112	11.0	1.7
CB01-6747	F	23	A	11	6	0	1	1	112	10.0	0.2
CB01-6749	F	23	A	13	6	0	1	1	112	11.0	6.0

Appendix A: Coded Lithic Debitage

no_especimen	sector	unidad	recinto	cuadro	corteza	huellas de uso	tipo plataforma	bordes	tipo techno	tamano	peso
CB01-6762	F	23	A	14	6	0	1	1	112	15.0	159.8
CB02-25-1015	A	25	A	39	6	0	1	1	112	10.0	0.7
CB02-25-1106	A	25	A	54	6	0	1	1	112	10.0	0.5
CB02-32-0197	F	32	A	7	6	0	1	1	112	10.0	0.9
CB02-32-0198	F	32	A	11	6	0	1	1	112	13.0	24.9
CB02-32-0215	F	32	A	18	6	0	1	1	112	11.0	10.2
CB02-32-0216	F	32	A	22	6	0	1	1	112	11.0	3.2
CB02-32-0202	F	32	A	27	6	0	1	1	112	11.0	9.5
CB02-32-0223	F	32	A	39	6	0	1	1	112	11.0	2.7
CB01-5999	L	19	A	1	6	0	1	1	112	11.0	2.7
CB02-09-1035	A	9	F	212	6	0	1	1	112	10.0	0.6
CB02-09-1113	A	9	F1	218	6	0	1	1	112	10.0	0.3
CB01-2717	A	9	A	2	6	0	1	1	112	11.0	4.2
CB01-2740	A	9	A	35	6	0	1	1	112	11.0	0.7
CB01-3575	A	9	B	90	6	0	1	1	112	11.0	1.9
CB01-3584	A	9	B	118	6	0	1	1	112	12.0	5.7
CB01-3553	A	9	B	119	6	0	1	1	112	12.0	4.8
CB01-3589	A	9	B	122	6	0	1	1	112	11.0	5.0
CB01-3593	A	9	B	136	6	0	1	1	112	12.0	8.2
CB01-3540	A	9	B	155	6	0	1	1	112	11.0	4.2
CB01-3561	A	9	B	164	6	0	1	1	112	11.0	3.4
CB01-3604	A	9	B	164	6	0	1	1	112	10.0	0.5
CB01-3604	A	9	B	164	6	0	1	1	112	11.0	1.2
CB01-3653	A	9	B	172	6	0	1	1	112	12.0	13.8
CB01-3654	A	9	B	172	6	0	1	1	112	15.0	110.4
CB01-4216	A	9	C	24	6	0	1	1	112	11.0	4.2
CB01-4226	A	9	C	43	6	0	1	1	112	11.0	4.5
CB01-4229	A	9	C	57	6	0	1	1	112	11.0	1.1
CB01-6379	H	21	A	1	6	0	1	1	112	11.0	9.1
CB01-6390	H	21	A	15	6	0	1	1	112	12.0	18.1
CB01-6763	F	23	A	4	6	0	1	1	112	11.0	1.3
CB01-6755	F	23	A	5	6	0	1	1	112	11.0	2.5
CB01-6758	F	23	A	10	6	0	1	1	112	12.0	24.3
CB01-6744	F	23	A	13	6	0	1	1	112	12.0	16.6
CB02-24-1790	A	24	A	4	6	0	1	1	112	11.0	7.3
CB02-25-1012	A	25	A	33	6	0	1	1	112	14.0	35.8
CB02-25-1097	A	25	A	42	6	0	1	1	112	11.0	4.0
CB02-25-1143	A	25	A	52	6	0	1	1	112	10.0	0.7
CB02-25-1054	A	25	A	99	6	0	1	1	112	12.0	5.5
CB02-25-1057	A	25	A	105	6	0	1	2	112	12.0	11.1
CB02-25-1061	A	25	A	110	6	0	1	1	112	12.0	6.9
CB02-25-1175	A	25	A2	78A	6	0	1	1	112	13.0	14.2
CB01-2745	A	9	A	66	6	0	1	1	112	11.0	1.8
CB01-4482	A	9	E	44	6	0	1	1	112	11.0	7.8
CB01-2131	A	7	F	73	6	0	1	1	112	11.0	2.1
CB01-3567	A	9	B	73	6	0	1	1	112	11.0	4.6
CB01-4479	A	9	E	30	6	0	1	1	112	11.0	11.8
CB02-09-1021	A	9	D	175	6	0	2	1	113	10.0	0.1
CB02-09-1081	A	9	F	247	6	0	2	1	113	10.0	0.2
CB02-24-1801	A	24	A	11	6	0	2	1	113	10.0	0.2

Appendix A: Coded Lithic Debitage

no_especimen	sector	unidad	recinto	cuadro	corteza	huellas de uso	tipo plataforma bordes	tipo techno	tamano	peso
CB02-25-0982	A	25	A	84	6	0	2	1	113	10.0	0.1
CB02-25-1121	A	25	A	86	6	0	2	1	113	10.0	0.1
CB02-25-0994	A	25	A	115	6	0	2	1	113	11.0	1.2
CB01-6401	H	21	A	11	6	0	1	1	113	10.0	0.2
CB02-09-1147	A	9	G	162	6	0	2	1	113	10.0	0.1
CB01-6406	H	21	A	18	6	0	2	1	113	10.0	0.1
CB02-09-1067	A	9	F	229	6	0	2	1	114	10.0	<0.1
CB02-25-1080	A	25	A	25	6	0	3	1	114	10.0	0.1
CB02-25-1086	A	25	A	31	6	0	3	1	114	10.0	0.1
CB02-09-0986	A	9	D	238	6	0	2	1	114	10.0	0.1
CB01-6763	F	23	A	4	6	0	1	1	117	11.0	2.1
CB01-4233	A	9	C	23	6	0	1	1	117	10.0	0.3
CB02-09-0995	A	9	D	141	6	0	1	1	117	10.0	0.1
CB02-09-1014	A	9	D	191	6	0	1	1	117	10.0	
CB02-09-0982	A	9	D	232	6	0	2	1	117	11.0	0.5
CB02-09-1067	A	9	F	229	6	0	1	1	117	10.0	0.1
CB02-09-1129	A	9	F2	252	6	0	1	1	117	10.0	0.7
CB02-24-1792	A	24	A	5	6	0	1	6	117	10.0	0.1
CB01-2745	A	9	A	66	6	0	1	1	117	11.0	0.5
CB02-09-0947	A	9	D	110	6	0	1	1	117	10.0	0.8
CB02-24-1855	A	24	A	1	6	0	1	1	117	10.0	0.1
CB02-09-0940	A	9	D	239	6	0	1	1	117	11.0	2.0
CB02-09-1000	A	9	D	157	6	0	2	1	118	10.0	
CB02-25-1115	A	25	A	75	6	0	2	1	118	10.0	0.1
CB01-2323	A	7	F	61	6	0	1	1	118	10.0	0.1
CB02-09-1024	A	9	D	95	6	0	1	1	120	10.0	1.7
CB01-2319	A	7	F	71	6	0	0	6	540	11.0	3.7
CB01-3567	A	9	B	73	6	0	1	1	110-1	10.0	0.1
CB02-09-1002	A	9	D	158	6	0	1	1	110-1	10.0	0.1
CB02-09-1007	A	9	D	173	6	0	1	1	110-1	10.0	0.1
CB02-09-1016	A	9	D	206	6	0	1	1	110-1	10.0	0.1
CB02-09-1133	A	9	F2	236	6	0	1	1	110-1	10.0	0.1
CB02-09-1135	A	9	F2	252	6	0	2	1	110-1	10.0	0.1
CB02-09-1144	A	9	G	147	6	0	2	1	110-1	10.0	0.1
CB02-24-1820	A	24	A	15	6	0	1	2	110-1	10.0	0.1
CB02-24-1821	A	24	A	16	6	0	1	1	110-1	11.0	0.1
CB02-27-0165	N	27	A	10	6	0	1	1	110-1	10.0	0.1
CB02-27-0169	N	27	A	15	6	0	2	1	110-1	10.0	0.1
CB02-27-0170	N	27	A	16	6	0	1	1	110-1	10.0	0.1
CB02-27-0171	N	27	A	17	6	0	1	1	110-1	10.0	0.1
CB02-24-1855	A	24	A	1	6	0	1	1	110-1	10.0	0.1
CB01-4214	A	9	C	22	6	0	1	1	110-1	10.0	0.1
CB02-24-1857	A	24	A	1	6	0	1	1	110-1	10.0	0.1
CB02-27-0216	N	27	C	54N	6	0	1	1	110-1	10.0	0.1
CB02-09-1094	A	9	F	215	6	0	1	1	110-1	10.0	0.1
CB02-09-1133	A	9	F2	236	6	0	1	1	110-1	10.0	0.1
CB02-09-1134	A	9	F2	252	6	0	1	1	110-1	10.0	0.1
CB02-09-1155	A	9	G	178	6	0	1	1	110-1	10.0	0.5
CB01-6770	F	23	A	11	6	0	1	1	110-1	10.0	0.2
CB02-09-1069	A	9	F	229	6	0	1	1	110-1	10.0	0.1

Appendix A: Coded Lithic Debitage

no_especimen	sector	unidad	recinto	cuadro	corteza	huellas de uso	tipo plataforma bordes	tipo techno	tamano	peso
CB01-3618	A	9	B	196	6	0	1	1	110-1	10.0	0.1
CB02-09-1044	A	9	F	197	6	0	2	1	110-1	10.0	0.1
CB01-3614	A	9	B	184	6	0	1	1	110-1	10.0	0.4
CB01-2747	A	9	A	89	6	0	1	1	110-1	10.0	0.3
CB02-32-0229	F	32	A	18	6	0	1	1	110-1	10.0	0.2
CB01-2319	A	7	F	71	6	2	1				
CB01-6394-3	H	21	A	2	7	0	0	1	110	12.0	59.4
CB02-25-1131	A	25	A	104	7	0	0	2	110	11.0	1.5
CB01-2328	A	7	F	71	7	0	0	1	110	11.0	8.2
CB01-2313	A	7	F	73	7	0	0	1	110	11.0	2.5
CB01-2321	A	7	F	81	7	0	0	2	110	11.0	1.3
CB02-09-0954	A	9	D	127	7	0	0	1	110	11.0	2.8
CB02-09-0931	A	9	D	143	7	0	0	6	110	11.0	1.8
CB02-09-0961	A	9	D	157	7	0	0	1	110	11.0	4.4
CB02-09-1015	A	9	D	205	7	0	0	1	110	11.0	9.3
CB02-09-1044	A	9	F	197	7	0	0	0	110	11.0	3.5
CB02-09-1085	A	9	F1	233	7	0	0	1	110	11.0	4.0
CB02-09-1156	A	9	G	179	7	0	0	1	110	11.0	7.3
CB02-09-1158	A	9	G	195	7	0	0	1	110	11.0	3.6
CB01-2322	A	7	F	82	7	0	0	0	110	10.0	0.3
CB02-09-0929	A	9	D	141	7	0	0	6	110	11.0	1.7
CB02-28-0018	N	28	A	11	7	0	0	0	110	13.0	14.3
CB01-2327	A	7	F	71	7	0	0	3	111	10.0	0.3
CB02-09-0952	A	9	D	126	7	0	1	6	111	10.0	1.3
CB02-09-1048	A	9	F	203	7	0	0	6	111	10.0	0.1
CB02-09-1094	A	9	F	215	7	0	0	6	111	11.0	5.1
CB02-25-1025	A	25	A	55	7	0	0	6	111	12.0	42.0
CB01-3607-6	A	9	B	167	7	0	0	6	111	14.0	146.9
CB02-24-1858	A	24	A	1	7	0	0	1	111	11.0	17.2
CB02-09-0933	A	9	D	190	7	0	0	6	111	10.0	
CB01-3650	A	9	B	168	7	0	0	6	111	11.0	5.8
CB01-3635	A	9	B	183	7	0	1	1	111	11.0	3.4
CB01-6763	F	23	A	4	7	0	1	1	112	12.0	24.7
CB02-09-0978	A	9	D	206	7	0	1	1	112	11.0	6.1
CB02-25-1025	A	25	A	55	7	0	0	6	121	13.0	71.8
CB01-3603	A	9	B	154	7	0	0	1	121	10.0	1.6
CB02-24-1832	A	24	A	8	7	0	0	6	540	10.0	1.1
CB02-09-1084	A	9	F	250	8	0	0	1	110	10.0	0.4
CB01-3603	A	9	B	154	8	0	0	1	110	11.0	3.6
CB02-09-1069	A	9	F	229	8	0	0	1	110	11.0	2.9
CB02-09-1121	A	9	F2	219	8	0	0	1	110	11.0	2.9
CB01-2732	A	9	A	17	8	0	0	1	110	11.0	6.4
CB01-3624	A	9	B	202	8	0	0	1	110	11.0	2.0
CB01-6399	H	21	A	10	8	0	0	1	110	10.0	1.5
CB01-6404	H	21	A	15	8	0	0	1	110	11.0	2.6
CB02-24-1841	A	24	A	11	8	0	0	1	110	10.0	0.1
CB02-25-1000	A	25	A	6	8	0	0	1	110	10.0	0.6
CB01-2321	A	7	F	81	8	0	0	0	110	12.0	12.4
CB01-2329	A	7	F	81	8	0	0	1	110	11.0	4.3
CB01-2729	A	9	A	2	8	0	0	1	110	10.0	0.5

Appendix A: Coded Lithic Debitage

no_especimen	sector	unidad	recinto	cuadro	corteza	huellas de uso	tipo plataforma bordes	tipo techno	tamano	peso
CB01-3607-8	A	9	B	167	8	0	0	1	110	13.0	29.7
CB02-09-0946	A	9	D	110	8	0	0	1	110	11.0	2.5
CB02-09-0928	A	9	D	127	8	0	0	1	110	11.0	3.4
CB02-09-1029	A	9	D	190	8	0	0	1	110	10.0	0.6
CB02-09-1052	A	9	F	213	8	0	0	1	110	11.0	3.8
CB02-09-1063	A	9	F	218	8	0	0	1	110	10.0	2.7
CB02-09-1112	A	9	F1	234	8	0	0	1	110	11.0	1.9
CB02-09-1119	A	9	F2	204	8	0	0	1	110	11.0	6.9
CB02-25-1091	A	25	A	36	8	0	0	1	110	10.0	2.9
CB02-24-1806	A	24	A	2	8	0	0	1	110	10.0	0.2
CB02-32-0221	F	32	A	33	8	0	0	1	110	10.0	0.6
CB02-09-1070	A	9	F	230	8	0	0	2	110	11.0	2.5
CB02-09-0924	A	9	D	79	8	0	0	6	110	10.0	0.1
CB02-09-0931	A	9	D	143	8	0	0	6	110	10.0	1.8
CB02-09-1103	A	9	F	232	8	0	0	1	110	10.0	0.3
CB02-09-1111	A	9	F1	232	8	0	0	1	110	10.0	0.2
CB01-2313	A	7	F	73	8	0	0	1	110	11.0	4.5
CB01-2759	A	9	A	146	8	0	0	1	110	11.0	2.0
CB02-09-0938	A	9	D	223	8	0	0	1	110	10.0	0.2
CB02-32-0224	F	32	A	43	8	0	0	1	110	11.0	5.3
CB01-2329	A	7	F	81	8	0	0	1	110	11.0	4.0
CB02-09-1025	A	9	D	95	8	0	0	1	110	11.0	6.6
CB02-09-1048	A	9	F	203	8	0	0	1	110	11.0	3.4
CB02-24-1857	A	24	A	1	8	0	0	1	110	10.0	0.3
CB02-25-1130	A	25	A	103	8	0	0	1	110	11.0	4.0
CB02-25-1131	A	25	A	104	8	0	0	1	110	12.0	5.1
CB02-25-1110	A	25	A	63	8	0	0	6	111	11.0	4.5
CB01-2759	A	9	A	146	8	0	0	6	111	11.0	5.3
CB02-24-1799	A	24	A	10	8	0	0	6	111	12.0	3.8
CB02-25-1058	A	25	A	106	8	0	0	6	111	12.0	11.1
CB01-2313	A	7	F	73	8	0	0	0	111	12.0	6.4
CB02-09-1061	A	9	F	216	8	0	0	6	111	10.0	2.6
CB02-09-1070	A	9	F	230	8	0	0	6	111	11.0	6.9
CB02-09-1158	A	9	G	195	8	0	0	6	111	10.0	3.8
CB02-09-1161	A	9	G	211	8	0	0	6	111	11.0	48.2
CB02-25-0999	A	25	A	2	8	0	0	6	111	11.0	2.0
CB02-25-1004	A	25	A	18	8	0	0	6	111	11.0	19.7
CB02-25-1075	A	25	A	19	8	0	0	1	111	10.0	0.5
CB02-09-1158	A	9	G	195	8	0	0	6	111	11.0	17.7
CB01-2748	A	9	A	82	8	0	0	6	111	12.0	11.1
CB02-09-1034	A	9	F	203	8	0	0	6	111	11.0	10.8
CB02-25-0983	A	25	A	86	8	0	0	6	111	10.0	0.8
CB02-25-0986	A	25	A	97	8	0	0	6	111	10.0	0.4
CB01-3661	A	9	B	203	8	99	99	96	111	11.0	2.3
CB01-3664	A	9	B	204	8	0	0	6	111	11.0	8.3
CB01-6414	H	21	A	6	8	0	0	1	111	11.0	1.3
CB01-2759	A	9	A	146	8	0	0	6	111	10.0	0.9
CB02-09-1141	A	9	G	146	8	0	0	6	111	10.0	0.5
CB02-09-1156	A	9	G	179	8	0	0	6	111	11.0	8.6
CB02-27-0181	N	27	B	28	8	0	0	6	111	10.0	1.1

Appendix A: Coded Lithic Debitage

no_especimen	sector	unidad	recinto	cuadro	corteza	huellas de uso	tipo plataforma	bordes	tipo techno	tamano	peso
CB02-32-0222	F	32	A	37	8	0	0	6	111	11.0	2.4
CB02-09-1052	A	9	F	213	8	0	0	6	111	10.0	0.5
CB02-27-0220	N	27	C	54E	8	0	0	6	111	10.0	0.2
CB01-2747	A	9	A	89	8	0	0	6	111	10.0	1.9
CB02-25-1011	A	25	A	32	8	0	1	1	112	14.0	112.4
CB01-3544	A	9	B	70	8	0	1	1	112	12.0	20.6
CB01-4224	A	9	C	40	8	0	0	1	112	13.0	37.7
CB02-09-1158	A	9	G	195	8	0	1	1	112	11.0	10.6
CB01-6379	H	21	A	1	8	0	0	1	112	12.0	33.6
CB01-2748	A	9	A	82	8	0	1	6	112	11.0	7.2
CB02-09-0942	A	9	D	62	8	0	1	0	112	11.0	1.4
CB01-2321	A	7	F	81	8	0	0	1	112	13.0	16.5
CB01-4227	A	9	C	55	8	0	0	1	112	12.0	7.2
CB02-09-1003	A	9	D	159	8	0	0	1	120	10.0	2.1
CB02-09-1163	A	9	G	227	8	0	0	6	540	10.0	0.7
CB01-3547	A	9	B	76	9	0	0	1	110	10.0	0.1
CB01-2330	A	7	F	81	9	0	0	1	110	10.0	0.1
CB01-3527	A	9	B	69	9	0	0	1	110	10.0	0.4
CB01-3567	A	9	B	73	9	0	0	1	110	10.0	0.1
CB01-3570	A	9	B	86	9	0	0	1	110	10.0	0.1
CB01-3574	A	9	B	89	9	0	1	1	110	10.0	0.1
CB01-3655	A	9	B	188	9	0	0	1	110	10.0	0.6
CB01-3659	A	9	B	203	9	0	0	1	110	10.0	0.3
CB01-3662	A	9	B	204	9	0	0	1	110	11.0	1.3
CB01-4216	A	9	C	24	9	0	0	1	110	11.0	0.8
CB02-09-0979	A	9	D	207	9	0	0	1	110	10.0	0.2
CB02-09-0939	A	9	D	237	9	0	0	6	110	11.0	2.1
CB02-09-1153	A	9	G	163	9	0	0	6	110	10.0	0.1
CB02-24-1817	A	24	A	9	9	0	0	1	110	10.0	0.1
CB02-24-1914	A	24	A	10	9	0	0	1	110	10.0	0.1
CB02-25-1069	A	25	A	15	9	0	0	1	110	10.0	0.1
CB02-25-1074	A	25	A	19	9	0	0	2	110	10.0	0.1
CB02-25-1102	A	25	A	47	9	0	0	1	110	11.0	0.1
CB02-09-1000	A	9	D	157	9	0	0	1	110	10.0	
CB02-09-1011	A	9	D	175	9	0	0	1	110	10.0	0.2
CB02-09-0974	A	9	D	191	9	0	0	2	110	10.0	0.1
CB02-09-1061	A	9	F	216	9	0	0	1	110	10.0	0.2
CB02-09-1120	A	9	F2	219	9	0	0	3	110	11.0	2.9
CB02-25-1032	A	25	A	25	9	0	0	1	110	11.0	1.3
CB02-25-1062	A	25	A	114	9	0	0	1	110	10.0	0.8
CB02-25-1139	A	25	A	115	9	0	0	1	110	11.0	1.5
CB02-27-0165	N	27	A	10	9	0	0	1	110	10.0	0.1
CB02-25-1115	A	25	A	75	9	0	0	1	110	11.0	0.4
CB01-3555	A	9	B	122	9	0	0	1	110	12.0	8.6
CB01-3616	A	9	B	187	9	0	0	1	110	11.0	2.7
CB02-09-0994	A	9	D	141	9	0	0	2	110	12.0	4.8
CB02-09-0984	A	9	D	237	9	0	0	2	110	11.0	1.8
CB02-09-1078	A	9	F	234	9	0	0	1	110	10.0	0.4
CB02-09-1087	A	9	F	245	9	0	0	1	110	11.0	1.1
CB02-09-1141	A	9	G	146	9	0	0	1	110	11.0	

Appendix A: Coded Lithic Debitage

no_especimen	sector	unidad	recinto	cuadro	corteza	huellas de uso	tipo plataforma	bordes	tipo techno	tamano	peso
CB02-24-1841	A	24	A	11	9	0	0	1	110	10.0	0.1
CB01-2309	A	7	F	75	9	0	0	1	110	11.0	0.7
CB01-2739	A	9	A	33	9	0	0	1	110	10.0	0.4
CB01-3617	A	9	B	188	9	0	0	1	110	12.0	9.0
CB02-09-1070	A	9	F	230	9	0	0	1	110	11.0	1.1
CB02-09-1161	A	9	G	211	9	0	0	1	110	11.0	5.2
CB01-6378	H	21	A	5	9	0	0	1	110	10.0	2.0
CB01-6399	H	21	A	10	9	0	0	1	110	11.0	1.2
CB01-6401	H	21	A	11	9	0	0	1	110	11.0	2.4
CB01-6401	H	21	A	11	9	0	0	1	110	10.0	0.4
CB02-24-1785	A	24	A	1	9	0	0	1	110	11.0	0.6
CB02-24-1857	A	24	A	1	9	0	0	1	110	11.0	1.0
CB02-25-1015	A	25	A	39	9	0	0	6	110	13.0	36.7
CB02-25-1116	A	25	A	79	9	0	0	1	110	11.0	3.7
CB01-2316	A	7	F	61	9	0	0	6	110	11.0	3.2
CB01-2327	A	7	F	71	9	0	0	1	110	10.0	3.2
CB01-2328	A	7	F	71	9	0	0	1	110	10.0	1.0
CB01-2313	A	7	F	73	9	0	0	10	110	12.0	10.1
CB01-2313	A	7	F	73	9	0	0	2	110	12.0	32.1
CB01-2131	A	7	F	73	9	0	0	1	110	11.0	4.4
CB01-2314	A	7	F	74	9	0	0	1	110	11.0	0.3
CB01-2321	A	7	F	81	9	0	0	1	110	11.0	1.5
CB01-2329	A	7	F	81	9	0	0	6	110	10.0	0.8
CB01-2743	A	9	A	51	9	0	0	1	110	11.0	2.1
CB01-2749	A	9	A	83	9	0	0	0	110	10.0	0.6
CB01-3651	A	9	B	169	9	0	0	1	110	11.0	4.5
CB01-4227	A	9	C	55	9	0	0	1	110	11.0	2.0
CB01-4228	A	9	C	56	9	0	0	1	110	11.0	2.1
CB02-09-0922	A	9	D	63	9	0	0	1	110	10.0	2.4
CB02-09-0923	A	9	D	77	9	0	0	1	110	11.0	
CB02-09-0927	A	9	D	125	9	0	0	1	110	10.0	0.2
CB02-09-0950	A	9	D	125	9	0	0	1	110	11.0	1.8
CB02-09-0952	A	9	D	126	9	0	0	1	110	11.0	1.8
CB02-09-0928	A	9	D	127	9	0	0	1	110	10.0	2.8
CB02-09-0986	A	9	D	238	9	0	0	1	110	10.0	0.8
CB02-09-1042	A	9	F	196	9	0	0	1	110	11.0	1.7
Cb02-09-1034	A	9	F	203	9	0	0	9	110	11.0	2.5
CB02-09-1049	A	9	F	204	9	0	0	1	110	11.0	2.7
CB02-09-1052	A	9	F	213	9	0	0	1	110	12.0	8.1
CB02-09-1052	A	9	F	213	9	0	0	1	110	11.0	1.4
CB02-09-1058	A	9	F	215	9	0	0	1	110	11.0	2.2
CB02-09-1061	A	9	F	216	9	0	0	1	110	10.0	2.2
CB02-09-1061	A	9	F	216	9	0	0	1	110	11.0	6.9
CB02-09-1062	A	9	F	217	9	0	0	1	110	10.0	1.1
CB02-09-1097	A	9	F	217	9	0	0	1	110	12.0	14.9
CB02-09-1066	A	9	F	228	9	0	0	1	110	10.0	0.1
CB02-09-1069	A	9	F	229	9	0	0	1	110	10.0	2.4
CB02-09-1078	A	9	F	234	9	0	0	1	110	10.0	1.3
CB02-09-1080	A	9	F	244	9	0	0	1	110	10.0	1.1
CB02-09-1124	A	9	F2	235	9	0	0	1	110	11.0	3.4

Appendix A: Coded Lithic Debitage

no_especimen	sector	unidad	recinto	cuadro	corteza	huellas de uso	tipo plataforma bordes	tipo techno	tamano	peso
CB02-09-1126	A	9	F2	236	9	0	0	1	110	10.0	1.1
CB02-09-1127	A	9	F2	251	9	0	0	1	110	10.0	1.2
CB02-09-1158	A	9	G	195	9	0	0	1	110	10.0	2.8
CB01-6362	H	21	A	1	9	0	0	1	110	11.0	5.2
CB01-6362	H	21	A	1	9	0	0	1	110	11.0	2.3
CB01-6370	H	21	A	13	9	0	0	1	110	11.0	3.9
CB02-25-1144	A	25	A	51	9	0	0	1	110	12.0	4.5
CB02-25-1106	A	25	A	54	9	0	0	1	110	10.0	2.1
CB02-25-1106	A	25	A	54	9	0	0	1	110	11.0	7.4
CB02-25-1136	A	25	A	108	9	0	0	6	110	11.0	0.9
CB02-25-0998	A	25	A	126	9	0	0	1	110	11.0	8.0
CB02-27-0168	N	27	A	15	9	0	0	1	110	11.0	1.9
CB01-6003	L	19	A	14	9	0	0	1	110	11.0	7.0
CB01-2748	A	9	A	82	9	0	0	1	110	11.0	2.7
CB01-3596	A	9	B	139	9	0	0	1	110	11.0	0.7
CB01-4225	A	9	C	42	9	0	0	1	110	11.0	1.6
CB01-6740	F	23	A	4	9	0	0	1	110	11.0	1.8
CB02-25-1087	A	25	A	32	9	0	0	1	110	10.0	0.5
CB02-27-0202	N	27	B	48	9	0	0	1	110	10.0	1.2
CB02-27-0202	N	27	B	48	9	0	0	1	110	11.0	2.5
CB02-27-0183	N	27	B	31E	9	0	0	1	110	10.0	0.2
CB02-27-0216	N	27	C	54N	9	0	1	1	110	11.0	3.1
CB02-27-0216	N	27	C	54N	9	0	0	1	110	10.0	0.1
CB02-09-1101	A	9	F	231	9	0	0	1	110	13.0	26.9
CB02-32-0223	F	32	A	39	9	0	0	1	110	10.0	1.0
CB01-2325	A	7	F	72	9	0	0	1	110	10.0	0.2
CB01-2741	A	9	A	49	9	0	0	1	110	11.0	6.6
CB01-2759	A	9	A	146	9	0	0	1	110	11.0	7.0
CB02-09-1086	A	9	F	229	9	0	0	1	110	10.0	0.2
CB01-6417	H	21	A	11	9	0	0	1	110	10.0	0.5
CB01-6417	H	21	A	11	9	0	0	1	110	10.0	0.4
CB01-6417	H	21	A	11	9	0	0	1	110	10.0	0.3
CB01-6417	H	21	A	11	9	0	0	1	110	10.0	0.7
CB01-6417	H	21	A	11	9	0	0	1	110	11.0	4.0
CB01-6371	H	21	A	14	9	0	0	1	110	11.0	2.9
CB01-6419	H	21	A	15	9	0	0	1	110	10.0	0.3
CB01-6773	F	23	A	14	9	0	0	1	110	11.0	1.0
CB02-24-1806	A	24	A	2	9	0	0	1	110	10.0	0.1
CB01-2131	A	7	F	73	9	0	0	0	110	11.0	2.0
CB01-2746	A	9	A	67	9	0	0	1	110	10.0	0.2
CB01-2754	A	9	A	114	9	0	0	1	110	10.0	0.1
CB02-09-0966	A	9	D	173	9	0	0	1	110	10.0	0.1
CB02-09-0984	A	9	D	237	9	0	0	6	110	10.0	0.1
CB02-09-0984	A	9	D	237	9	0	0	1	110	11.0	2.3
CB02-09-1042	A	9	F	196	9	0	0	1	110	10.0	0.2
CB02-09-1061	A	9	F	216	9	0	0	1	110	10.0	1.0
CB02-09-1108	A	9	F	217	9	0	0	1	110	10.0	0.1
CB02-09-1147	A	9	G	162	9	0	0	1	110	10.0	0.1
CB02-25-1093	A	25	A	38	9	0	0	0	110	10.0	1.4
CB02-32-0226	F	32	A	3	9	0	0	6	110	11.0	1.9

Appendix A: Coded Lithic Debitage

no_especimen	sector	unidad	recinto	cuadro	corteza	huellas de uso	tipo plataforma bordes	tipo techno	tamano	peso
CB02-32-0222	F	32	A	37	9	0	0	1	110	10.0	1.3
CB01-3654	A	9	B	172	9	0	0	1	110	10.0	0.2
CB02-09-0992	A	9	D	126	9	0	0	1	110	10.0	0.1
CB02-09-1052	A	9	F	213	9	0	0	1	110	10.0	0.2
CB02-09-1069	A	9	F	229	9	0	0	1	110	10.0	0.6
CB02-09-1138	A	9	G	242	9	0	0	1	110	10.0	0.3
CB01-2311	A	7	F	44	9	0	0	1	110	11.0	0.4
CB01-2314	A	7	F	74	9	0	0	0	110	10.0	0.3
CB02-09-1105	A	9	F	246	9	0	0	0	110	10.0	0.1
CB02-27-0222	N	27	C	54N	9	0	0	1	110	10.0	0.2
CB01-2746	A	9	A	67	9	0	0	1	110	10.0	0.3
CB02-09-1061	A	9	F	216	9	0	0	1	110	10.0	0.4
CB02-09-1069	A	9	F	229	9	0	0	1	110	10.0	0.3
CB02-09-0921	A	9	D	62	9	0	0	1	110	10.0	0.9
CB02-09-0959	A	9	D	143	9	0	0	1	110	10.0	1.1
CB02-32-0219	F	32	A	27	9	0	0	1	110	10.0	1.3
CB02-32-0203	F	32	A	28	9	0	0	1	110	11.0	1.9
CB02-32-0232	F	32	A	29	9	0	0	2	110	10.0	0.6
CB02-32-0221	F	32	A	33	9	0	0	1	110	11.0	2.4
CB01-2313	A	7	F	73	9	0	0	1	110	10.0	0.6
CB01-2131	A	7	F	73	9	0	0	1	110	11.0	1.0
CB01-2321	A	7	F	81	9	0	0	1	110	10.0	0.7
CB01-2329	A	7	F	81	9	0	0	1	110	10.0	0.2
CB02-09-0922	A	9	D	63	9	0	0	1	110	11.0	1.6
CB02-09-0922	A	9	D	63	9	0	0	1	110	10.0	0.5
CB02-09-0928	A	9	D	127	9	0	0	1	110	10.0	0.2
CB02-09-1029	A	9	D	190	9	0	0	1	110	10.0	0.4
CB02-09-1048	A	9	F	203	9	0	0	1	110	12.0	9.6
CB01-6763	F	23	A	4	9	0	0	1	110	11.0	1.0
CB01-2739	A	9	A	33	9	0	0	1	110	11.0	5.0
CB01-2739	A	9	A	33	9	0	0	1	110	10.0	1.1
CB01-3638	A	9	B	75	9	0	0	1	110	11.0	0.4
CB01-3604	A	9	B	164	9	0	0	1	110	12.0	1.0
CB01-3604	A	9	B	164	9	0	0	1	110	10.0	0.2
CB01-4228	A	9	C	56	9	0	0	1	110	11.0	4.0
CB02-25-1021	A	25	A	51	9	0	0	1	110	10.0	1.3
CB02-25-1111	A	25	A	64	9	0	0	1	110	10.0	0.9
CB02-25-1057	A	25	A	105	9	0	0	1	110	11.0	3.3
CB02-27-0164	N	27	A	10	9	0	0	1	110	12.0	6.6
CB02-27-0168	N	27	A	15	9	0	0	1	110	10.0	0.7
CB01-3528	A	9	B	71	9	0	1	1	110	11.0	6.5
CB01-3590	A	9	B	86	9	0	0	1	110	11.0	0.6
CB01-3599	A	9	B	150	9	0	1	1	110	10.0	1.7
CB01-4227	A	9	C	55	9	0	0	6	110	10.0	0.5
CB02-09-0995	A	9	D	141	9	0	0	6	111	11.0	1.6
CB02-27-0221	N	27	C	54E	9	0	0	6	111	10.0	0.1
CB01-2737	A	9	A	33	9	0	0	6	111	10.0	3.7
CB01-3619	A	9	B	197	9	0	0	6	111	10.0	0.4
CB01-4242	A	9	C	22	9	0	0	1	111	10.0	0.8
CB01-4204	A	9	C	24	9	0	0	6	111	10.0	0.1

Appendix A: Coded Lithic Debitage

no_especimen	sector	unidad	recinto	cuadro	corteza	huellas de uso	tipo plataforma	bordes	tipo techno	tamano	peso
CB01-4236	A	9	C	38	9	0	0	6	111	12.0	8.8
CB01-4209	A	9	C	42	9	0	0	1	111	10.0	0.1
CB02-09-1013	A	9	D	190	9	0	0	6	111	10.0	0.3
CB02-24-1817	A	24	A	9	9	0	0	6	111	10.0	0.4
CB01-3575	A	9	B	90	9	0	0	6	111	11.0	3.2
CB01-3696	A	9	B	139	9	0	0	6	111	10.0	0.3
CB01-3656	A	9	B	188	9	0	0	6	111	10.0	0.7
CB02-09-1065	A	9	F	220	9	0	0	1	111	10.0	0.2
CB02-24-1882	A	24	A	3	9	0	0	1	111	10.0	0.1
CB02-25-1163	A	25	A	114	9	0	0	1	111	10.0	0.4
CB02-25-0997	A	25	A	125	9	0	0	6	111	11.0	0.6
CB02-09-1126	A	9	F2	236	9	0	0	6	111	10.0	0.4
CB02-24-1799	A	24	A	10	9	0	0	6	111	12.0	4.4
CB02-25-1049	A	25	A	95	9	0	0	6	111	13.0	28.5
CB02-25-0988	A	25	A	104	9	0	0	1	111	11.0	2.1
CB02-09-0984	A	9	D	237	9	0	0	1	111	11.0	2.0
CB01-6416	H	21	A	10	9	0	0	1	111	11.0	2.1
CB02-25-1140	A	25	A	116	9	0	0	1	111	12.0	16.7
CB01-2318	A	7	F	71	9	0	0	6	111	12.0	6.2
CB01-2314	A	7	F	74	9	0	0	0	111	11.0	1.5
CB02-09-0924	A	9	D	79	9	0	0	6	111	10.0	1.2
CB02-09-1027	A	9	D	175	9	0	0	6	111	11.0	9.7
CB01-4484	A	9	E	46	9	0	0	1	111	11.0	3.5
CB02-09-1035	A	9	F	212	9	0	0	6	111	10.0	1.1
CB02-09-1052	A	9	F	213	9	0	0	6	111	10.0	0.2
CB02-09-1150	A	9	G	163	9	0	1	6	111	11.0	6.5
CB02-09-1158	A	9	G	195	9	0	0	6	111	11.0	14.0
CB01-6412	H	21	A	2	9	0	0	1	111	11.0	3.8
CB02-25-1050	A	25	A	96	9	0	0	1	111	11.0	0.7
CB02-25-1065	A	25	A	116	9	0	0	1	111	11.0	2.4
CB02-25-0980	A	25	A	79	9	0	0	1	111	10.0	0.8
CB01-6407	H	21	A	18	9	0	0	1	111	10.0	1.3
CB02-25-1064	A	25	A	115	9	0	0	1	111	11.0	1.9
CB02-27-0194	N	27	B	40	9	0	0	6	111	11.0	9.5
CB02-27-0194	N	27	B	40	9	0	0	6	111	12.0	25.6
CB01-2747	A	9	A	89	9	0	0	6	111	10.0	0.5
CB01-3649	A	9	B	167	9	0	0	6	111	11.0	9.6
CB01-4206	A	9	C	26	9	0	0	6	111	11.0	6.0
CB02-09-1163	A	9	G	227	9	0	0	6	111	10.0	1.1
CB01-6382	H	21	A	5	9	0	0	0	111	10.0	1.2
CB01-6416	H	21	A	10	9	0	0	1	111	10.0	0.5
CB01-6742	F	23	A	10	9	0	0	1	111	11.0	1.5
CB02-24-1875	A	24	A	2	9	0	0	6	111	11.0	1.5
CB02-25-1118	A	25	A	83	9	0	0	6	111	10.0	0.1
CB02-25-1060	A	25	A	108	9	0	0	1	111	11.0	4.7
CB01-6001	L	19	A	8	9	0	0	6	111	12.0	3.0
CB01-2749	A	9	A	83	9	0	1	6	111	10.0	3.4
CB02-09-1069	A	9	F	229	9	0	0	6	111	10.0	0.4
CB02-09-1148	A	9	G	162	9	0	0	6	111	10.0	1.0
CB01-6392	H	21	A	18	9	0	0	6	111	10.0	2.7

Appendix A: Coded Lithic Debitage

no_especimen	sector	unidad	recinto	cuadro	corteza	huellas de uso	tipo plataforma bordes	tipo techno	tamano	peso
CB01-6742	F	23	A	10	9	0	0	1	111	10.0	0.5
CB02-09-1049	A	9	F	204	9	0	0	6	111	10.0	0.1
CB01-2757	A	9	A	131	9	0	0	6	111	10.0	0.5
CB02-24-1846	A	24	A	16	9	0	0	1	111	10.0	0.3
CB02-09-1103	A	9	F	232	9	0	0	6	111	10.0	0.2
CB02-09-1104	A	9	F	233	9	0	0	6	111	10.0	0.2
CB01-6382	H	21	A	5	9	0	0	1	111	10.0	0.8
CB02-27-0163	N	27	A	9	9	0	0	1	111	10.0	0.1
CB01-2747	A	9	A	89	9	0	0	6	111	10.0	0.8
CB01-3620	A	9	B	198	9	0	0	6	111	10.0	0.3
CB01-2318	A	7	F	71	9	0	0	6	111	10.0	0.7
CB01-2747	A	9	A	89	9	0	0	6	111	10.0	1.4
CB02-09-0940	A	9	D	239	9	0	0	6	111	10.0	1.9
CB01-6160	L	20	A	35	9	0	0	1	111	12.0	3.6
CB02-25-1097	A	25	A	42	9	0	0	6	111	12.0	37.9
CB02-25-1143	A	25	A	52	9	0	0	1	111	10.0	0.4
CB02-25-1040	A	25	A	81	9	0	0	1	111	11.0	1.7
CB01-6412	H	21	A	2	9	0	0	1	111	11.0	1.2
CB01-3581	A	9	B	108	9	0	0	1	111	11.0	5.0
CB02-24-1813	A	24	A	7	9	0	0	1	112	10.0	0.4
CB02-24-1851	A	24	A	1	9	0	1	1	112	10.0	0.1
CB02-24-1870	A	24	A	1	9	0	1	2	112	10.0	0.1
CB01-3529	A	9	B	90	9	0	1	1	112	11.0	1.4
CB01-2310	A	7	F	92	9	0	0	1	112	11.0	1.5
CB02-24-1792	A	24	A	5	9	0	1	1	112	11.0	1.8
CB02-25-1011	A	25	A	32	9	0	1	1	112	11.0	1.5
CB02-25-1023	A	25	A	53	9	0	0	1	112	12.0	18.5
CB02-25-1038	A	25	A	79	9	0	0	1	112	10.0	0.5
CB01-2720	A	9	A	81	9	0	1	1	112	13.0	34.6
CB01-3651	A	9	B	169	9	0	0	1	112	11.0	1.1
CB01-4213	A	9	C	21	9	0	0	1	112	10.0	1.0
CB01-4220	A	9	C	36	9	0	0	1	112	12.0	2.8
CB01-4220	A	9	C	36	9	0	0	1	112	11.0	0.7
CB02-09-0924	A	9	D	79	9	0	0	6	112	12.0	7.3
CB01-4482	A	9	E	44	9	0	0	1	112	11.0	4.6
CB02-09-1095	A	9	F	216	9	0	0	1	112	11.0	2.1
CB01-6379	H	21	A	1	9	0	0	1	112	12.0	11.5
CB01-6408	H	21	A	19	9	0	0	1	112	11.0	3.3
CB02-27-0182	N	27	B	29	9	0	1	1	112	11.0	9.7
CB02-27-0182	N	27	B	29	9	0	1	1	112	12.0	15.9
CB02-27-0189	N	27	B	34	9	0	0	1	112	11.0	2.4
CB02-27-0189	N	27	B	34	9	0	0	2	112	12.0	9.0
CB02-27-0192	N	27	B	38	9	0	0	1	112	12.0	8.7
CB02-27-0208	N	27	B	44	9	0	1	1	112	10.0	0.3
CB01-4478	A	9	E	29	9	0	0	1	112	11.0	4.7
CB02-27-0202	N	27	B	20	9	0	1	1	112	10.0	0.3
CB02-09-1148	A	9	G	162	9	0	0	1	112	10.0	1.0
CB02-09-1108	A	9	F	217	9	0	1	1	112	10.0	0.1
CB01-3663	A	9	B	204	9	0	0	1	112	11.0	0.8
CB01-6160	L	20	A	35	9	0	0	1	112	11.0	9.0

Appendix A: Coded Lithic Debitage

no_especimen	sector	unidad	recinto	cuadro	corteza	huellas de uso	tipo plataforma bordes	tipo techno	tamano	peso
CB01-6742	F	23	A	10	9	0	0	1	112	12.0	11.7
CB01-2752	A	9	A	99	9	0	1	1	112	10.0	0.5
CB01-6396-7	H	21	A	6	9	0	1	1	112	11.0	2.8
CB02-24-1892	A	24	A	7	9	0	1	1	112	13.0	31.3
CB01-2751	A	9	A	98	9	0	0	1	113	11.0	1.6
CB01-3623	A	9	B	201	9	0	0	1	117	10.0	0.6
CB01-4207	A	9	C	27	9	0	0	1	117	10.0	0.2
CB01-4206	A	9	C	26	9	0	0	6	540	11.0	2.3
CB02-09-1002	A	9	D	158	9	0	0	6	110-1	10.0	0.1
CB01-3577	A	9	B	103	9	0	0	1	110-1	10.0	0.1
CB01-3577	A	9	B	103	9	0	0	1	110-1	10.0	0.1
CB02-25-1078	A	25	A	21	9	0	0	1	110-1	10.0	0.1
CB01-6399	H	21	A	10	9	0	0	1	110-1	10.0	0.1
CB01-2317	A	7	F	62	10	0	0	6	111-1	11.0	5.2
CB01-2317	A	7	F	62	10	0	0	6	111-1	12.0	30.0

Appendix B: Coded Lithic Implements

no especimen	sector	unidad	recinto	materia prima	condition	corteza	tipo techno	termina distal	termina proximal	forma	largo (mm)	ancho (mm)	grosor (mm)	peso (gr)	tipo de lascas	bordes	retoque
CB01-2323	A	7	F	133	12	10	331	50	0	0	8.2	1.0	2.6	0.1	2	10	300
CB01-2316-1	A	7	F	153	30	10	511	0	0	500	66.5	0.0	0.0	218.0	1	11	0
CB01-2317	A	7	F	152	10	10	500	6	0	0	0.0	0.0	0.0	5.2	1	0	0
CB01-2317	A	7	F	152	10	10	500	6	0	0	0.0	0.0	0.0	2.5	1	0	0
CB01-2319	A	7	F	221	30	10	210	70	360	230	27.1	18.1	12.5	6.5	2	20	210
CB01-2320	A	7	F	152	0	10	510	0	0	0	0.0	0.0	0.0	4736.0	1	0	0
CB01-2329	A	7	F	133	0	10	400	0	0	0	26.6	25.7	8.0	4.4	2	0	0
CB01-2336	A	7	G	411	30	10	510	0	0	510	9.1	6.4	3.0	0.2	1	11	0
CB01-2337	A	7	G	153	30	10	510	0	0	511	128.5	88.7	36.2	533.8	1	11	0
CB01-2338-3	A	7	G	152	30	14	511	0	0	500	93.6	84.8	65.2	777.2	1	0	0
CB01-2343-3	A	7	G	156	30	14	511	60	141	512	118.2	58.6	59.6	661.5	1	0	0
CB01-2347-2	A	7	G	100	30	10	510	0	0	510	121.8	142.2	46.7	1457.6	1	0	0
CB01-2334	A	7	G	156	30	11	410	0	0	0	107.5	75.1	53.6	374.1	2	0	0
CB01-2726	A	9	A	150	30	13	440	0	0	519	108.1	73.4	64.5	876.4	0	0	0
CB01-2727	A	9	A	152	30	13	450	0	0	530	110.5	106.2	62.9	850.1	2		0
CB01-2769	A	9	A	411	30	10	510	0	0	510	4.9	4.8	2.4	0.1	0	0	0
CB01-2755	A	9	A	152	30	14	700	0	0	530	130.2	91.7	67.5	1014.7	0	0	0
CB01-2757	A	9	A	152	0	13	470	0	0	530	132.7	90.8	102.2	1905.1	0	0	0
CB01-2764	A	9	A	412	30	10	510	0	0	510	4.3	4.2	1.6	0.1	0	0	0
CB01-2735	A	9	A	151	30	12	340	0	0	510	13.9	137.5	48.4	904.4	0	0	0
CB01-2763	A	9	A	134	30	10	331	10	141	200	40.4	23.5	5.6	4.8	8	10	340
CB01-2761	A	9	A	133	30	10	331	10	130	210	19.8	9.1	1.6	0.3	3	10	330
CB01-2739	A	9	A	133	11	10	331	30	0	0	8.3	4.7	2.8	0.1	2	10	360
CB01-2767	A	9	A	133	30	10	300	10	100	200	21.0	12.0	2.8	0.6	2	10	360
CB01-2742	A	9	A	133	40	10	300	0	0	0	5.0	12.2	4.2	0.3	2	10	340
CB01-2768	A	9	A	133	22	10	331	0	132	110	14.9	9.2	3.4	0.3	7	10	340
CB01-2744	A	9	A	152	30	12	410	0	0	515	86.3	85.5	60.1	540.1	2	0	0
CB01-2744	A	9	A	155	30	13	470	0	0	530	118.1	77.3	39.3	364.8	2	0	0
CB01-2747	A	9	A	133	11	10	331	10	0	200	12.9	13.0	2.9	0.3	2	10	330
CB01-2747	A	9	A	152	0	11	400	0	0	530	86.2	78.3	40.5	302.3	2	0	0
CB01-3627	A	9	B	133	11	10	300	10	0	200	18.1	19.6	3.7	0.9	7	10	340
CB01-3681-2	A	9	B	134	30	10	331	30	132	210	17.8	8.6	2.5	0.3	2	10	330
CB01-3580-2	A	9	B	100	30	14	520	0	0	530	134.8	85.3	61.8	716.0	0	0	0
CB01-3675	A	9	B	133	11	10	300	30	0	0	11.5	5.7	3.3	0.1	7	10	340
CB01-3583	A	9	B	152	30	14	470	0	0	510	139.9	121.5	51.1	977.9	0	0	0
CB01-3640	A	9	B	134	12	10	300	0	100	0	19.8	7.5	3.9	0.5	2	10	340
CB01-3589-7	A	9	B	310	30	14	470	0	0	530	106.7	80.1	53.5	632.5	0	0	0
CB01-3560	A	9	B	221	30	10	340	10	360	270	64.9	49.7	18.2	45.1	0	10	330
CB01-3605-E	A	9	B	411	0	0	510	0	0	520	18.7	13.0	6.4	1.6	0	0	0
CB01-3671	A	9	B	134	30	10	331	10	130	110	27.7	8.5	3.9	0.8	2	10	340
CB01-3682-1	A	9	B	133	30	10	331	10	100	200	29.9	21.6	4.0	2.3	4	10	330
CB01-3666	A	9	B	134	30	10	331	10	100	211	43.3	22.7	3.9	3.4	2	10	330
CB01-3651	A	9	B	221	30	11	400	0	0	400	30.7	21.3	20.1	17.1	2	0	0
CB01-3677	A	9	B	134	30	10	331	10	130	100	17.0	11.7	2.6	0.4	2	10	330
CB01-3684	A	9	B	111	0	10	510	0	0	514	51.3	47.4	9.6	37.2	0	11	0
CB01-3683	A	9	B	133	30	10	331	10	130	110	20.8	12.5	3.2	0.5	2	10	340
CB01-3686	A	9	B	133	30	10	331	10	130	110	24.4	9.2	3.2	0.5	7	10	340
CB01-3685	A	9	B	222	30	10	331/33	10	200	110	17.8	10.3	4.9	0.5	7	10	340
CB01-3688	A	9	B	221	30	11	331	10	130	110	19.0	9.8	3.3	0.5	2	30	330
CB01-3680	A	9	B	133	30	10	331	10	130	200	22.6	10.5	3.9	0.7	2	10	340

Appendix B: Coded Lithic Implements

no especimen	sector	unidad	recinto	materia prima	condition	corteza	tipo techno	termina distal	termina proximal	forma	largo (mm)	ancho (mm)	grosor (mm)	peso (gr)	tipo de lascas	bordes	retoque
CB01-3564	A	9	B	160	30	14	511	0	0	500	98.9	92.9	69.7	938.1	0	0	0
CB01-3621	A	9	B	221	30	11	340	70	400	210	43.9	32.1	120.0	27.0	2	20	310
CB01-4246	A	9	B	240	30	11	540	0	0	500	14.9	12.2	14.9	2.6	0	0	0
CB01-3690	A	9	B	221	30	10	331	50	130	211	23.5	11.7	3.6	0.9	2	10	330
CB01-3691	A	9	B	300	0	10	510	0	0	519	16.1	11.9	2.2	0.6	0	11	0
CB01-3692	A	9	B	411	20	10	510	0	0	510	70.5	12.8		0.2	0	11	0
CB01-3693	A	9	B	133	22	10	331	0	100	100	17.0	11.8	4.9	0.6	2	10	340
CB01-3687	A	9	B	134	30	10	331	30	132	110	22.8	9.0	3.6	0.5	7	10	340
CB01-3638-2	A	9	B	999	30	14	520	0	0	530	25.2	20.1	14.6	12.4	0	0	0
CB01-3672	A	9	B	227	30	10	331	30	130	110	29.5	9.9	3.7	0.8	2	30	330
CB01-4231	A	9	C	133	0	10	320	0	0	221	58.8	51.7	8.8	31.4	2	20	330
CB01-4241	A	9	C	181	30	14	520	0	0	530	46.0	45.8	37.4	122.8	0	0	0
CB01-4247	A	9	C	227	21	10	331	10	200	110	29.9	8.4	3.5	0.8	7	10	340
CB01-4253-A	A	9	C	133	30	10	331	10	130	200	19.1	10.2	2.4	0.4	2	10	330
CB01-4242	A	9	C	152	30	14	520	0	0	530	47.4	39.6	38.6	102.4	0	0	0
CB01-4232	A	9	C	160	30	14	511	0	0	510	40.8	38.7	26.9	62.2	0	0	0
CB01-4251	A	9	C	223	21	10	331	10	0	110	15.6	5.5	2.6	0.2	3	10	340
CB01-4212	A	9	C	227	30	12	210	60	400	270	39.8	28.6	14.7	13.8	2	20	240
CB01-4248	A	9	C	240	30	10	540	0	0	500	15.8	14.3	13.8	2.9	0	0	0
CB01-4252	A	9	C	133	20	10	331	30	131	230	32.5	13.4	3.3	1.0	7	10	340
CB01-4249	A	9	C	135	30	10	331	10	131	200	17.6	9.3	2.9	0.3	7	10	330
CB01-4240	A	9	C	412	30	10	510	70	142	100	40.2	24.9	5.1	7.2	0	11	0
CB01-4245	A	9	C	134	40	10	331	0	0	0	16.9	12.5	3.4	1.1	3	10	330
CB01-4253	A	9	C	134	20	10	336	50	100	211	59.5	31.7	7.3	12.7	2	10	330
CB01-4253-B	A	9	C	134	30	10	331	50	141	220	33.8	21.0	4.6	2.7	2	10	330
CB01-4250	A	9	C	240	30	10	540	0	0	500	12.7	12.7	13.2	2.0	0	0	0
CB01-4239	A	9	C	160	30	14	511	0	0	530	54.4	37.7	36.9	105.8	0	0	0
CB02-09-0948	A	9	D	134	0	10	210	0	0	0	22.7	11.6	3.9	0.7	2	20	240
CB02-09-0951-A	A	9	D	133	30	10	331	10	132	110	25.0	12.6	4.3	0.8	2	10	230
CB02-09-0991	A	9	D	133	40	10	300	0	0	0	15.2	16.4	5.7	1.8	2	10	330
CB02-09-0951-B	A	9	D	134	30	10	331	50	130	200	31.4	21.5	4.7	2.6	7	10	330
CB02-09-0953	A	9	D	133	30	10	331	10	131	200	33.7	19.5	3.4	2.3	2	10	330
CB02-09-0957	A	9	D	133	30	10	331	10	131	100	20.1	12.6	1.5	0.3	2	10	330
CB02-09-0960	A	9	D	133	30	10	331	10	132	100	19.8	9.3	3.9	0.3	2	10	340
CB02-09-0962-A	A	9	D	133	40	10	331	0	0	110	16.0	12.4	1.7	0.4	4	10	240
CB02-09-0962-B	A	9	D	133	22	10	331	0	130	100	11.3	9.7	2.2	0.2	2	10	340
CB02-09-1001	A	9	D	133	30	10	331	10	130	110	24.9	11.6	3.5	0.8	4	10	340
CB02-09-1002	A	9	D	133	12	10	336	0	131	200	21.1	20.4	5.0	2.2	2	10	360
CB02-09-0932	A	9	D	133	40	10	331	0	0	0	11.8	14.4	3.9	0.7	2	10	330
CB02-09-0964	A	9	D	133	30	10	336	50	100	211	57.7	28.7	5.2	9.0	2	10	340
CB02-09-0969	A	9	D	132	21	10	334	10	0	211	37.0	22.1	6.3	2.9	2	10	360
CB02-09-0967	A	9	D	133	30	10	331	10	130	100	21.8	14.0	2.0	0.5	3	10	330
CB02-09-0968	A	9	D	226	30	11	420	0	0	0	25.0	39.5	26.5	32.4	8	0	0
CB02-09-1022	A	9	D	151	30	11	230	70	100	280	29.7	37.9	18.7	19.6	2	20	270
CB02-09-0973	A	9	D	133	0	10	310	0	0	0				1.2	2	10	330
CB02-09-0934	A	9	D	133	40	10	331	0	0	0	16.8	14.2	4.3	1.0	2	10	360
CB02-09-1014	A	9	D	133	40	10	300	0	0	0	11.0	16.4	4.8		2	10	330
CB02-09-0936	A	9	D	133	12	10	331	0	131	0	21.7	14.4	2.3	0.9	2	10	330
CB02-09-0976	A	9	D	152	30	11	410	0	0	0	25.3	30.4	22.2	21.4	2	0	0
CB02-09-0937	A	9	D	300	30	10	500	60	100	100	18.8	16.5	2.5	1.4	1	11	0

Appendix B: Coded Lithic Implements

no especimen	sector	unidad	recinto	materia prima	condition	corteza	tipo techno	termina distal	termina proximal	forma	largo (mm)	ancho (mm)	grosor (mm)	peso (gr)	tipo de lascas	bordes	retoque
CB02-09-1017	A	9	D	181	20	14	511	0	0	500	58.5	43.2	48.9	174.0	0	0	0
CB02-09-0985	A	9	D	133	30	10	331	10	130	100	28.9	13.0	3.4	1.0	2	10	330
CB02-09-0987	A	9	D	134	12	10	331	0	131	220	14.5	10.8	3.4	0.5	3	10	330
CB02-09-0988	A	9	D	133	30	10	331	10	131	100	15.7	9.5	2.2	0.5	2	10	360
CB02-09-0988	A	9	D	133	30	10	331	10	100	100	15.6	9.7	2.2	0.3	2	10	330
CB02-09-0943	A	9	D	133	40	10	331	0	0	0	12.8	19.1	5.1	1.8	2	10	330
CB02-09-1019	A	9	D	133	30	10	331	10	132	110	22.8	9.5	2.5	0.4	7	10	330
CB01-4490	A	9	E	133	30	10	331	10	130	110	16.9	8.9	2.3	0.3	2	10	340
CB01-4489	A	9	E	133	30	10	331	10	132	210	23.5	15.3	3.4	1.0	2	10	330
CB01-4480	A	9	E	133	12	10	331	0	141	0	18.5	27.7	8.4	1.9	3	10	330
CB01-4488	A	9	E	151	30	10	331	10	220	100	16.0	9.6	2.9	0.3	7	30	330
CB02-09-1043	A	9	F	133	30	10	331	50	132	220	15.8	11.4	1.9	0.2	2	10	330
CB02-09-1047-A	A	9	F	133	40	10	300	0	0	0	4.6	14.7	4.4	0.3	2	10	330
CB02-09-1047-B	A	9	F	133	30	10	331	10	160	110	18.2	9.3	3.4	0.4	2	10	340
CB02-09-1033	A	9	F	133	12	10	336	0	100	0	17.0	23.5	4.3	1.9	3	10	340
CB02-09-1049	A	9	F	412	10	10	510	0	0	510	8.5	13.6	4.3	0.7	1	11	0
CB02-09-1050	A	9	F	226	40	10	230	0	0	221	23.6	21.9	7.8	3.3	2	10	240
CB02-09-1053	A	9	F	133	11	10	331	10	0	0	19.3	17.9	3.7	0.8	2	10	340
CB02-09-1052	A	9	F	151	30	10	331	50	131	220	21.5	14.1	2.8	1.0	3	10	330
CB02-09-1056	A	9	F	133	30	10	331	10	160	110	18.8	9.4	2.5	0.3	2	10	330
CB02-09-1059	A	9	F	133	30	10	331	10	130	100	20.9	13.6	3.0	0.4	2	10	330
CB02-09-1096	A	9	F	134	30	10	331	50	130	220	14.5	11.3	3.2	0.3	3	10	340
CB02-09-1037	A	9	F	223	30	10	331	10	130	210	21.1	9.6	3.6	0.5	2	10	330
CB02-09-1115	A	9	F	150	30	14	520	0	0	500	?	?	?	1243.6	0	11	0
CB02-09-1064	A	9	F	224	11	11	334	30	0	110	22.3	15.3	7.0	1.0	2	10	360
CB02-09-1069	a	9	F	224	30	10	331	10	100	100	17.3	11.5	3.9	0.5	2	10	370
CB02-09-1116	A	9	F	110	30	14	511	0	0	500	79.8	70.2	60.3	520.6	0	11	0
CB02-09-1071	A	9	F	133	40	10	336	0	0	0	17.4	22.8	4.3	2.0	3	10	340
CB02-09-1100	A	9	F	133	30	10	331	10	130	100	14.1	8.1	2.6	0.3	2	10	340
CB02-09-1030	A	9	F	134	30	10	331	10	131	210	27.8	15.2	3.2	1.3	7	10	330
CB02-09-1072	A	9	F	133	40	10	300	0	0	0	19.0	11.8	4.6	0.8	2	10	360
CB02-09-1039	A	9	F	223	30	10	331	10	200	110	21.6	11.7	4.5	0.8	7	10	340
CB02-09-1075-B	A	9	F	152	30	10	310	20	400	270	39.9	27.7	4.3	5.3	2	40	330
CB02-09-1075	A	9	F	223	30	10	331	50	100	100	27.2	16.9	2.2	1.0	3	10	330
CB02-09-1075-A	A	9	F	223	30	10	310	50	141	100	27.2	16.8	2.3	0.9	3	10	230
CB02-09-1040	A	9	F	151	30	10	331	50	150	230	21.7	14.3	2.9	0.7	2	10	210
CB02-09-1089	A	9	F	151	21	10	310	10	0	270	32.8	16.2	4.4	1.9	2	10	330
CB02-09-1090	A	9	F	240	0	10	510	0	0	0	85.2	71.4	47.3	312.9	1	0	0
CB02-09-1068	A	9	F	227	30	10	331	30	130	100	19.2	11.8	3.0	0.4	3	10	330
CB01-2331-A	A	9	F	133	30	10	335	60	100	210	32.5	19.5	4.7	2.9	2	40	330
CB01-2331-B	A	9	F	133	30	10	335	60	100	210	40.1	20.6	4.5	3.8	2	20	340
CB01-2332	A	9	F	133	30	10	331	10	130	210	22.6	10.7	2.4	0.5	3	10	330
CB01-2333	A	9	F	133	30	10	331	10	130	210	22.0	12.7	2.4	0.5	2	10	230
CB02-09-1114	A	9	F1	111	30	10	511	0	0	513	101.0	73.8	47.0	645.6	0	11	0
CB02-09-1096	A	9	F1	134	30	10	331	10	130	100	14.5	11.6	3.2	0.5	2	10	360
CB02-09-1108	A	9	F1	226	11	10	331	10	0	100	18.2	10.6	3.3	0.5	2	10	300
CB02-09-1106	A	9	F1	160	20	10	510	0	0	510	136.2	110.1	34.1	834.3	0	11	0
CB02-09-1117	A	9	F1	110	30	10	510	0	0	510	128.3	110.9	39.4	925.8	0	11	0
CB02-09-1100	A	9	F1	133	30	10	331	10	132	110	14.1	8.1	2.7	0.2	2	10	360
CB02-09-1118	A	9	F1	110	30	10	510	0	0	510	102.3	91.6	57.9	836.2	0	11	0

Appendix B: Coded Lithic Implements

no especimen	sector	unidad	recinto	materia prima	condition	corteza	tipo techno	termina distal	termina proximal	forma	largo (mm)	ancho (mm)	grosor (mm)	peso (gr)	tipo de lascas	bordes	retoque
CB02-09-1092	A	9	F1	412	30	14	500	0	0	510	29.4	27.4	10.0	9.0	1	0	0
CB02-09-1120	A	9	F2	133	10	10	331	0	0	0	14.9	12.8	3.9	0.7	2	10	330
CB02-09-1122	A	9	F2	226	10	10	310	0	100	270	8.7	12.8	4.3	0.5	2	10	330
CB02-09-1124	A	9	F2	141	30	10	331	10	130	220	16.1	10.9	2.9	0.5	2	10	210
CB02-09-1125	A	9	F2	152	30	10	230	10	130	210	21.4	11.6	3.2	0.6	3	10	240
CB02-09-1124	A	9	F2	154	30	10	331	10	130	210	21.4	11.4	3.4	0.7	3	10	210
CB02-09-1136	A	9	F2	110	30	13	511	0	0	511	100.0	77.9	58.6	731.4	1	11	0
CB02-09-1142	A	9	G	150	30	12	511	0	0	530	84.0	88.0	57.7		0		0
CB02-09-1444	A	9	G	134	30	10	331	10	100	100	16.4	12.3	2.9	0.5	2	10	360
CB02-09-1146	A	9	G	151	30	13	511	0	0	530	290.0	192.0	111.0	7000.0	0	11	0
CB02-09-1149	A	9	G	133	30	10	331	10	130	110	28.4	11.4	3.6	0.8	2	10	330
CB02-09-1150	A	9	G	141	30	11	410	0	0	530	70.1	51.6	41.2	132.0	2	0	0
CB02-09-1154	A	9	G	154	0	10	511	0	0	516	200.9	156.6	46.9	2448.6	0	11	0
CB02-09-1151	A	9	G	160	30	14	520	0	0	500	64.7	49.6	40.1	188.9	0	1	0
CB02-09-1155	A	9	G	141	30	10	450	0	0	530	81.2	27.2	29.3	81.8	2	0	0
CB02-09-1157	A	9	G	160	30	14	511	0	0	500	49.9	39.6	21.0	60.4	0	11	0
CB02-09-1159	A	9	G	412	30	101	510	0	0	250	15.6	12.3	2.7	0.8	0	11	0
CB02-09-1161	A	9	G	152	30	03,(1	200	10	100	270	85.7	83.8	24.2	157.3	0	20	240
CB02-09-1139	A	9	G	226	40	10	340	0	0	250	16.3	11.7	4.8	1.0	2	10	360
CB02-09-1164	A	9	G	152	30	11	450	0	0	530	119.4	135.7	110.0	1698.0	2	0	0
CB02-09-1140	A	9	G	227	30	11	331	30	131	230	18.2	12.3	4.4	0.4	2	10	340
CB02-09-1138	A	9	G	151	12	06, 1(	310	0	10	270	21.9	21.1	5.1	2.5	1	10	310
CB02-09-1166	A	9	G	451	30	10	510	0	0	515	13.7	12.0	8.6	2.8	0	11	0
CB01-5993	L	19	A	151	30	11	450	0	0	520	41.8	40.6	27.3	52.3	0	0	0
CB01-5997	L	19	A	151	30	10	450	0	0	520	72.5	63.7	39.2	154.4	0	0	0
CB01-5995	L	19	A	151	30	11	230	60	142	270	63.1	39.0	6.9	19.6	3	10	240
CB01-6162	L	19	A	111	30	12	511	0	0	513	77.9	56.1	36.6	245.3	0	0	0
CB01-6161	L	20	A	151	30	10	410	0	0	270	65.2	40.9	27.6	71.7	0	0	0
CB01-6148	L	20	A	221	30	11	230	0	0	270	47.3	30.0	19.7	23.4	0	10	250
CB01-6421	H	21	A	133	30	10	331	10	210	100	18.7	10.7	5.3	0.8	2	10	360
CB01-6422	H	21	A	227	30	10	331	30	330	110	19.7	10.3	2.7	0.4	5	10	330
CB01-6386	H	21	A	155	30	10	410	0	0	510	83.0	59.5	26.5	142.3	0	10	0
CB01-6439	H	21	A	223	30	10	331	10	330	110	21.0	10.3	3.4	0.6	3	30	340
CB01-6439	H	21	A	227	30	10	331	10	330	100	16.8	10.7	2.8	0.3	3	30	330
CB01-6430	H	21	A	300	30	10	510	0	0	518	5.0	5.1	3.6	0.5	0	11	0
CB01-6424	H	21	A	111	30	10	510	0	0	510	6.4	6.3	2.6	0.1	0	11	0
CB01-6433	H	21	A	152	30	10	510	0	0	510	6.0	5.9	2.3	0.1	0	11	0
CB01-6388	H	21	A	160	30	12	511	0	0	270	194.0	111.2	40.6	1199.2	0	0	0
CB01-6431	H	21	A	222	30	10	331	10	220	100	15.2	11.0	2.8	0.6	2	10	330
CB01-6423	H	21	A	227	30	10	331	10	220	100	18.7	10.6	3.3	0.5	2	10	360
CB01-6432	H	21	A	400	0	10	510	0	0	510	0.0	0.0	0.0	0.3	0	11	0
CB01-6442	H	21	A	412	30	10	510	0	0	518	5.7	5.8	4.1	0.2	0	11	0
CB01-6432	H	21	A	420	30	10	510	0	0	510	5.2	5.2	3.9	0.2	0	11	0
CB01-6433	H	21	A	420	30	10	510	0	0	510	6.7	6.4	3.2	0.1	0	11	0
CB01-6442	H	21	A	420	30	10	510	0	0	518	5.2	5.2	3.1	0.2	0	11	0
CB01-6425	H	21	A	133	30	10	331	30	220	110	18.2	10.0	2.8	0.3	3	10	330
CB01-6436	H	21	A	133	22	10	331	0	220	110	17.9	10.7	3.3	0.5	2	30	340
CB01-6426	H	21	A	223	30	10	331	30	330	100	17.6	10.3	3.9	0.4	4	30	340
CB01-6426	H	21	A	223	30	10	331	30	220	110	22.5	11.3	3.7	0.6	2	10	330
CB01-6440	H	21	A	227	30	10	331	10	220	110	19.9	10.6	3.1	0.4	4	30	330

Appendix B: Coded Lithic Implements

no especimen	sector	unidad	recinto	materia prima	condition	corteza	tipo techno	termina distal	termina proximal	forma	largo (mm)	ancho (mm)	grosor (mm)	peso (gr)	tipo de lascas	bordes	retoque
CB01-6434	H	21	A	400	30	10	510	0	0	510	6.8	6.7	2.9	0.1	0	11	0
CB01-6434	H	21	A	400	10	10	510	0	0	510	0.0	0.0	0.0	<0.1	0	11	0
CB01-6435	H	21	A	420	30	10	510	0	0	510	4.9	4.9	2.9	0.1	0	11	0
CB01-6441	H	21	A	227	30	10	331	10	330	110	19.2	11.2	2.9	0.4	3	30	330
CB01-6437	H	21	A	412	30	10	510	0	0	518	4.6	4.6	3.9	0.1	0	11	0
CB01-6438	H	21	A	133	30	10	331	50	220	100	17.6	9.3	3.0	0.3	3	10	330
CB01-6380	H	21	A	152	30	10	450	0	0	530	110.5	49.0	29.9	147.4	2	0	0
CB01-6380	H	21	A	152	30	10	310	60	120	100	34.7	24.4	6.8	3.4	2	20	240
CB01-6427	H	21	A	222	30	10	331	10	210	110	18.6	10.5	3.1	0.5	3	30	330
CB01-6443	H	21	A	222	30	10	331	10	210	100	17.5	9.7	3.2	0.3	3	10	330
CB01-6428-11	H	21	A	240	30	14	510	0	0	500	13.8	13.2	16.1	2.7	0	11	0
CB01-6429	H	21	A	133	30	10	331	10	220	100	18.5	11.2	3.1	0.4	2	10	360
CB01-6585	H	22	B	151	30	11	410	0	0	511	89.1	69.5	45.7	366.9	0	0	0
CB01-6586	H	22	B	154	0	10	530	0	0	510	146.7	126.2	11.8	374.3	0	0	0
CB01-6586	H	22	B	181	30	10	511	0	0	500	50.9	47.0	42.5	140.1	0	11	0
CB01-6586	H	22	B	181	30	10	511	0	0	500	56.4	55.3	49.0	211.5	0	11	0
CB01-6759	F	23	A	160	0	10	511	0	0	500	14.3	100.8	50.1	1129.8	0	0	0
CB01-6758	F	23	A	420	30	0	520	0	0	530	18.8	10.6	7.9	2.6	0	0	0
CB01-6780	F	23	A	300	10	10	510	0	0	518	4.9	6.9	4.0	0.1	0	11	0
CB01-6776	F	23	A	152	30	10	510	0	0	500	16.9	15.4	13.5	4.6	0	10	0
CB01-6777	F	23	A	152	30	10	510	0	0	500	13.5	15.1	16.2	4.1	0	11	0
CB01-6781	F	23	A	223	30	10	331	10	210	100	18.7	9.5	3.9	0.5	3	10	330
CB01-6778	F	23	A	133	22	10	331	0	130	200	14.4	11.4	2.8	0.4	6	11	340
CB01-6765	F	23	A	160	30	14	511	0	0	514	73.5	57.3	34.9	231.6	0	0	0
CB01-6779	F	23	A	133	30	10	331	30	100	110	18.9	9.9	2.3	0.3	8	10	340
CB01-6766	F	23	A	152	30	11	320	0	0	510	81.8	70.1	26.0	189.4	0	0	0
CB01-6741	F	23	A	221	30	10	440	0	0	530	40.3	22.7	16.6	16.5	0	0	0
CB02-24-1859	A	24	A	133	30	10	336	50	130	211	59.4	23.3	5.9	8.0	3	10	340
CB02-24-1865	A	24	A	134	30	10	336	50	100	211	45.6	22.7	5.7	5.5	2	10	330
CB02-24-1858	A	24	A	150	30	0	531	0	0	510	150.8	110.3	39.6	1183.8	0	0	0
CB02-24-1781	A	24	A	134	30	10	331	10	360	120	16.0	15.9	3.7	0.7	7	10	330
CB02-24-1926	A	24	A	411	30	10	510	0	0	510	3.4	3.6	2.0	0.1	0	11	0
CB02-24-1930	A	24	A	412	30	10	510	0	0	518	9.7	7.4	7.5	0.8	0	11	0
CB02-24-1917	A	24	A	414	30	10	510	0	0	510	5.4	5.3	2.3	0.1	0	11	0
CB02-24-1929	A	24	A	414	30	10	510	0	0	518	2.6	2.6	2.6	0.1	0	11	0
CB02-24-1929	A	24	A	414	30	10	510	0	0	510	3.8	3.8	1.2	0.1	0	11	0
CB02-24-10?5	A	24	A	133	30	10	331	10	131	100	21.3	10.4	2.1	0.4	3	10	330
CB02-24-1937	A	24	A	133	0	10	331	0	0	200	15.6	11.0	3.2	0.4	0	10	0
CB02-24-1842	A	24	A	111	30	14	511	0	0	500	47.4	39.1	37.5	94.8	0	0	0
CB02-24-1940	A	24	A	133	30	10	336	70	100	211	41.2	25.7	5.1	6.5	2	10	340
CB02-24-1844	A	24	A	133	30	10	336	50	100	211	44.1	22.9	5.7	5.7	2	10	340
CB02-24-1943	A	24	A	133	0	10	331	0	0	100	15.2	12.6	3.9	0.5	0	10	0
CB02-24-1848	A	24	A	133	40	10	331	0	0	0	8.9	14.5	3.8	0.5	2	10	330
CB02-24-1849	A	24	A	154	0	10	531	0	0	510	135.0	61.2	15.1	178.3	0	11	0
CB02-24-1874	A	24	A	134	0	10	300	0	0	200	6.0	5.0	2.0	0.1	0	10	0
CB02-24-1874	A	24	A	134	30	10	300	0	0	530	19.8	15.1	9.1	2.5	0	10	0
CB02-24-1877	A	24	A	134	21	10	310	60	0	250	35.8	28.3	7.8	8.8	2	10	370
CB02-24-1788	A	24	A	111	30	13	440	0	0	530	102.5	82.7	42.4	431.0	0	0	0
CB02-24-1789-A	A	24	A	133	30	10	331	10	132	100	18.3	10.8	2.3	0.3	2	10	330
CB02-24-1789-B	A	24	A	133	30	10	331	10	131	100	19.9	11.9	4.0	0.6	3	10	330

Appendix B: Coded Lithic Implements

no especimen	sector	unidad	recinto	materia prima	condition	corteza	tipo techno	termina distal	termina proximal	forma	largo (mm)	ancho (mm)	grosor (mm)	peso (gr)	tipo de lascas	bordes	retoque
CB02-24-1884	A	24	A	133	30	10	331	10	130	100	18.9	10.9	3.2	0.4	7	20	340
CB02-24-1794	A	24	A	133	40	10	331	0	0	0	13.9	13.1	2.5	0.4	2	10	330
CB02-24-1890	A	24	A	134	30	10	336	0	13	130	47.9	29.4	6.3	8.1	5	10	340
CB02-24-1889	A	24	A	150	30	14	520	0	0	530	137.0	103.4	65.7	1064.3	0	0	0
CB02-24-1904	A	24	A	111	30	14	511	0	0	500	43.1	42.2	28.9	72.0	OO	11	0
CB02-24-1798	A	24	A	133	22	10	331	0	360	110	12.3	14.6	3.1	0.6	2	10	340
CB02-24-1906	A	24	A	134	30	10	200	0	0	530	24.2	17.9	6.7	2.4	0	10	0
CB02-24-1902	A	24	A	223	22	10	336	0	220	110	16.2	7.6	3.4	0.3	3	30	330
CB02-24-1875	A	24	A	221	30	10	410	0	0	530	19.5	33.4	21.3	14.6	2	0	0
CB02-24-1875	A	24	A	221	30	10	210	70	360	270	39.9	32.5	8.9	14.6	03(1)	10	250
CB02-25-1055	A	25	A	154	0	12	511	0	0	516	159.0	99.8	31.6	1050.0	0	11	0
CB02-25-1098	A	25	A	133	30	10	310	10	142	210	31.1	11.4	5.4	1.6	5	10	330
CB02-25-1058	A	25	A	152	30	10	310	10	360	270	62.0	53.6	22.7	39.1	1	20	310
CB02-25-1137	A	25	A	132	0	10	230	0	0	0	12.1	12.3	6.1	1.0	2	0	220
CB02-25-1008	A	25	A	133	30	10	331	10	130	110	24.1	13.1	2.5	0.6	7	10	330
CB02-25-1083	A	25	A	133	30	10	331	10	130	100	15.6	11.7	3.8	0.3	2	20	340
CB02-25-1086	A	25	A	134	0	10	300	0	0	0	12.2	16.6	4.3	0.5	1	10	240
CB02-25-1094	A	25	A	133	30	10	331	10	130	110	11.0	9.5	2.5	0.3	7	10	340
CB02-25-1095	A	25	A	160	30	13	511	0	0	500	98.5	98.1	81.5	1103.2	0	0	0
CB02-25-1155	A	25	A	221	30	10	200	70	360	270	25.4	13.2	2.6	0.8	0	10	220
CB02-25-1103	A	25	A	111	20	10	510	0	0	517	21.6	29.5	30.0	18.0	0	11	0
CB02-25-1103	A	25	A	182	30	10	510	0	0	517	21.6	30.4	28.7	18.0	0	11	0
CB02-25-1108	A	25	A	133	30	10	331	10	131	220	13.3	12.9	2.2	0.4	7	10	330
CB02-25-1107	A	25	A	160	30	10	511	0	0	510	151.5	114.4	67.0	1804.5	0	11	0
CB02-25-1027	A	25	A	154	0	14	530	0	0	530	203.0	134.1	35.9	1846.2	0	0	0
CB02-25-1029	A	25	A	134	30	10	331	50	131	200	23.4	14.9	2.8	0.8	2	10	330
CB02-25-1145	A	25	A	133	22	10	331	0	130	220	13.3	13.4	1.9	0.4	2	10	330
CB02-25-1112	A	25	A	154	0	10	531	0	0	510	230.4	148.2	53.5	3500.0	0	11	0
CB02-25-1157	A	25	A	160	30	10	511	0	0	500	89.2	79.1	70.0	714.1	0	11	0
CB02-25-1035	A	25	A	227	30	10	336	10	240	100	26.1	9.8	3.2	0.6	3	30	340
CB02-25-1036	A	25	A	150	30	10	510	0	0	513	99.6	78.7	37.6	486.4	0	11	0
CB02-25-1120	A	25	A	133	40	10	300	0	0	0	8.3	8.7	3.8	0.2	2	10	360
CB02-25-1044	A	25	A	100	30	14	511	0	0	530	47.7	30.0	30.7	77.5	0	11	0
CB02-25-1123	A	25	A	134	40	10	300	0	0	0	11.9	1.2	4.7	0.4	2	10	360
CB02-25-1067	A	25	A	154	0	12	531	0	0	510	230.0	122.7	63.1	2790.4	0	0	0
CB02-25-1052	A	25	A	160	30	10	511	0	0	510	109.1	102.2	46.8	867.6	0	11	0
CB02-25-1162	A	25	A2	412	30	10	510	0	0	510	4.9	5.0	1.8	0.1	0	11	0
CB02-25-1176	A	25	A2	181	30	10	511	0	0	500	102.2	88.8	84.5	1185.0	0	11	0
CB02-25-1173	A	25	A2	133	12	10	331	0	100	0	19.1	23.4	11.4	2.7	2	10	330
CB02-25-1152	A	25	A2	133	11	10	331	0	100	0	18.8	14.5	3.3	0.9	2	10	340
CB02-25-1158	A	25	A2	133	40	10	331	0	0	0	13.7	1.0	4.9	0.5	2	10	330
CB02-25-1174	A	25	A2	133	11	10	331	10	0	0	16.6	12.9	3.2	0.4	2	10	330
CB02-25-1170	A	25	A3	135	11	10	335	10	0	0	22.6	27.8	5.8	2.6	2	10	360
CB02-27-0184	N	27	B	152	30	10	200	70	400	270	57.3	125.1	28.3	174.6	2	20	240
CB02-28-0015	N	28	A	222	0	10	210	0	0	530	16.9	16.0	10.7	2.2	0	10	0
CB02-32-0201	F	32		152	30	11	410	0	0	515	74.8	60.4	36.7	180.3	0	0	0
CB02-32-0219	F	32		221	0	12	400	0	0	520	35.6	31.0	19.8	24.8	0	0	0
CB02-32-0222	F	32		152	30	11	210	60	100	280	65.8	60.4	31.8	125.6	2	20	250
CB02-32-0224	F	32		133	40	10	331	0	0	0	16.2	10.6	4.4	0.6	2	10	360

Appendix B: Coded Lithic Implements

no especimen	sector	unidad	recinto	materia prima	condition	corteza	tipo techno	termina distal	termina proximal	forma	largo (mm)	ancho (mm)	grosor (mm)	peso (gr)	tipo de lascas	bordes	retoque
CB02-28-0015	N	28	A	222	0	10	210	0	0	530	16.9	16.0	10.7	2.2	0	10	0
CB02-32-0201	F	32		152	30	11	410	0	0	515	74.8	60.4	36.7	180.3	0	0	0
CB02-32-0219	F	32		221	0	12	400	0	0	520	35.6	31.0	19.8	24.8	0	0	0
CB02-32-0222	F	32		152	30	11	210	60	100	280	65.8	60.4	31.8	125.6	2	20	250
CB02-32-0224	F	32		133	40	10	331	0	0	0	16.2	10.6	4.4	0.6	2	10	360

www.ingramcontent.com/pod-product-compliance
Lightning Source LLC
Chambersburg PA
CBHW041704290426

44108CB00027B/2850